Economics and Management of Education: Emerging Themes

CONTEMPORARY ANALYSIS IN EDUCATION SERIES
General Editor: Philip Taylor, University of Birmingham

Contemporary Analysis in Education Series

Economics and the Management of Education: Emerging Themes

Edited by
Hywel Thomas
University of Birmingham

and

Tim Simkins
Sheffield City Polytechnic

 The Falmer Press
(A member of the Taylor & Francis Group)
London New York and Philadelphia

UK   The Falmer Press, Falmer House, Barcombe, Lewes, East Sussex,
         BN8 5DL

USA   The Falmer Press, Taylor & Francis Inc., 242 Cherry Street,
         Philadelphia, PA 19106-1906

First published 1987

Library of Congress Cataloguing-in-Publication Data

Economics and the management of education.

(Contemporary analysis in education series; 15)
Proceedings of a research seminar.
Bibliography: p.
Includes indexes.
1. Education—Economic aspects—Great Britain.
2. School management and organization—Great Britain.
I. Thomas, Hywel. II. Simkins, Tim. III. Series.
LC67.G7E27 1987   338.4′73712′00941   87–15604
ISBN 1–85000–208–8
ISBN 1–85000–209–6 (pbk.)

Jacket design by Leonard Williams

Typeset in 11/13 Garamond by
Imago Publishing Ltd, Thame, Oxon

Printed and bound in Great Britain by
Redwood Burn Limited, Trowbridge, Wiltshire

Contents

Contents

Acknowledgements

The chapters included in this volume were prepared initially for a research seminar designed to explore the contribution which economics can make to educational management as a field of study. The invitation to the editors of this volume to organize such a seminar came from Peter Ribbins, Chairman of the Research Committee of the British Educational Management and Administration Society (BEMAS). We wish to acknowledge our thanks to him and the Committee for the proposal and the invitation. We would also wish to thank Gareth Williams for his advice and support at an early stage in preparing the seminar. We much appreciated the advice and support given by others in preparing for the seminar and, at the seminar itself, the response of all the participants certainly convinced the organizers that their efforts had been worthwhile.

We wish to thank Meredydd Hughes, Head of the Department of Social and Administrative Studies in Education, University of Birmingham, for making a grant to assist the funding of the seminar and his support of our use of the Department's secretarial and other resources. In particular, we acknowledge the considerable secretarial help and advice given by Penny Lowe, who undertook the considerable work related to the seminar and this book with patience, good humour and care.

General Editor's Preface

Education costs money. Education consumes about one-fifth of this country's gross national product. It makes sense, therefore, to exhibit a nice sense of the economic when considering how best to manage our educational system. It is just this that the several contributors to this volume do and Hywel Thomas and Tim Simkins are to be congratulated in orchestrating their efforts.

What is achieved for the reader in addition to a carefully orchestrated collection of papers is a sharp awareness of the complexity of the relationships between economics, social aspirations, education and the opportunities of individuals. Nothing is plain nor, to paraphrase Oscar Wilde, is it ever as simple as our political masters would want it to be. Unintended consequences of policy abound. Benefits there are. Costs too arising from every decision. Perhaps it was ever so but that does not detract from the value of this collection of papers. It brings us back to a very tangible reality which educationists are at times only too willing to ignore.

Philip Taylor
University of Birmingham 1987

Part One

Education Management: The Potential Contribution of Economics

Hywel Thomas and Tim Simkins

Introduction

Even the idea of an economic perspective on education and its management seems inappropriate to many educationists, who appear to believe that education lies beyond an economic calculus which, if applied, debases its cultural processes. This view was well summarized by Woodhall and Blaug nearly twenty years ago, in discussing the applicability to education of the concept of 'productivity'.

> Educationalists are afraid that measurement of the productivity of schools will involve emphasizing quantity at the expense of quality, if only because the quality of education is so difficult to measure. In fact, some critics go further and suggest that the most important educational objectives are in principle immeasurable, concerned as they are with a child's whole personality and character. In the words of one writer, 'anything measurable enough to satisfy the economist is likely to appear disgustingly mundane to an educationalist who is more concerned with the soul ...' (Woodhall and Blaug, 1968, p. 3).

Such fears are undoubtedly still to be found among many educationists. Indeed, this may explain in part why the economics of education has suffered something of a relative eclipse in the United Kingdom since the high point of the 1960s. We suggest that such a view is based upon a misunderstanding of the nature of economics and, therefore, of the nature of its potential contribution to education. Indeed, one of the pleasures of teaching in this area is observing a change in the attitudes of many students, from an initial suspicion about the relationship between economics and education

3

to a recognition of its usefulness in helping to answer certain kinds of questions.

A principal aim of this book, therefore, is to illustrate the nature and usefulness of an economic perspective for education and the field of education management in particular. We hope to demonstrate this usefulness in three ways. First, in a later section of this chapter we shall briefly describe the ways in which economists view education and, in so doing, emphasize a prevalent concern with the quality of education. Second, several chapters present and review current research in the economics of education, in both academic institutions and government agencies, with a particular concern to appraise their relevance for the study and practice of educational management and administration. And, third, throughout the book, the issue of how economics can assist in tackling particular problems in the management of education is addressed from a variety of perspectives and in relation to a number of different areas of education.

We also hope the book acts as a stimulus for readers to take further any interest they are developing in this area. For reasons we discuss later, economic approaches are likely to become increasingly prominent in the management of the education service. In such circumstances, it would seem to be appropriate that educationists become more knowledgeable about economics because, as Cumming (1971) has remarked:

> There need be no fears of naive productivity experts dominating the teachers' work if the teachers and educationists take pains to learn more of economics than economists know of education (p. 232).

In this respect we hope that readers will find helpful guidance for further reading from the bibliography collected at the end of the volume.

For much the same reason we hope this book may encourage and assist the introduction and development of economic and resource management perspectives into long and short courses in educational management. We hope that it is significant that the origin of this book, or more particularly the seminar on which it draws, was an initiative by the Research Committee of the British Educational Management and Administration Society (BEMAS) whose Chairman, Peter Ribbins, first extended an invitation to organize a seminar for exploring the contribution which economics can make to educational management as a field of study.

It may be that such an invitation reflects a growing recognition that education managers need a better understanding of the techniques of economics, their strengths and weaknesses, for analyzing and evaluating the problems they face. Indeed, it is our contention that improved understanding would seem to be particularly important for those who are concerned with the well-being of the education service. There are two sets of reasons for this. The first is related to the changing economic, demographic and ideological context within which the education system works. It will be argued in the next section of this chapter that these changes are so substantial that it is no longer open to education managers to prevent the application of techniques derived from economics to certain problems of educational policy and practice. The second set of reasons is concerned with the applicability of economics to the circumstances perennially faced by educationists of making choices in conditions of scarcity and uncertainty; they represent positive reasons why economics is a valuable aid for the better management of education. An initial consideration of these reasons is provided in the third section of this chapter, although they are the prime focus of the book as a whole and are deeply embedded in all the chapters which follow.

Economy, Demography and Ideology

On economy, the international recession precipitated by the oil price rises beginning in 1973 worsened the United Kingdom's existing problems of low economic growth and rising unemployment caused by the chronic relative uncompetitiveness of its manufacturing sector. In addition, there is widespread agreement that the nature of the economic policies adopted by successive UK governments since 1976, which have given overwhelming priority to controlling inflation, have contributed to the continuing low rate of economic growth and rising levels of unemployment. These problems have had a considerable effect upon the education service and many other public sector activities. One reason for this is that the unemployed pay no income tax and reduce the scarce public revenue resources for which education must compete. A second reason is that welfare payments to the unemployed add to the demands upon those same public revenue resources. Fortunately for education and other public sector activities the tax revenue from North Sea

oil has, to some degree, compensated for the revenue and welfare payment implications of unemployment. However, this has
not been sufficient to protect public sector activities from the
straitened circumstances of the economy and from increasing demands for improved 'efficiency' and better 'value for money'. Indeed, it is understandable that at times of low growth in public
revenue and increased demands by many social welfare programmes,
there comes also a heightened awareness of the need to maximize
the benefits obtained from scarce public resources which have alternative uses.

The greater awareness of resource scarcity helps to explain the
search both for means of assisting and legitimizing the process of
choice among competing public sector wants, and for ways of
identifying areas of inefficiency in resource use which have the
potential for releasing scarce resources for use in areas of greater
impact. Both assessing the welfare impact of choices concerning
resource allocation and identifying areas of inefficiency in resource
utilization are *prima facie* more difficult in the public sector where
the signals of the price system are muffled by administered markets,
and where consumer choices are mediated through the decisions of
elected representatives and elected and non-elected public officials.
This is not to argue that the competitive market model offers a
ready-made solution to problems of choice, but rather to suggest
that the absence of markets does help to explain the search for, and
use of, measurable criteria for guiding public sector policy choices.
Such developments have been occurring over recent years at all
levels in the public policy system: at national level (Thomas, 1983);
at local government level, particularly through the work of the
Audit Commission (1984a, 1985a and 1986); and at institutional
level, for example the Jarratt Report in the university sector
(CVCP, 1985). Furthermore, unlike earlier work in this area with
respect to education, much of which was undertaken by academics
and had little perceptible policy impact, current developments are
largely taking place through organizations and processes which seem
designed to ensure their institutionalization as an important dimension of education policy-making and management.

However, in recognizing the pressures upon many public sector
programmes to demonstrate their internal efficiency in terms of
measurable criteria, we should note that education may be a special
case in that there are particular demographic circumstances which
have intensified its need to find such criteria to justify its perform-

ance and hence its continuing entitlement to an adequate supply of public funds.

On demography, education suffers on account of its own contracting numbers and because of the growing welfare demands represented by increasing numbers of retired people. Their needs, let alone those of more than three million unemployed, are likely to be seen as more urgent than those of an education system in which the numbers of pupils in the maintained schools sector in England and Wales are expected to fall to 7.2 million in 1990 from a peak of 9.2 million in 1977 (ACSET, 1981, annex, table 1). This fall changes fundamentally the basis of discussion concerning the resourcing of education. Indeed, education is here hoisted by the petard of its own favoured criteria for determining resourcing levels. Such criteria have traditionally emphasized the use of *input* measures, such as the pupil-teacher ratio, or *per capita* expenditure on pupils and students, for determining resource requirements for whole sectors of education and for particular institutions. This ensured not only that resource provision increased at least in proportion to pupil or student numbers, but also that any desired improvements in standards were themselves specified in resource terms through improving staffing ratios and increasing levels of *per capita* expenditure. With the resourcing question defined historically in these terms, it is hardly surprising that few outside education readily understand why 'First and foremost, falling rolls do not automatically require fewer teachers . . .' (Williams, S. 1979, p. 456), and why, more generally, standards cannot be maintained by reducing resourcing levels proportionately with pupil and student numbers. Such concerns can only be addressed by developing new criteria which demonstrate the inadequacy of the old. Such criteria need to embody a more truly *economic* perspective on resource allocation which recognizes the importance of relating inputs in some way to the educational value which these inputs produce. Movements in this direction can be identified in all sectors of education: the movements towards curriculum-based staffing of secondary schools (Simkins, 1984; Walsh *et al*, 1985) and towards discriminatory financing of universities by the UGC using, in part, indicators of research performance are examples which illustrate the trend. Both recognize that the pressures of contraction significantly reduce the viability of traditional incrementalist resource allocation mechanisms (Lindblom, 1959) and provide considerable incentives for relating expenditure decisions to more clearly specified concepts of purpose and priority.

Such developments often require new conceptual and technical questions to be resolved, but they also give rise to conflicts of value and interest which earlier resource allocation procedures concealed. Indeed, the resource allocation criteria which emerge from such developments are commonly the subject of at least as much contention and controversy as those they replace. They do, however, force the consideration of certain key economic questions which earlier resource management methods may have largely ignored.

The potent combination of economy and demography would seem to be problem enough for the education service, requiring it to demonstrate its effectiveness in using public resources, but changes in ideology add to its beleaguered position.

On ideology, there have been three related sets of changes which have altered the perceived purpose of education, the autonomy of its teaching force and the perceived propriety of using certain techniques for evaluating educational activity. The major ideological change is a move away from the former idea that spending on virtually any form of education was a 'good' thing, because it was believed to contribute to economic growth and the creation of a society where lifetime opportunities did not depend upon family background. In the government of education in Britain, a more circumspect view now prevails. While academic analysis, usefully reviewed by Blaug (1976, *passim*), questions the human capital assumptions about the relationship between education and economic growth, British governments have remained committed to the positive nexus between these two factors. However, this nexus is now characterized by a specific formulation which is profoundly altered, emphasizing vocational and technical preparation oriented to the needs of the economy's industrial, manufacturing and commercial sectors at the expense, as necessary, of liberal education. In this view of the world, the economic relevance of education depends upon its content and method. Thus, the altered emphasis on the purpose of education has brought in train a challenge to the autonomy of the teaching profession to define courses and teaching styles. It is an ideological shift which can be represented in the words of two prime ministers. Waddington (1985, p. 101) cites Edward Heath in a speech to the Society of Education Officers in 1973:

> We try as a society to indicate to the professionals the human values, the social attitudes, the cultural traditions, the range of skills we wish them to foster ... Thereafter we leave it to their professional responsibility and expertise to

decide how to translate our wishes into courses and sylla-
buses.

Thus Heath leaves teachers a substantial area of professional discretion. In contrast, James Callaghan in his Ruskin College speech
(1976, p. 333), while recognizing '. . . the need to cater for a child's
personality . . .' warns that 'There is no virtue in producing socially
well-adjusted members of society who are unemployed because they
do not have basic skills,' and then enters the arena of methods,
courses and evaluation.

> Let me repeat some of the fields that need study because
> they cause concern. There are the methods and aims of
> informal instruction; the strong case for the so-called 'core
> curriculum' of basic knowledge; next, what is the proper
> way of monitoring the use of resources in order to maintain
> a proper national standard of performance; then there is the
> role of the inspectorate in relation to national standards; and
> there is the need to improve relations between industry and
> education.

The comments on monitoring standards represent the third
strand of ideological change. For some, measuring the performance
of the education system is viewed not only as necessary and legitimate but also as fairly straightforward. Representative of this view is
Carlisle's (1979a) view that complaints about levels of achievement
in basic skills can be dealt with by setting national standards and
using the APU to monitor performance. For others, the political
and practical issues involved are more complex. In general, however, the 'accountability' movement in education (Kogan, 1986) has
created pressures which point towards the development both of
more clearly specified, instrumental — and hence measurable —
goals for education, and of new mechanisms, often financial, for
ensuring that both patterns of provision and the quality of that
provision can be more readily influenced and more tightly controlled by those outside the immediate professional community of
education.

Such developments provide clear opportunities for economists
to develop a greater involvement in the processes of educational
policy-making and management. There are a number of reasons for
this. First, the emphasis on clear specification of objectives and
outcomes attempts to reduce the ambiguity attached to educational
goals which is such a major problem in much of educational econo-

mics. Secondly, the renewed emphasis on resource allocation and control as policy tools focusses very much in a realm where economists feel that their methods of analysis have something of value to offer. And thirdly, such developments generate new kinds of data, both on outcomes and expenditure patterns, which greatly facilitate economic analysis. Thus economic, demographic and ideological developments provide a whole context of change in the environment of the education system and create circumstances where the relevance of economics to pressing concerns of educational policy and management is increasingly recognized. The reasons why educationists should respond positively to these developments is the theme of the next section.

Education and Economics: The Case for Cooperation

If educationists have little opportunity for preventing the intrusion of economic techniques into their world, they retain choice over how they respond to their entry. These choices appear to lie between an uncooperative hostility, which probably threatens the best interests of the education service, or a cooperative approach. Cooperation might entail only an apparent welcome where the real purpose is to become sufficiently well informed as to have the ability to recognize and, using appropriate economic terms, to resist improper application by 'outside experts' of partially digested quasi-economic techniques to half-understood educational problems. More constructively, it could entail becoming sufficiently confident and competent to utilize the strengths of a perspective particularly well-suited to the analysis of problems of choice. A more positive approach such as this will recognize that the challenges outlined in the previous section cannot be met without a much greater and, in many cases, deeper consideration of the resource dimensions of educational questions than practitioners in schools and colleges will often allow; and that modes of analysis which facilitate the better understanding of how educational resources are used, and how their use might be improved, are essential elements in the armoury of the educationist today.

Conversely, economists can respond to the challenge of applying their skills and techniques to education in a variety of ways. At one extreme — and too many examples of this can be found — it is possible to apply economic principles to education in ways which so reduce and simplify the educational process that the fears of educationists expressed at the beginning of this chapter are amply justified. In the current economic and political climate, with educationists generally on the defensive, there is perhaps greater opportunity for economists to do this than ever before. However, in the longer-term interests both of education and of the credibility of educational economics, this really will not do. If economic analysis is to be seen to have value in helping to solve problems of policy and management in education, it must be applied in ways which recognize and are sensitive to the nature of educational institutions and processes and the concerns of educational practitioners. This means, first, that economic models developed to analyze quite different circumstances and problems outside education should not be applied widely and unquestioningly in the educational sector, and second, that economists should cultivate a degree of modesty about what their techniques can and cannot do in the area of education. It is perhaps this final point that provides the key to increased and more productive cooperation between educationists and economists. One of the key preconditions for an intelligent application of economic concepts to education is an increased understanding by educationists and economists of each other's methods of thought. The remainder of this section attempts to outline briefly the framework of analysis which economists bring to educational problems and which hence underpins the rest of this book.

Economists would argue that Robbins' well-known definition of economics as 'the science which studies human behaviour as a relationship between ends and scarce means which have alternative uses' (Robbins, 1935, p. 16), is as applicable to education as to any other area of human activity. The implications of this definition, however, can be developed in a variety of ways, drawing on a range of theoretical perspectives to address a multitude of conceptual and practical problems. There is no room here to review in any detail the full range of issues explored in the literature on the economics of education, although we hope the bibliography at the end of the book provides a useful starting point for further exploration in this area. However, two particular aspects of the contribution of economics to educational policy-making and management must be briefly mentioned here. First, because economists are concerned to ask questions about choice in an educational world of scarce means and many wants, economic analysis may assist both in enhancing our understanding of how and why resource allocation and other decisions are made in education, and in providing guidance for policy-makers and managers on how best to influence such decisions through appropriate financial and other mechanisms. In doing this economists seek to burrow beneath policy and management rhetoric in order to understand the decision-making world which individuals and groups actually inhabit; and to explore how decisions emerge from the interactions of individual and group preferences, and conceptions of the opportunities and constraints which limit the choices available. The importance of the insights provided by this kind of analysis for policy-makers and managers in education lies in its implications for the prediction of responses to various policy mechanisms, particularly in the area of finance and resource management. Examples relating to the allocation of funds from central to local government, to the financing of students through fees, grants and loans, and to the rapid expansion of direct or 'categorical' funding of educational initiatives are to be found in later chapters of this book.

The second major potential contribution of economics to educational policy-making and management concerns the analysis of how resources are actually utilized within the education service and to provide guidance for decision-makers on the resource allocations which are more likely to secure greater educational outcomes in the future. To facilitate such analysis economists commonly view education as a productive process in which the various human and physical resources, which they call inputs, are mixed together, or processed, in various ways. Out of these processing activities come educational outcomes or outputs, though no economist would suggest that these outputs are by any means as predictable and measurable as in more conventionally understood manufacturing processes. It is a framework which is, nevertheless, useful in two major ways. First, by distinguishing inputs from process and outputs, it clarifies the differing nature and status of variables often discussed as though they were somehow the same. For example, the pupil-teacher ratio is clearly identified as a ratio of one input (pupils) to another input (teachers) and is not, as is so often claimed, a measure of educational quality, which presumably needs to be measured by output indicators of various kinds. The specification and measure of such indicators, however, is not easy. Educational programmes have many outcomes, some of which are intended and some not. Furthermore, any attempt to specify the desirability of particular outcomes runs up against problems of conflict between the preferences and deeply held values of individuals and groups within society. As Miles has argued about schools:

> Because schools are people-changing systems, their goals
> cannot be articulated on narrowly technical, pragmatic or
> obvious grounds, but involve normative and ideological
> choices ... In sum the goals of schools, manifest and latent,
> represent a sort of multi-level value tangle, and goal conflict
> is thereby claimed as inevitable. (Miles, 1981, p. 61)

Nevertheless, despite these profound difficulties, an economic
approach to education would insist that questions of outcome be
addressed. Indeed, it may be argued that two important potential
contributions of economics to educational management and policy-
making lie, on the one hand, in its ability to highlight the difficulties
involved with any attempt to measure satisfactorily educational outcomes, and, on the other, in an insistence that any assessment of
outcomes is related to some measures of the costs involved in
achieving them. Two examples of this way of thinking to be found
later in this book relate to the question of assessing the desirable
level of subject provision in higher education and to the relative
cost-effectiveness of different patterns of 'A' level provision.

Beyond this, though, a more dynamic application of the input-
process-output framework would emphasize the interrelationships
of the variables involved. At best, this would lead to an examination
of how changes in the availability of certain inputs affect the nature
of certain process variables and how these in turn affect educational
outcomes. An example of this would be appraisal of the implication
of changes in quantitative and qualitative aspects of the teaching
force, during a period of contraction, upon educational processes
and outcomes (see Thomas, 1984).

This brief statement may serve to emphasize that, properly
applied, economics is concerned with the quality of education. An
economic education is not to be equated with a cheap education; the
emphasis is not on financial outlays alone but on financial and
other resource expenditures in relation to educational outcomes.
The case for using economics to study educational problems of
choice and efficiency would seem to be overwhelming. What virtue
can there be in wasting resources on an inefficient way of achieving
given ends if those same ends can be achieved more cheaply, thereby
releasing resources to achieve some other educational goal which
otherwise would have to be ignored for absence of resources? Clearly, there is a need for caution in applying economic analysis, both in
ensuring that it does not become an input-focussed, finance-

controlling exercise masquerading as an economic approach and in recognizing that quantifying many educational outcomes *is* very difficult. This serves to emphasize both the appropriateness of Cumming's comments quoted earlier as to why educationists must become more knowledgeable about economics; and also why economists need to consider carefully exactly where, how and to what degree their methods of analysis can best contribute to education management and policy-making. The chapters which follow attempt to address these issues in a variety of ways.

The Structure of the Book

Part 2 contains four chapters which reflect the concepts and literature of the economics of education which have a particular relevance to education management. Chapter 2 by John Mace discusses the relationship between education and the economy and examines the conflicting explanations offered of the relationship between education, the economy and the labour market by a number of major theoretical perspectives. These several perspectives have sharply contrasting implications for the education system and, specifically, for the management of the curriculum. As indicated earlier in this introductory chapter, the ideological perspective to which policy makers may be attached has considerable consequence for those working within the education system.

Chapter 3 by Gareth Williams focusses upon financial mechanisms and their implications for educational provision. It identifies the different means available for regulating the flow of resources to education and their significance as a channel for sending messages between providers and users of finance. It is suggested that the nature of the mechanisms affects the relative influence of client and provider groups on the nature of provision; and that the mechanisms can also influence the comparative significance upon provision for particular sub-groups of clients against other client sub-groups. In sum, financial mechanisms have crucial consequences for who gets what resources: a critical issue for those concerned with problems of distribution and equity in educational provision.

Chapters 4 and 5, by John Pratt and Tim Simkins respectively, deal with the internal economics of educational institutions, the first considering the literature and problems in the post-compulsory sector and the second discussing relevant problems in the compulsory sector. Both chapters examine approaches to, and limitations of, attempts at assessing the internal efficiency of educational institutions. The discussions also examine processes of internal resource allocation, the use of indicators of performance, information and control systems and their implications for provision, process and performance.

Part 3 of the book reflects the issues which are discussed in part 2 but is organized sectorally, enabling readers to locate sets of chapters of more immediate relevance to their own circumstances. However, the first three chapters (chapter 6 by Judith Marquand, chapter 7 by Paul Ryan and chapter 8 by John Gibson and Peter Watt) deal with problems which relate to the whole service. Marquand offers a challenging analysis, arguing that curriculum managers in all sectors must design their provision in such a way that learners develop and maintain an ability to cope with and respond to change. Ryan draws attention to the discrepancy between the government's emphasis on the importance of investment in education and its public expenditure decisions. He argues that only limited gains can be achieved through efficiency maximizing policies. The nature of the 'cost disease' which influences service activities like education mean that even policies of level funding will lead to a decline in educational output. The pattern of expenditure is analyzed separately for the primary, secondary and university sectors. Gibson and Watt report preliminary findings of a research project on the effects of changes in the mechanisms by which local authorities receive grants from central government, providing empirical support for the proposition that different mechanisms influence spending decisions. The examination of the data is prefaced by a helpful account of the complex series of changes to which local government has been subject since 1980.

Five chapters on the higher education system follow. Andrew Gurney (chapter 9) and Jason Tarsh (chapter 10) develop the theme of the relationship between education and the economy, showing how economic analysis can be applied to inform policy on the selective management of subject provision in universities and polytechnics. Gurney reports on empirical work on the determinants of graduate supply in different subjects, suggesting that the data can be used to guide government policy on the supply of student places. The case for firmer government intervention into the pattern of subject provision is reinforced by Tarsh's chapter. Drawing on information from the first destination survey of graduates he suggests that evidence on unemployment levels and narrowing pay differentials between graduates and less qualified manpower offers a cogent case for reducing spending on higher education, although such cuts should be selective and aim at protecting those subject areas where demand remains buoyant.

Maureen Woodhall (chapter 11) considers the effects of alternative financial mechanisms on the distribution of educational opportunities. Her discussion on loans and grants and on overseas students fees is evidence of the contribution which economists of education should be making to policy in this area. It is an analysis which illustrates the subtle effects of financial mechanisms in influencing access and underlines the view that the issues relating to policy in these areas are more complex than many of the ideological debates allow.

The internal efficiency of higher education institutions is the focus of the contributions from John Sizer (chapter 12) and Rob Cuthbert (chapter 13). Sizer is concerned to emphasize the challenge to manage for excellence and not just for survival. Among other suggestions, he argues that economists have a role in developing appropriate performance indicators to assist the internal management of higher education institutions and to engage in scenario analysis leading to the development of strategies for resource mobility. Economists also have a role in developing cost-curve analyses in relation to questions of departmental size. Cuthbert's chapter is a discussion of the appropriate form of organizational structure in conditions where the selection of criteria to assess efficiency involves ambiguity and disagreement.

Keith Drake (chapter 14) and Rachel Britton (chapter 15) discuss issues in the management of provision in the training sector, but also raise questions of much more general relevance. In addition to considering the appropriate balance of training between government and employer-funded provision, Drake emphasizes the unreliability of data in this area and the problems created thereby for making soundly-based policy decisions. The difficulty of obtaining reliable and appropriate data is also raised by Britton, whose chapter is an account of developments in the relationship between LEAs and the MSC over the non-advanced further education and and training (NAFE) initiative.

The following six chapters deal with the schools' sector from the three perspectives identified by the keynote chapters in part 2. Chapter 16 by David Ashton and Malcolm Maguire deals with the relationship between schools and the economy. Drawing on research into the nature of the youth labour market they discuss the implications of this relationship for the school curriculum, suggesting that it could undergo fairly radical change without affecting the employment chances of many young people. The optimism which this engenders must be tempered by findings that for some jobs, employers put an emphasis on a readiness to accept the discipline of routine and often boring work, where evidence of personal initiative and leadership qualities are negatively valued. This chapter provides an important counterweight to the argument advanced in Judith Marquand's chapter.

The means by which funds are made available and their consequences for teachers and clients in schools are the focus of three chapters by, respectively, Brian Knight, Oliver Fulton and Hywel Thomas. Brian Knight (chapter 17) outlines the many different ways in which funds, or 'honeypots' as he graphically names them, are made available and offers an appraisal of their possible advantages and disadvantages. Oliver Fulton (chapter 18) reports preliminary research findings into the effects of the direct funding by the MSC of the Technical and Vocational Education Initiative (TVEI). He suggests that while changing the funding mechanisms may alter the rules of play the relative strengths of the participants in the making of educational policy are not necessarily radically altered. Chapter 19 by Hywel Thomas reports research findings on the consequences of treating schools as cost centres, where heads are given much more control and freedom in allocating their budgets. It describes some of the changes which have arisen from such 'autonomy' schemes but, in analyzing their underlying assumptions, warns of the dangers of expecting too much from them if personnel are inadequately prepared for thinking about their educational implications and potential.

In chapter 20 David Reeson outlines an approach to the assessment of cost-effectiveness in education. Specifically, it isolates the budgetary costs of providing 'A' level courses in different types of educational institutions and links them to indices of performance based on examination results. Given the earlier discussion in this chapter, it may be significant that here we have an officer of the Audit Commission seeking to devise some measure of performance which do not focus exclusively on costs.

Chapter 21, by Chris Cumming, is rather different from the others in that it draws directly on experience from overseas in relating economics to the management of education. In presenting an account of the challenges of working as a cost consultant in the Third World, it underlines the problems of data collection and validation which arise in other chapters. It also acts as a warning of the ephemeral consequences which may beset some research, particularly in circumstances where funding agencies do not have an adequate information system into which research findings may be properly disseminated.

Conclusion

Economics provides an example of a social science discipline whose potential contribution to education management has tended to be underdeveloped. We have argued that in the current climate economics will be less on the sidelines than hitherto and we hope that this book contributes in moving the discipline more into the centre of discussions concerning the theory and practice of managing education.

The chapters contained in parts 2 and 3 demonstrate that the concerns of economists with education and its management spread across many areas. There is work in progress to further clarify important problems about the education system and its economic purposes, about the funding of educational opportunities and about the internal economics of institutions. We hope this book may serve to encourage further work in these areas. This is not to suggest that economics has an entitlement to a special place in educational policy analysis, but to a place alongside other social sciences in analyzing alternatives and providing better information for the decisions about provision, process and performance that are taken daily in one part or another of our educational system.

Part Two

Education, the Labour Market and Government Policy

John Mace

Introduction

The present government is pursuing education (and training) policies which clearly imply an understanding of how the education system and the labour market are linked. As the precise nature of this link has exercised the minds of economists of education for years it would seem worth examining what assumptions about the relation between education and the labour market underpin government policy to see whether they are supported by empirical and conceptual work in the economics of education. It seems reasonable to examine government policy in this way because there has been no suggestion from the government that it has developed any original theories of the education/labour market relationship to replace the current theories or, indeed, that it has access to any empirical results that show why any of the existing theories is to be preferred to any other as a basis for education policy making.

To some extent my choice of topics to discuss is arbitrary — a necessarily limited selection from the almost endless series of questions about the goverment's education policy that are worth exploring. However, I will discuss three that are all linked by the underlying notion that education and training make people more productive in the labour market. I continually allude to training and education together because they are becoming increasingly linked in government policy. Indeed, there is recurrent discussion that they may be combined in one super-department. There may be some conceptual sense in such a move if it results in greater cohesion in the policies to develop human capital and also reduces inefficiency in the use of scarce educational and training resources. But it may make less sense if education and training serve different purposes and the links between both and the labour market are inadequately understood by policy makers.

My, admittedly, arbitrary choice of topics to discuss is thus: education, the labour market and economic growth; human capital and 'screening'; and the economics of training.

Under the first heading I will consider the way in which education is perceived by the government as being linked to the labour market and to the economic performance of the UK economy. Under the second heading I will examine the way in which education is related to earnings and review the current state of the debate between those who consider that education increases the *productivity*, and thus the earnings of individuals, and those who hold the view that education merely 'screens' for those with *pre-existing* abilities. In the last section I will examine, albeit briefly, the current policy of vocationalizing the curriculum in order to prepare individuals better for productive employment. In that section I will consider the changes in education/training policy at all levels of the system, from YTS to university level. There will, of necessity, be some overlap between the three sections of the chapter.

Education and Economic Performance

Education imbues individuals with skills and attitudes, human capital, which will affect the labour market in a number of ways. First, it will alter the employment pattern through its effect on the supply of differently qualified people. Employers will alter their hiring, firing and pricing strategies as the supply of human capital changes. Richard Freeman (1976) in the *Over-educated American* shows the changes in relative wages that have been caused by the increase in supply of more educated Americans. In addition changes in the supply of educated labour will affect the organization and structure of work. The increased supply of human capital will increase the pace of technological change and innovation bringing about a change in the nature of jobs and, consequently, in the employment prospects of differently qualified workers. For example, technological change will make some skills obsolescent and increase the demand for others. Whether the effect of these changes is to increase or reduce employment prospects generally cannot be predicted with any certainty. What should increase is the level of national output and, *ceteris paribus*, the level of employment. This government, like so many before it, argues that one of the keys to enhanced economic performance is investment in education. What is the basis for this view?

Economists have analyzed education's contribution to growth in three ways: growth accounting, cost-benefit analysis and cross country comparisons. I shall deal briefly with the first and the second. The most famous exemplar of this approach is Denison (1962 and 1979) who finds that education accounted directly for 11 per cent of the USA economic growth between 1948 and 1973 and indirectly, 'advances in knowledge and miscellaneous determinants', for a further 29 per cent. There is no evidence that the government has been influenced by this growth accounting method which is just as well as it is fundamentally flawed (see Blaug, 1970, for a destructive critique of Denison's methodology).

The government in the recent White Paper and its Green Paper on higher education cites the results of social rate of return calculations. For 1982 they show a social rate of return of 8 per cent for first degrees if research costs are excluded and if it is assumed that all of the increased earnings of graduates over 'A' level holders are due to their extra education.

Now there are a number of reasons for doubting whether the government actually knows how to use rate of return results as a guide to policy formulation. First, as Robin Marris (1985) points out, if rate of return is indeed this high then the government should be expanding, not contracting, the university system — labour market signals should be bringing about change in educational policy. Second, calculations of social rates of return should be made for different degrees. The government believes that the economy 'needs' more engineers. Why, then, does it not demonstrate this fact by showing that the social rate of return to an engineering degree is higher than, for example, a sociology or an arts degree? Maybe it is because it places no credence in the signals received from the market. Certainly there is evidence that industry places a high value on the 'generalist skills of non-science based degree courses'. As Bill Hughes, Chairman of the CBI (Scotland) 1985 stated 'The precise discipline is less significant than the abilities which are tested and proved in a good honours degree', and more generally of degrees he said 'quality is enhanced or diminished by the extent to which personal qualities are developed'.

On top of all this remain the well rehearsed problems of using rate of return results as a guide to policy making. Very briefly they are: that they take no account of externalities or the consumption benefits of education, that they are based on cross-sectional data which may be no guide to the future, and that, as we have said, they assume earnings are an adequate proxy for productivity, and that the increased earnings of the more educated are a result of their education rather than class, ability or luck.

The government seems much more influenced by international comparisons in its education policy making. It appears to believe — as did the early Science Committees, Lord Crowther-Hunt and Sir Monty Finniston — that we are economically outperformed by our industrial competitors because they have invested more wisely, in qualitative and quantitative terms, in education generally, and in higher education in particular. This naive faith in the value of international comparisons flies in the face of all the available empirical evidence and lacks any theoretical validity.

At the heart of this belief of the value of international comparisons lies the idea that there is a world 'manpower growth path'. But the massive OECD study of 1970 and other studies, such as Layard and Saigal's (1966), establish that there is no systematic link between education, however measured, and economic growth. The most recent study by Hicks of LDC's (1980) which examines the relationship between life expectancy and literacy and economic growth turns out, as so many similar studies before it, to merely establish a correlation but not a causal relationship between literacy rates and growth.

The government and industry are fond of asserting that one area in which this country lags behind competitors, and thus in economic performance, is in the number of qualified engineers. But it is by no means certain that this country does suffer from a shortage of engineers as is claimed so often by industry and the government. As Hansard shows (29 January 1986) our output of engineering graduates compares favourably with most of our competitors. However, even if we had relatively fewer engineers and educated workers than in other countries this would not mean that we could infer any educational policy implications, unless there is a 'world manpower growth path'.

For all economies to be on the same 'manpower growth path' we must assume similar factor endowments, that price and wage relativities are either the same or have no effect on employment patterns, that countries operate with the same production functions, that productivity changes will occur at the same rate, and that social, cultural and political differences have no impact on production patterns between countries. It seems hardly surprising that the empirical evidence lends so little support for the validity of this approach when it is so obviously conceptually invalid.

Is the government aware of this? It does not appear so from its public statements about the need to emulate our competitors' education (and training) policies.

The Economic Value of Education

One of the central questions in the economics of education concerns the relationship between education, earnings and productivity. On the one hand there is the human capital notion that more educated people earn, on average, more than less educated people (supported by empirical evidence from countries around the world) and that these higher earnings result from their additional education because it has raised their relative productivity. On the other hand there is the 'screening hypothesis' which accepts the first part of the human capital proposition, that the more educated earn more, but asserts that this is because the more educated possess greater innate productive skills and this is why they are more productive and are paid more. All that education does is to identify for the employer those with greater natural abilities, hence the name — 'screening hypothesis'.

The difference between the two views of education's role can be expressed diagramatically.

Figure 1

(a) Human Capital Model   (b) Screening Model

Education → Productivity earnings   Education ---→ Productivity earnings
                                          ↖   ↗
                                          Ability

In model (a) education leads directly to greater productivity and earnings. In model (b) the solid lines are from ability to education and to productivity. The role of education is merely to identify these abilities for potential employers, hence the broken arrow.

The 'screening hypothesis' presents a serious challenge to educational policy makers because it implies that the vast expenditure on education, and higher education in particular, is adding nothing to the labour market value of graduates. Its only function is to screen, at enormous expense, for students with pre-existing abilities. The net social value of education then turns out to be the difference between the social costs of education and the costs that would have been incurred, by society and by employers, had no sorting been provided by the education system.

A great deal of attention has been given in the literature to the problem of how to 'test' for 'screening'. The problem of testing stems principally from the fact that the predictions of the 'screening hypothesis' are the same as the predictions of human capital theory — higher earnings result from additional education. Thus to refute, or confirm, the competing explanations of the education-earnings relationship economists have had to devise subtler and, often, indirect tests of the models. A further complication arises because the 'screening model' comes in a number of similar, but not identical, forms: 'certification', 'signalling', the 'diploma disease', 'educational inflation'. For simplicity we will confine discussion here to the model described earlier, namely, that education screens for pre-existing, innate abilities and it is these abilities that make the educated more productive, and thus paid more, in the labour market (see Arrow, 1973, for an elaboration of the model).

We will not discuss all of the attempts to test the 'screening' model, but will briefly describe and comment on the more important of them. The first and most obvious 'test' that was attempted made use of existing empirical work on earnings functions. Earnings functions attempt to identify the independent effects on earnings of such factors as schooling, ability and social class. If innate ability is measured in these tests then it should be possible to disentangle its independent effect on earnings from that of schooling. Psacharopoulos (1975) reviews a large number of studies and concludes that education accounts, on average, for nearly 80 per cent of the variance of earnings. 'The overall average value of alpha is equal to 0.77. In other words, regardless of the level of education or the ability — plus other factors distinction, education is responsible for over three-quarters of observed earnings differentials' (p. 54). There are two reasons why these results cannot be taken as a refutation of the screening model. The first concerns the validity and reliability of ability tests themselves. Hindley and Owen (1978), using data from a longitudinal study, found very wide variations in the IQ scores of their sample, 'half the children will change by more than 10 points, and a quarter by 20 points or more' (p. 346). The second reason for rejecting these findings as a satisfactory test and refutation of screening stems from the use of such ability tests as a proxy for innate *productive ability.* It is this innate ability whose effect must be tested and nobody has yet devised an adequate measure of it.

Let us turn to other empirical tests of screening. Layard and Psacharopoulos (1974) derive inferences from Arrow's model and devise three tests 'in the spirit' of the screening model. First, the Arrow model postulates that education provides two principal screens — admission of the student to a course of study and successful (or unsuccessful) completion of that course of study. If education screens in this fashion, the rate of return to dropouts should be lower than the return to individuals who successfully complete their course of study. Surveying a number of empirical studies, Layard and Psacharopoulos could find no strong support for this proposition. While this finding does not support the screening model as put forth by Arrow it is not necessarily inconsistent with models which include an entire vector of schooling activity, including years of education, as potential signals to employers. We might add that it lends little support to the human capital model either.

A second inference Layard and Psacharopoulos draw from screening models is that, controlling for ability, the effect of education credentials on earnings should diminish as the employer gains first-hand experience of the employee, while the returns to productive ability should rise. This inference implies that employers systematically overpredict the effect of education on the productivity of the average worker. Rather, one might expect to observe increased variance in pay over time, though not necessarily decreased average pay.

Their survey of the empirical literature suggests that just the opposite is true. This finding, however, is not necessarily injurious to the screening hypothesis if employers in addition to offering high starting pay to individuals with more education also provide them with more specific on-the-job training. No conclusive evidence is available on this point but evidence of the existence of internal labour markets, for example, among the more educated, would make it probable that firms would be prepared to pay for the training of their workers. There is some evidence for the existence of internal labour markets in the USA (see Doeringer and Piore, 1971) and in the UK (see Mace, 1979).

A third inference from Arrow's model is that if education acts merely as a screening device then ultimately it will not be demanded when alternative, cheaper methods of screening are developed. In fact, the prediction is that it is in the interests of employers to develop these cheaper methods as with the prevailing system they have to pay enhanced salaries to graduates and other highly qualified people. If the cost of providing an alternative screen was less than the discounted earnings differentials between, say, graduates and non-graduates, then it should be in the employer's interests to provide this screen.

The employer, though, does not have to pay for the screening provided by education. It is a public subsidy. It may also be that the costs of devising such an alternative screen are prohibitively expensive — Wiles (1974) inclines to this view. It might also be that, as Layard and Psacharopoulos argue, no test has been devised because it is education itself that augments workers' productivity and any test prior to graduation would thus be an irrelevance.

There may be another reason why we have not seen the development of large-scale alternative screening devices, particularly those designed to select non-graduates. This is that more and more socio-economic class A and B occupations now expect the minimum entry requirement to be an honours degree. Selection then occurs afterwards by a series of employer-devised tests and observation of graduate competence in performing work functions. In these circumstances, the non-graduates are excluded from the outset.

It is certainly true, as Lazear (1977) states, that 'valid methods for separating screening from productivity-augmenting views of education are hard to come by' (p. 254). But it is necessary that some attempt to devise such a method is made, for as Winkler (1984) points out 'Screening models suggest that both efficiency and equity may be adversely affected by screening. Under some assumptions, the models have extreme policy implications such as the abolition of higher education or the imposition of taxes to secure the private cost of education'.

For myself I think considerable insight into the importance of the productivity augmenting effects of education can be gleaned in ways that have received far too little treatment in the screening literature. In the first place direct evidence of the skills used in the work place and their relationship to skills, cognitive and affective, acquired through education could be obtained. Some evidence of this relationship is intuitively obvious in professional education and there is some empirical evidence for this in, for example, Mace and Taylor (1975) who examined the education and work skills relationship for engineers. Such studies will provide only minimum evidence of the productivity effects of education since they will take no account of all the productive attributes developed by education, particularly 'trainability'. (Thurow, 1972, argues that this is *the* most important function of education).

Another line of enquiry would be to examine the competitiveness of labour markets. The importance of this line of enquiry is that if competition does exist in labour markets, it will certainly answer the question as to whether the higher earnings of the more educated are because they are more productive — an assumption made by both screenists and human capital theorists. The establishment of competition in the labour market will also strengthen the point made by Psacharopoulos and Layard that in such labour market conditions there is every incentive for employers, or agents on their behalf, to devise tests of ability prior to attendance at university. Thus they could secure the innately able more cheaply and for a longer period than is currently the case. Blaug (1972) suggests this line of enquiry.

The question of the competitiveness of labour markets is important in consideration of the government's training policies so we shall leave further discussion of it until the next section.

Government Training Policy

The MSC is receiving some billion pounds annually in the expectation that money spent by it will provide training/education opportunities that will increase the employment prospects, mainly of the young, and concomitantly increase national output. (Incidentally, since those on MSC courses are not registered as unemployed it also dramatically improves unemployment figures). The government is also compelling universities, and public sector higher education, to alter the relative proportions of arts and science students; the numbers on science and engineering courses are to rise relative to the total. Within schools, TVEI and CPVE are being introduced to ensure that pupils doing these courses are provided with vocationally relevant skills.

Quite clearly the government considers that the education system has failed to provide the industrial fodder that employers' opinions, international comparisons and government ideology consider desirable. The education system has, it would appear, failed and the government, or its agents, are now compelled to become more directive in terms of the school curriculum and the ways in which money is allocated between LEAs, the DES and MSC — the fact that the MSC has become such an important educational spender implies that schools, further education colleges, local education authorities and the DES have all failed. The fact that the University Grants Committee (UGC) and the National Advisory Body (NAB) are being given more precise instructions by the government means that they too, and their servants, the universities and polytechnics, have also failed.

A number of questions about this switch in educational spending policy need to be answered. Is it that the education system is failing to provide the required manpower because it is inculcating the wrong abilities, or skills, or both? A cursory glance at labour market indicators contained in the New Earnings Survey, results from the General Household Survey, and UCCA reports on the first destination of graduates suggests that both employment and earnings prospects increase with educational qualifications. Moreover, qualifications not only increase these prospects but also the prospect for future training. 'The LFS (Labour Force Survey) showed that those in employment with a previous qualification were ten times more likely to receive training than those with no previous qualification' (Labour Market Quarterly, February, 1986).

It would appear from the behaviour of firms that educational qualifications indicate enough for them to offer higher pay and greater training opportunities to those who possess them than to those who do not. Perhaps, on the other hand it is that the education system is doing something useful, but that it is not doing it well enough. Hence the need to reallocate resources within education and between education and training. There appears from government policy to be a 'need' to vocationalize education. If this merely means providing better information about labour market prospects and broadening the range of experience of pupils and students this may be acceptable. However, if it means changing the curriculum, structure and control of education in the country it needs to be carefully examined.

The Economist of 21 March 1986 suggests that changes are needed. It argues that academic education needs to improve in order to ensure that we have a more 'educated' workforce. (This country is compared to a number of our competitors which raises the problem of the value of international comparisons that we discussed earlier.) However, this does not seem to be what lies behind present government policy which is not to improve academic skills, but to improve vocational skills. It appears that the 'vocational school fallacy' so brilliantly exposed by Foster twenty years ago is looming larger that ever in Britain in the 1980s (Foster, 1961).

The fallacy essentially concerns three, not unrelated, factors in education: student aspirations, educational facilities and the way that labour markets operate. Student educational aspirations will be determined by labour market signals (see Williams and Gordon, 1982) and by the consumption aspects of education. As pointed out earlier the signals from the labour market suggest students should get more academic education to improve their labour market prospects, and not necessarily in science based subjects. We will ignore the fact, as the government always does, that education might serve more than the narrowly defined 'economic needs' of the economy.

Secondly, can education provide the vocational and training experience that employers seek? To do so requires a massive injection of retrained teaching staff, school buildings and teaching equipment. This the government has not provided and even if it did, as employers readily concede, no 'specific' training provided will usually compare with training on the job. Training on the job, of course, includes more than learning specific skills. It is also an induction into the ethos of the firm and it also provides employers with an opportunity to evaluate their employees.

The government would find it of interest to examine the results of a recent World Bank study of diversified curricula (Psacharopoulos and Loxley, 1985). Although it relates to LDCs it does point up the need to examine very carefully the costs and benefits involved in vocationalizing the curriculum. There is no evidence that the government has done this.

Finally, to turn to the labour market itself. We have already discussed the importance of labour market signals: unemployment rates, vacancy rates and, of course, earnings. But there is a more important question: how does the labour market operate? If no substitution possibilities exist for changing occupational/education ratios and capital/labour ratios, if employment practices are determined by technology and not by relative prices, if the supply of educated labour does not influence existing manpower practices, if future technological changes are predictable and will not alter existing education/occupation relationships, if the future growth of the economy is known, if international exchange rate movements, interest rates and goods and service markets are predictable — if in the highly unlikely event that all these assumptions hold, then there would perhaps be some sense in pursuing a training policy which is based on the 'vocational school fallacy' and, more fundamentally, on the totally discredited 'manpower requirements' type of approach to educational planning.

Ahamad and Blaug (1973) present all the theoretical arguments and much empirical evidence for rejecting this method of planning. Is the government cognizant of their arguments and evidence or does it have new evidence and arguments to refute theirs? If so, many of us in the field of educational planning would love to hear of it.

Concluding Comments

In this chapter we have considered three questions concerning education/training and its links with the labour market. The link between these three questions was the underlying assumption of education/training as a generator of *productive* attributes within individuals. If the government is genuinely interested in pursuing educational policies that will promote economic development it is clear that the primary question it must address is how the labour market functions. Once this has been done the potential for education/training to raise productivity, employment and economic growth will be better understood. All of the questions raised in this chapter will not be answered by such analysis, but it will be a great deal better than the current position of pursuing policies which are often contradictory and rarely, if ever, based upon any systematic analysis, conceptual or empirical, of human capital and labour market theories.

If we did discover by labour market analysis that the human capital explanation of the link between education, earnings and productivity held, then this would certainly be a help in the formulation of educational policies to promote economic growth. However, it should be regarded as only *one* input into the educational policy making process. We must never lose sight of the fact that education may serve other functions, such as those related to equity, socialization and political interests whose importance to the creation of a 'worthwhile' society may often take precedence over the 'narrower' questions with which economists tend to be obsessed.

Changing Patterns of Educational Finance and Their Anticipated Effects on Institutional Behaviour and Educational Outcomes

Gareth Williams

Adam Smith and Milton Friedman

The education 'cuts' between the mid-1970s and mid-1980s have been widely discussed and are the subject of numerous studies. Although there is far from universal agreement about the causes of financial stringency, it is broadly accepted that a combination of falling school rolls, government attempts to limit public expenditure generally and a lessening of the political priority accorded to education, confronted by rigidities in staffing and buildings, brought acute financial problems and loss of morale to most sectors of the education service. Much less widely discussed are the diversification of the sources of income for educational institutions and the changes in the mechanisms through which schools, colleges and universities receive their funds. These changes in the sources and mechanisms of finance are likely to be more significant for educational policy and institutional management in the long run than restrictions on overall expenditure levels. Changes in the arrangements for sharing the financial burdens between central and local government, the increased use of specific funding by both the MSC and the DES, and some shift towards private sources of funds are having, and are likely to continue to have, marked effects on incentives within education and, hence, on the patterns of pupil and student demand and the organizational behaviour of schools, universities and colleges.

In this chapter three main models of finance for educational institutions are outlined and this is followed by a discussion of the patterns of financial and other incentives likely to be associated with each. Subsequently, some important recent changes in schools, further education and higher education are summarized and predictions are made about the likely effects of these changes.

The effect of different models of finance on the behaviour of educational institutions was first discussed by Adam Smith in his essay, 'Of the expense of the institutions for the education of the youth', which forms one of the many appendices to Book V of *The Wealth of Nations*. Smith identifies three ways in which schools and universities may receive their income. First, they can be financed 'from the interest of some sum of money allotted and put under the management of trustees for this particular purpose'. Second, educational institutions can be subject to the authority of, and by implication financed by, what Smith describes as 'an extraneous jurisdiction'. Third, they may depend on the 'fees or honoraries of the scholars'.

The world has, of course, changed considerably during the past 200 years. However, Smith's analysis of these three models, despite the eighteenth century language, still has considerable relevance to the finance and management of the education service today. Of institutions which receive guaranteed sources of funding independently of their performance he writes: 'The endowment of schools and colleges have necessarily diminished more or less the necessity of application in their teachers. Their subsistence ... is evidently derived from a fund altogether independent of their success and reputation in their particular professions. If (the teacher) is naturally active and a lover of labour, it is his interest to employ that activity in any way from which he can derive some advantage rather than in the performance of his duty from which he can derive none'. He then goes on to make the well known remark that 'in the University of Oxford, the greater part of the public professors have, for these many years, given up altogether even the pretence of teaching'. Smith was, of course, not the only observer to notice the sloth and apathy of eighteenth century Oxford. Edward Gibbon, for example, tells that his tutor 'neither gave nor sought to give him more than one lesson'. However, Smith was the first to conclude that 'the stagnation of learning which prevailed in the wealthy universities of England was due at bottom to nothing but their wealth, because it was distributed on a bad system' (Rae, 1895).

Smith's strictures on 'extraneous jurisdiction' over the resources of educational institutions are less frequently quoted but no less pertinent.

If the authority to which he (the teacher) is subject resides, not so much in the body corporate of which he is a member, as in some other extraneous persons — in the Bishop of the Diocese for example; or the Governor of the Province; or, perhaps in some Minister of State — it is not indeed in this case very likely that he will be suffered to neglect his duty altogether. All that such superiors can, however, force him to do, is to attend upon his pupils a certain number of hours, that is, to give up a certain number of lectures in the week or in the year. What these lectures shall be must still depend on the diligence of the teacher ... an extraneous jurisdiction of this kind, besides, is liable to be exercised both ignorantly and capriciously. In its nature it is arbitrary and discretionary, and the persons who exercise it, neither attending upon the lectures of the teacher themselves, nor perhaps understanding the sciences which it is his business to teach, are seldom capable of exercising it with judgment ... the person subject to such jurisdiction is necessarily degraded by it, and, instead of being one of the most respectable, is rendered one of the meanest and most contemptible persons in the society. It is by powerful protection only that he can effectually guard himself against the bad usage to which he is at all times exposed ....

Smith was much more impressed by those educational institutions in which

the salary makes but a part, and frequently but a small part, of the emoluments of the teacher, of which the greater part arises from the honoraries or fees of his pupils. The necessity of application, though always more or less diminished, is not in this case entirely taken away. Reputation in his profession is still of some importance to him, and he still has some dependency upon the affection, gratitude and favourable report of those who have attended upon his instructions.

On this basis Smith speaks highly of the old dame schools, depending as they did partly on the fees paid by pupils. He also remarked upon the greater enthusiasm of both students and teachers in schools of music and dancing and schools for riding and fencing which were no doubt popular forms of continuing education in eighteenth century Scotland. However, Smith was probably most influenced by his early experiences in Edinburgh as a successful public lecturer whose income depended almost entirely on what he could earn from his students. In contrast to England, higher education was very popular in the Edinburgh of the eighteenth century. 'As the lectures of the professors are open to everyone and the expense of attending them very trifling, it is in the power of almost every tradesman to furnish his son with that instruction which is most adapted to his taste and capacity' (E Topham, Letters from Edinburgh, cited in Fay, 1956).

Modern discussion of the effects of different financial mechanisms on the economic behaviour of educational institutions derives from Friedman's *Essays in Positive Economics* (1953) and was given a boost in Britain with the publication of E G West's *Education and the State* (1965) which drew a distinction between state *finance* of education and state *provision* of education. Broadly West's case was that while there may be case on equity grounds for some state subsidy of pupils and students, there was not a strong case in either equity or efficiency for public provision of education. It is more efficient, claimed West, to subsidize students, if necessary, and to let them purchase places from institutions that competed for their services. Clearly, this case was heavily influenced by the earlier work of Friedman (for example, Friedman, 1953) which led to the almost continuous debate from 1960 onwards about the likely benefits from a scheme of vouchers for school pupils and loans as the most efficient and equitable form of financial support for students in higher education. These arguments have been periodically reviewed by Woodhall (1970, 1977, 1982a and 1982b). Much of the debate about vouchers and loans has concentrated on the equity issues involved and the related issues of allocative efficiency. Broadly, it is claimed by the proponents of vouchers and loans that subsidy of individuals rather than subsidy of institutions leads to a pattern of provision that is more likely to accord with the real wishes of the community as a whole. However, there are also effects on technical efficiency. Competition between institutions for students who are consciously seeking value for money will, it has been claimed, result in greater efficiency by the institutions in the use of their physical plant, academic staff and other resources.

Financing Mechanisms and Models of Resource Allocation

A financing mechanism is both a means of allocating resources so that learning can occur and a channel for messages between providers and users of finance. Budget estimates and accounts of expenditure are among the most useful indicators of the intentions and performance of an educational institution. It is possible to identify numerous different ways by which resources are allocated from the ultimate users of educational services — families and households — to the ultimate supplier, the teacher in the classroom. At the national level Peacock *et al* (1968) set out the flows by which schools and higher education institutions can receive funds (see figure 1). More recently, there has been a growth of interest in the different forms of resource allocation within schools, for example, Simkins (1986).

As in their management styles generally, heads can be authoritarian, consultative or democratic in their allocation of school resources regardless of where the funds come from. However, despite this complicating factor it is convenient and useful to follow Adam Smith and group the external funding mechanisms into three main groups, and we may also follow Smith in his hypothesis that the mechanisms of external funding have a considerable effect on the organizational behaviour of institutions and on the educational activities that take place within them.

In the first model the institution has control over a significant part of its expenditure and can determine its own educational priorities. In its extreme form this is the model of the endowed university or school which has a considerable amount of financial and hence educational freedom as a result of its ownership of property or other investments. Usually this model involves the existence of a Board of Trustees or Governors whose main responsibility is to ensure that the school or college conforms to the requirements of the various bequests that constitute the source of its endowment income and that the management acts in accordance with the regulations governing the charitable status that educational institutions usually find it convenient to acquire. In most cases also there is a Charter or a Statute which establishes the legal basis of the endowed institution which must be adhered to. Within these constraints, which are usually in practice pretty broad, the endowed school or college has very considerable freedom over its use of resources.

This is the model which in broad terms the UGC adopted for the funding of universities in Britain in 1920–1980. Universities were given their recurrent funds in the form of block grants which, within broad limits, they were free to spend as they wished within the terms of their charters. It is also the model for resource allocation in voluntary-aided and the former direct grant schools. Within overall limits set by local education authorities (and nationally by

Gareth Williams

Figure 1: Flows of Funds in Education

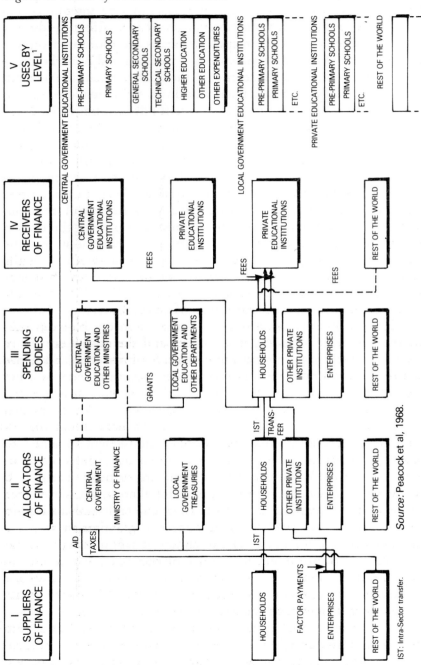

Source: Peacock et al, 1968.

the government) schools were able to allocate resources largely in accordance with their own curricular and other priorities.

In the second model a powerful external funding agency allocates resources to several institutions and has considerable monopoly power with respect to any one of them. Often, but not always, the external agency owns the institution. This is broadly the model of the local authority maintained schools and colleges. The external agency has responsibility for ensuring that public funds are properly used and establishes regulatory mechanisms to assure itself that the public interest is being met. These regulatory mechanisms are likely to be seen as bureaucratically intrusive within the institutions.

In the third model there are many sources of finance, and academic institutions in effect sell services to them. In the extreme the services are sold to individual students. Each school or college receives income from several different sources so no single external agency can control its internal activities. An institution must respond to some outside influences in order to survive but within broad limits it can determine its own strategies about which services it will sell at which combination of price and quality. This is broadly the model of the independent sector of education.

There is clearly not a one-for-one relationship between these models of external funding mechanisms and the machinery for resource allocation within school or college. Simkins (1986) has shown that secondary schools with the same mechanisms of external funding can adopt 'creeping incrementalism', 'benevolent despotism', 'open market arrangements' or 'formulae' as ways of allocating their capitation allowances. However, there can be little doubt that the methods by which institutions receive their finance do affect the power relationships within them. Broadly our hypothesis is that the endowment or block grant form of funding is most likely to be associated with collegial forms of management within the institution (see, for example, Clark, 1984). The regulatory external funding agency is likely to favour bureaucratic or authoritarian forms of management and, finally, if the institution derives a substantial part of its income from the sale of services market relationships are also likely to be prominent in its internal organization. For example, in a university a professor who secures large research grants usually carries more weight than his less entrepreneurial colleagues.

It is to be expected that educational institutions that control their own resource allocation decisions will evolve participatory styles of management in which resource allocation decisions have an authority legitimized by consensus, or at least compromise, amongst those to whom they apply. Any organization such as a school or university which depends on high-level professional skills will operate most smoothly if there is a substantial measure of participation in its management procedures. Independence in financial matters frees it both from dependence on consumers and from external regulatory agencies. Of course there are problems in consensus-building: these have often been illustrated in academic novels. The departmental meeting, the college council, the Senate, are all standard literary set pieces. Constructing a consensus is time-consuming and erratic in its outcomes. It can sharpen conflicts, or it can lead to mutual toleration of incompetence and to a neglect of the interests of those who are not part of the consensus. However the fundamental weakness of collegial forms of management is their ability to resist innovation and change.

If a collegial model is working well, a professional ethos and high academic standards would be prominent. If working less well, the protection of vested interests within the institution will be more evident. Adam Smith took the cynical view: 'The discipline of colleges and universities is in general contrived, not for the benefit of students, but for the interest, or more properly speaking, the ease, of the masters. Its object is, in all cases, to maintain the authority of the master, and whether he neglects or performs his duty, to oblige the student in all cases to behave to him as if he performed it with the greatest of diligence and ability'. In short, pupils and students are privileged to be at such an institution and they must accept what it offers. However, there is also one great advantage of financial independence. The basic truth that 'there is no such thing as a free lunch' is likely to be apparent to all members of any institution which controls its own resources. If the Science Department has more equipment there is less available for the Craft Department. If the professor travels first-class on the train, fewer lecturers can travel and so on.

Problems are particularly apparent when resources are not increasing. Where expansion ensures that innovations do not damage the existing interests of others, consensus can mean simply the aggregation of individual claims for increased resources. When resources are scarce, decisions must be more consciously collective since expansion of some activities can occur only if there is reduction in others. In general, collegial forms of management are most likely to be successful in institutions which do not comprise too wide a range of interests. The greater the variety of interests within a school or college, the more it is likely that compromise can be achieved only around the existing balance of power, and the more likely it is that some individuals or groups will see themselves as being in conflict with the institution as a whole. In such a situation resource allocation decisions must be taken in the light of a responsible assessment of their possible implications for the institution as a whole. Collective decision-making in a period of adaptation without growth requires high quality, proactive management to ensure both that decisions are reached and that once taken they are implemented.

The bureaucratic model also, has advantages and disadvantages. Good academic leadership, supported by centralized management structures and an effective bureaucracy, can mean efficient resource use and rapid response to a changing environment. Bureaucratic procedures can protect the quality of education by ensuring that resources are adequate for the tasks which operating units are asked to perform. In recent years the activities of the Schools Inspectorate and the CNAA have helped to protect the financial situation of schools and colleges by showing that resources were inadequate for the tasks which the institutions were being expected to perform. The possible disadvantages are, however, no less obvious. For example, authoritarian management can impose innovation but in so doing it neglects the stage of the innovation process in which proposed changes are tested in debate with colleagues, which can be a valuable part of the process of selecting ideas which are worth pursuing. Debating change and trying to build coalitions to promote it help to distinguish innovations which are worthwhile from those which are merely a convenient response to some temporary external pressure.

There are particular problems in organizations such as schools and colleges where there is specialist expertise throughout the bureaucratic hierarchy. The relationship between managers and managed in a bureaucracy is frequently one of conflict. Students and teachers use the bureaucratic rules to serve their own interests, and the management, with equal justification, makes new rules to close what are seen as loopholes. However, if professional expertise is concentrated near the base of the bureaucratic pyramid it is almost impossible to implement effective resource allocation rules without a substantial measure of positive support from those who have to conform to the regulations. This can be seen clearly in the purchase of specialized equipment. Only specialists are likely to know which type of pottery kiln or photo-spectrometer is the most appropriate for the task. Since, in general, there is some relationship between price and quality the natural tendency will be to claim the highest quality and therefore probably the most expensive equipment for which authorization can be obtained, unless there are obvious financial benefits to close colleagues from financial restraint. In general, under bureaucratic allocation procedures claims for resources will be made with little concern or awareness of the nature of overall resource constraints.

The obvious weaknesses of collegial and bureaucratic models of organizational behaviour have led several observers to propose the market as a way of avoiding the inertia of the former and the conflict of the latter. The intellectual attraction of the market is that resource allocation decisions are taken out of the hands of both politicians and self-interested professionals. They are determined instead by independent decisions of many different consumers of educational services. The market circumvents the technical problem of efficient resource allocation in education, namely that the 'outputs' are almost impossible to define and measure in any operational way. Output becomes what consumers are prepared to buy. Effectively, the power which is in the hands of the politicians and administrators in the bureaucracy and of professional educationists in the collegial model, is possessed in the market by students and pupils, and their families.

One issue is the extent to which it is desirable that such power should be in the hands of consumers of educational services. If access to education was simply bought and sold, only students with substantial incomes would be able to afford to buy it. This difficulty can be overcome through subsidy. Pupils can pay fees but have them reimbursed by the state. That is the essence of the voucher system which is proposed from time to time and which has been the subject of experiments in various countries. However, a more intractable difficulty with the market model results from lack of information about the implications of educational decisions. If markets are to operate properly, consumers must be well-informed about the likely outcomes of their purchases, the effects on the decisions of one individual must be independent of decisions of other individuals, and consumers must have the opportunity of learning from experience. In education most decisions are open to any individual once only and they are irreversible, ultimate outcomes are not apparent for a considerable length of time, and they are strongly affected by decisions taken at the same time by other pupils and students. Supporters of the market in education claim that the provision of advisory and counselling services independent of schools and colleges would enable students to make better informed decisions. However, even professional counselling cannot fully overcome the problems of the irreversibility and interdependence of individual education decisions. For example, if students are advised that there will be plenty of job opportunities for information technologists in the 1990s but no other steps are taken to plan numbers the end result may well be a surplus of information technologists and much wasted investment, as well as personal frustration.

The main advantages claimed for the market is the incentive it provides to respond to changing external circumstances. This can, however, result in deterioration of quality where it is difficult to specify the quality of output and where purchasers of services are not well informed about the technical specification of the product they are buying. This danger may be particularly acute when institutional survival is at stake and universities, colleges and schools need to compete fiercely to ensure the use of their capacity at an economic level. The present efforts of heads of many secondary schools to maintain their recruitment from their local primary schools and the emerging competition amongst non-advanced further education colleges for the dwindling number of 16–19-year-olds provide examples of cases where the requirements of institutional survival may be put above the best interests of individual pupils and students.

A Programme of Empirical Research

Research in this area needs to be developed on three main points.

The first is an examination of the extent of changing patterns of educational finance since the mid-1960s and a comparative review of different patterns of finance in other countries. In the schools sector the most obvious shifts in funding of recent years have been the trend towards increasing school autonomy with regard to the use of capitation allowances, the TVEI programme, the increased use of parental contribution to supplement capitation allowances and the new specific grants of the DES. In recent years a number of LEAs (ILEA, Cambridgeshire, East Sussex, Kingston-upon-Thames and Solihull) have experimented with delegation of financial control as a means of enhancing educational performance. The Audit Commission Handbooks (1983 and 1984a) stressed that value for money is more likely to be achieved if budgets are linked to cost centres — of which individual schools form by far the largest component. They proposed that cost centre 'managers' should be held accountable for achieving the agreed service standards within budgeted costs. External auditors as part of their mandatory value for money (VFM) work will be following up in the Audit Commission Report and examining the scope for increased financial delegation — particularly in secondary schools. The government's Green Paper of May 1984 (DES, 1984a) *Parental Influence at School* added a slightly new dimension to the debate by proposing that governors should also be involved in ensuring value for money. Another significant innovation is the way in which the Manpower Services Commission monitors expenditure by LEAs and schools contracted into the Technical and Vocational Education Initiative. For example LEA-appointed project coordinators for TVEI have clear financial control procedures to follow based on principles established by MSC.

Within further and higher education there are several examples of more fundamental shifts in the balance between public and private finance. These include full-cost fees for overseas students, industrial support for research, the creation of 'science parks' with significant private funding and the development of short, mainly vocational, courses for external sponsors. These all represent new or expanded sources of funds. There have also been important changes in the mechanisms by which public funds are allocated to universities, polytechnics and colleges. For example, the funding of advanced further education has been fundamentally changed as a result of the capping of the pool for advanced further education (AFE), the creation of the National Advisory Body (NAB) and the adoption of a programme-weighted unit of resource as a basis for the allocation of finance. A substantial part of the income of further education colleges is now channelled through the Manpower Services Commission on the basis of criteria different from those normally used by local education authorities. An increasing proportion of the income of universities, polytechnics and some colleges is now derived from full-cost fees, either from overseas students or for short courses, especially post-experience vocational courses which are likely to grow considerably in importance during the next ten years.

Simple descriptive studies will have considerable value simply in mapping the changing patterns of educational finance and illustrating the extent of the changes and their effects on patterns of pupil and student demand. In addition, the following practical policy issues need to be explored: (a) the effects on demand and institutions' response to it if subsidy is channelled through students rather than given directly to institutions; (b) how financial burdens are shared between central and local government, individual students and their families, employers and other funding sources; (c) the effects of 'secret' and 'open' formulae as a basis for the funding of institutions.

The second constituent of the research programme being advocated would consist of independent, but ideally comparable, empirical case studies which examine the effects of changing sources and mechanisms of finance and methods on individual institutions or groups of institutions. These studies should throw light on the question of whether changes in funding mechanisms have had identifiable effects on the internal allocation of resources, on the manageability of institutions, and on their degree of response to outside influences including pupil and student demand, the needs of employers and the national interest as expressed through public policy-making bodies.

The arrangement whereby overseas students now pay full-cost fees illustrates the changes that can be anticipated and the advantages and disadvantages of market mechanisms in education. On the one side, full-cost fees have produced many examples of entrepreneurial activity in further and higher education. There is no doubt that universities and colleges are making much greater efforts to meet the needs of their overseas students than they were in 1979. On the other hand, there have been suggestions that some establishments are sacrificing academic integrity for the income that is generated by increased numbers of overseas students. Representatives of universities and other colleges deny this but one interesting indicator is that the proportion of overseas applicants accepted by the universities through UCCA has increased from 24 per cent in 1979 to 35 per cent in 1985. This suggests, but by no means proves, that universities may now be less rigorous in the qualifications they require from overseas students who pay high fees.

The need for research on the methods of funding higher and further education and the effects of alternative financial mechanisms on institutions and on students is nowhere more obvious than in the confused debate on the role of fees and student financial support. The Robbins Report recommended significant increases in the level of fees in order to expose universities and colleges to the influence of market forces, and thus to increase their efficiency. In general, Robbins believed that it is better to subsidize individuals than institutions and that ultimately greater dependence on fees would protect the autonomy of universities. At the other extreme, the Jarratt Report (CVCP, 1985) has recently expressed doubts about the administrative complexity of the present arrangement for the payment of fees and the arbitrary level at which they are set. Jarratt suggested that it might be preferable if fees were abolished altogether. There is clearly considerable uncertainty about the proper role of fees as a means of financing post-compulsory education but this is a symptom of a more fundamental uncertainty about how costs should be shared and about the desirability and likely effects of alternative ways of raising and distributing finance for post-compulsory education. It is to be hoped that the enquiry into student financial support announced in the summer of 1986 will examine these issues as well as the more obvious question of loans to support the maintenance costs of students.

In fact, since 1970 there have been several important changes in the levels of fees paid by home and overseas students and decisions about them have been taken with no explicit reference to the economic, administrative and educational issues involved. There can be no doubt that full-cost fees for overseas students have had a marked effect on universities' behaviour and that the universities' response has been markedly different from that in the public sector where financial mechanisms are very different. In broad terms, the difference is that universities are able to retain the income generated by the recruitment of overseas students whereas many public sector institutions must surrender this income to their funding bodies and therefore have little incentive to try to expand their recruitment of foreign students.

The trend towards more diversified sources of funding and increased institutional autonomy in the use of resources and the greater institutional competition to obtain them seems likely to continue in Britain, as in many other countries where cost pressures are causing all public education budgets to be examined very carefully. It is important, therefore, to establish reliable procedures for evaluating the effects of changes in the way institutions are funded and resources allocated so that objections to the changes which result merely from the defence of vested interests can be distinguished from those which arise from genuine concern about academic and educational standards.

The third focus for study should be a strengthening of the conceptual models outlined in the first part of this chapter. This theoretical work must both precede and succeed the empirical studies. One practical outcome of the theoretical work once it has been backed up by empirical evidence is to provide a rigorous framework for examining the relationship between policy intentions and policy outcomes. Frequently policy interventions fail to have their intended effects because financial and other incentives encourage activities that were not part of the policy intention. Ultimately, it ought to be possible to draw general empirically verified conclusions about the relationship between financial incentives and educational outcomes. All three of the models outlined in the first two sections can be shown to have both advantages and disadvantages on *a priori* grounds from the point of view of equity, efficiency, institutional autonomy and educational standards. The ultimate aim of the research programme outlined in the third section is to provide a robust, analytical framework and sound empirical evidence to test claims that are made in the economic and policy analytic literature and in the policy debates about the effects of new funding arrangements on the quality, equity and efficiency of educational provision.

The Economics of Post-Compulsory Education

John Pratt

Introduction

No one who has read Paul Johnson's *A History of the Modern World* (Johnson, 1983) can doubt the power of ideas in human affairs. In looking at the present state of post-compulsory education this power is evident, particularly of notions which, if not wholly economic derive from — or are alleged to be derived from — economic principles. The sector has suffered major financial reductions; institutions have merged and closed; government has increasingly directed resources; a new sub-sector concerned with training rather than education has emerged as a major force; and the future holds the prospect of yet more, and more radical development (DES, 1985b).

Whilst it sometimes seems that these developments have been the work of economizers rather than economists, a new range of issues is faced by those who manage, work or study in the institutions and many new terms have entered their daily vocabulary. Amongst these are the problems of managing contraction and financial constraint; the concepts of vocational relevance, of efficiency and value for money; performance indicators; the notion of resource management; the pressures for income generation and entrepreneurialism.

The emergence of issues such as these on the education agenda is evident in research into post-compulsory education. The Society for Research into Higher Education *Abstracts* over the past three years, for example, report more than a dozen references to papers on the problems of planning, resource allocation and management within institutions, and only slightly fewer considering national funding mechanisms, and the (mainly economic) assumptions on which they are based. There are also major research projects financed by the DES in these areas. A study under the direction of Kogan at Brunel University examined the relationship between higher education and the labour market (Roizen and Jepson, 1985); two other studies, under Sizer at Loughborough University and Pratt from North East London Polytechnic and Gill at Sheffield City Polytechnic (Pratt and Gill, 1986) are examining the effects of constraint upon the universities and public sector institutions.

This chapter discusses the impact of these developments on institutions of post-compulsory education. It begins by discussing the effect of economic ideas on national policy for post-compulsory education, which constitutes the context within which institutions have to operate. Because of these developments, concern within institutions has had to concentrate on what might be called the economics of constraint, and the economics of education has reflected this concern too: the literature on the economics and management of constraint is discussed, but most of this chapter discusses the empirical and theoretical studies in this area. The chapter concludes with a consideration of the major issue that these experiences raise.

It is worth noting the areas that have little mention in this chapter — reflecting the emphasis of the economics of education. Most people in post-compulsory education are not found in the universities or the polytechnics, nor even in non-advanced further education but in adult education. This part of the sector has suffered more than most from the chill winds of economies, but there are few studies of the effects. Equally, there are few studies of the large non-advanced FE sector and there is also the vast area of training with its more obvious links with the labour market and different instructional models and financing. Whilst Derbyshire (1985) discusses some of the issues here, it is with higher education that the economics of education has been mainly concerned.

The Economics of Education

In the last few years, the study of the economics of education has been undergoing if not a spiritual crisis at least a period of critical self-analysis.

Blaug, who may reasonably be identified as the main promoter of the economics of education in the UK in the 1960s was, by the early 1980s asking 'Where are we now in the economics of education?' (Blaug, 1985). He identified a ' profound change' in the role

John Pratt

of economists in educational policy making from the 'golden years' of the 1960s when 'no self respecting minister of education would have dreamed of making educational decisions without an economist sitting at his right hand' (well, he is entitled to a little nostalgic exaggeration) to a period of 'new pessimism' when it appeared that many of the optimistic (and mainly egalitarian) theories of the 'first generation' economists of education were refuted by experience. As a result, the 'second generation' emerged prompted by Bowles and Gintis (1976) and other radical economists of education. The notion of the socialization function of the education system and the 'screening hypothesis' became accepted — to varying extents as Blaug shows — and concentrated attention on the relationship between education and the labour market.

Not all economists of education share Blaug's views. Mincer (1984) for example rejects the assertion that education does not contribute to economic growth. Mace (1984) feels that Blaug's view is unduly pessimistic, though he recognizes some of the excessive optimism of the first generation.

Over-pessimistic or over-optimistic, there is scant comfort from these analyses of the recent history of the economics of education for those in the post-compulsory sector. The 'screening hypothesis', even in the 'weak' form accepted by Blaug, suggests that they could be seen merely as ciphers — tools in a system used by employers and society to allocate people to their proper (?) position in the labour market (and society itself) — a scenario the Victorians would have recognized and celebrated. But more significantly for policy in post-school education, the sense that Blaug conveys that education has not delivered the goods, and the change in emphasis of the economics of education to the relationship between higher education and the labour market have not been restricted to economists of education; both have been reflected in government policy, and this in turn affects individual institutions.

Financial Stringency

The sense of disillusion with education, and higher education in particular, has been allied with a distaste for public expenditure, and a concern about efficiency and 'value for money' in the public sector. Post-compulsory education has suffered from stringency as a result. However, although there are few countries in Western Europe where public spending is not being reduced, there is none where it has attained what Neave has called 'such a suicidal level' as in Britain (Neave, 1982). For the universities this programme culminated in the now notorious letter of 1 July 1981 when their recurrent grants were cut by about 17 per cent, with individual institutions losing up to 44 per cent of their grant over the period to 1983/84. For the public sector the period of constraint that began with the 'capping' of the advanced further education (AFE) pool in 1980 was continued and heightened by the planning exercise for 1984/85 of the National Advisory Body for Local Authority Higher Education (as it then was). Spending on polytechnics in real terms was calculated as falling by 17.6 per cent between 1979/80 and 1983/84 (CIPFA, 1984).

The Direction of Education

The increased interest by government in the relationship between education and the labour market is seen in the way that it has become concerned not only with controlling the level of spending on education but also its direction. It has increasingly sought to achieve a closer relationship between the output of post-school institutions and the needs of the economy (see Tarsh, in this volume), and to direct and control spending to achieve better 'value for money'.

It is often forgotten how early these changes began. As Shattock and Rigby (1983) have noted, the universities were surprisingly reluctant to recognize that the golden years for them ended in the early 1970s. By 1972, hence well before Bowles and Gintis, the White Paper (DES, 1972) (mischievously called *Education: A Framework for Expansion*) expressed concern that students should be given skills and knowledge 'related more directly to the decisions that will face them in their careers'. The strictures became more specific in ensuing years: 'Government, industry and the higher education system must work together to match the output of qualified personnel with industry's needs,' according to the Junior Education Minister in 1982 (Waldegrave, 1982). When he appeared before the Select Committee in 1980 the Deputy Secretary at the DES went further, speaking of the idea of a 'broad steer' by government which would 'translate somehow the very specific requirements of the market into very broad subject areas ...' and the hope to be able to 'try to work out from such messages as can be derived from the employment market a subject profile which would be a guiding principle for institutions . . .' (House of Commons, 1980). Although by early 1981 the concept was, at least for the public sector, modified to one of 'delivery' reflecting a concern less for a particular output of particular kinds of manpower, or indeed any particular output in detail' (Jones, S., 1984) than with the management of an efficient and effective system from a national point of view, the tendency to direct was continued and heightened in subsequent policy for both sectors. For universities, the steerage became brutally apparent in the July 1981 cuts, one of whose aims was to achieve a shift of provision towards science and technology. Similarly, in allocating additional funds to universities through 'new blood' posts and in specific initiatives in, for example, biotechnology and information technology, the University Grants Committee (UGC) exercised further central control of university development. There is also increased control of universities' subsequent actions. Institutions which recruited more students in specific subjects than the UGC planned have been told that the Committee 'will require severe reduction in admissions' and may be penalized. Other universities are being told to close departments (UGC, 1983; *THES*, 25 February and 16 December 1983). Similar redirection of research towards the needs of the economy was also announced by the Secretary of State for Education and Science (Joseph, 1983) and the Science and Engineering Research Council (SERC) has indicated that projects with an industrial slant will have the best chance of support even in basic research (*THES*, 18 May 1984). A similar attempt to direct research in the social sciences was evident in the renaming of the Social Science Research Council and its restructuring in 1983 to facilitate the development of research more directly related to social policy and problems.

Within the public sector, the policy of central direction was reflected in the creation of, and implemented through, the National Advisory Body (NAB) in 1982. The creation of the NAB marked a watershed for the public sector bringing together in one body responsibility for advising on both funding and the distribution and approval of courses.

NAB implemented its joint responsibilities nationally for the first time in its planning exercise conducted from September 1982 for the 1984/85 AFE pool allocation, amongst whose aims of the exercise were a wish to give favourable treatment to particular areas of provision in line with the guidance given by the Secretary of State; achieve some geographical redistribution of provision; and protect provision of part-time and sub-degree level courses (NAB,

1985). This too marked a watershed for institutions, with allocations of target student numbers for each institution in each of 14 'programme areas' in line with these criteria, favouring certain subject areas, and an elaborate unit funding mechanism allocating funds to institutions in line with these targets, whilst seeking to improve efficiency and reduce the costs of high spending institutions through a system of subject weightings based on 'best practice' student/staff ratio figures derived from an exercise by Her Majesty's Inspectorate (HMI).

It is also worth recalling that whilst the government was attempting to control the direction of the higher education system and heighten its relationship to the needs of the economy, it was also seeking new and even more direct ways outside the higher education system of intervening and controlling the relationship between qualified people and the labour market. It began to bypass the education system altogether, following to a conclusion the logic of the argument that the system had failed. Whilst finances for higher education have become increasingly scarce, funds have been increasingly devoted to the Manpower Services Commission (MSC) for industrial training. From the point of view of central control, the MSC, as an agency of the central government established in 1973, has obvious advantages, and none of the problems of the dispersed responsibility in the systems of further or higher education. At first this provision could be seen as additional to that of the education system, reflecting the traditional distinction between 'education' and 'training'. But the White Paper *Training for Jobs* (DE/DES, 1984) made clear the government's intention to go further and begin to challenge the primacy of LEAs in further education by allocating — and therefore automatically directing — funds for training on courses hitherto run by local authorities as part of their further education provision.

Implications for Institutions

These developments raise important questions about the economic assumptions on which policy is based, but with which willy-nilly institutions have to cope. We need not detail these here; Mace (in this volume) examines these issues in greater depth; but we can note some of the contradictions that they present for institutions.

It is clear that the concern that higher education should contribute to the economy accepts much of the theory of human capital, that there is a relationship between education and economic growth, and seeks to relate the two factors more closely. But the theory does not imply that such a relationship can be established by directing students and institutions to subjects which are — or are thought should be — in demand. It is not as simple, simplistic or as specific as that, as shown by the 'screening hypothesis' and the history of efforts to relate these variables through manpower planning.

The government has shown that it was aware of the lessons of the economics of education about manpower planning, acknowledging that 'Precise manpower planning is no longer considered feasible' (Carlisle, 1979b). But the increasing dirigisme introduced into the system (paradoxically by a free market government) means that institutions have suffered a substantial loss of autonomy, and find themselves funded for subjects for which they cannot recruit students, and have to reject applicants in disciplines for which there is evident demand.

Notwithstanding (in fact largely because of) the contradictions and complexities, these developments at national level have challenged many of the basic educational, financial and constitutional assumptions on which the system had been operating. The 'rules of the game' for institutions have changed significantly. They face contraction of resources with new constraints upon their ability to respond. This is compounded by uncertainty as planning horizons have been reduced and resource allocation mechanisms have been changed often at short notice to reflect new policy directions, and increasing selectivity in allocation of resources to them.

In the face of these developments, institutions have been forced to direct their attention to their internal management, their strategies for responding to constraint, methods of resource allocation and control, the improvement of efficiency and income generation.

The Economics of Institutions

These issues, too, have been the subject of research and study by economists of education. Indeed, Mace (1984) chides Blaug for omitting the work carried out in these areas in his review of the subject. He goes on to claim that, whilst it may have been overshadowed by the emphasis on external efficiency, the economic value of education, equity effects and education's effect on income, studies on such questions as internal efficiency may be of more value to people working in the field of education planning. He cites work on production function analysis and cost analysis to illustrate this point. But most of the studies of education as a production function, attempting to relate output (such as achievement) against inputs (such as class size) have been of schools; when the Council for National Academic Awards (CNAA) recently tried to prepare a paper on the effect of financial constraint on educational quality it found the research evidence disconcertingly scarce. Cost analyses, concerned with the way costs and outputs are related, have again concentrated more on schools than post-compulsory education. However, there are a number of studies on, for example, optimum sizes of institutions (producing in one case a result for the optimum for USA universities to four significant figures). A conference organized by the SRHE and the DES examined this concept in some detail, and Goodlad (1983), discussing the findings, pointed to a need for further research into mergers and closures, an exploration of the relationship between size of institution and quality and for more data on financial economies. There has been a number of studies of the costs of higher education, most recently by Woodhall and Towse (n.d.) on the effect of cuts in higher education spending on access and costs. As Lockwood (in Lockwood and Davies, 1985) points out, such studies usually reveal the complexity of the inputs, the low substitutability of labour, and the problems of inseparable joint effects of key acts of labour on different outputs. Thus as Mace (1984), Snell (1982) and others have pointed out, they usually rely on inadequate measures of output — indeed use inputs (such as student numbers) as proxies. The proxies give indications of the existence (and occasionally absence) of economies of scale and in the form of student-staff ratios, are widely used as a basis for measuring the 'efficiency' of institutions of post-school education and for allocating resources to them, raising the kinds of problems raised by Cuthbert (in this volume). Woodhall and Towse show that the absence of information on long-run average and marginal costs and concentration in a period of contraction on short-run costs is likely to lead to the wrong planning decisions. Lockwood, nonetheless, argues that 'the use of the economist's approach has improved the understanding of elements in the complexity of the university'. He similarly suggests that economist's idea of the 'market' is of increasing relevance, 'and indicates the complexity of the university', and exemplifies the functioning of a growing number of universities. He sees further insights in the form of open systems theory advocated by Katz and Kahn (1966), viewing institutions in 'constant commerce with their environment' — a concept still often new to some academic bodies.

Whilst this literature offers some useful insights and some awful warnings about the misuse of concepts and may in the long run be 'the most important contribution to education that economists can make' (Cohn, 1979), institutions facing contraction have to manage the problems of the present. In doing this they can draw on a further substantial management literature and on empirical studies of their own responses. What these studies reveal is considerable discrepancy between the advice of the literature and the actual responses of institutions to constraint.

The Management of Constraint

Advice on responding to constraint is not hard to find. The OECD Institutional Management in Higher Education Programme, for example, has produced numerous studies from across the Western world (for example, Jadot *et al*, 1980). The SRHE/Leverhulme series of seminars considered the future of the UK higher education system in the aftermath of the UGC July 1981 cuts and in the run up to the NAB planning exercise for 1984/85, and more recently Lockwood and Davies (1985) produced a substantial book on the 'management challenge' facing universities.

The common advice of these studies is that institutions should plan their responses to constraint; that they should have a clear and agreed set of goals, perhaps a 'mission statement', and allocate their resources and organize their activities in the light of these. The problems of doing this are, of course, recognized. Sizer (1982) remarks that as non-profit organizations universities exist to provide a service rather than make money, so the outcome is not only more difficult to measure but even agreeing what this outcome should be is problematical. But as Norris (1978) argued, taking a management by objectives approach, 'Until the goal question is resolved and meaningful priorities set for institutional policy as a whole, it is impossible to say what is really important for that institution and hence where resources should be allocated.' Lockwood (in Lockwood and Davies, 1985) proposes a corporate planning approach involving statements of institutional mission and objectives, the structuring of activities to meet these broad goals, definitions of timescales, an attempt to forecast future developments particularly outside the institution and a means for implementing these decisions. Sizer (1982; and in this volume) proposes that institutions undergo a stage of portfolio analysis in which they attempt to relate their historic and current performance against likely future needs in society for their services, and draws attention to Doyle and Lynch's (1979) work in applying product portfolio concepts to universities.

Responses to Constraint

There are few signs that institutions implement these suggestions, certainly to the full. Most of the studies of institutional responses to constraint show that institutions tend to react conservatively. Davies and Morgan (1982), drawing on experiences in UK and US universities, discuss the responses in terms of the politics of institutional change, showing how, because of the kinds of institutions they are, universities are reluctant to make far-reaching radical decisions. At first indeed there tends to be a belief that contraction if it occurs will happen elsewhere. Later, as decisions become inevitable, the institution generally moves toward a 'political' model of organizational behaviour from the bureaucratic or collegial model on which it previously operated. The decisions that are reached are usually partial, short range and based on compromise. A study of resource allocation in British universities by Shattock and Rigby (1983) broadly confirms this, though more radical developments are seen in universities which have suffered from substantial budget reductions such as Aston and Salford and which are currently the subject of research by Sizer.

Strategic Planning

The Jarratt Committee offered a very critical description of strategic planning in universities, noting that their aims and objectives were defined only in very broad terms and restricted to subjects at present established in the institution (CVCP, 1985). Long-term planning was largely ignored and in some institutions plans for even a few years ahead were not produced: Jarratt said somewhat inscrutably 'such limited forward planning as exists is generally at the margin'. There was no evidence of a thorough consideration of options but a reluctance to set priorities and discuss academic strengths and weaknesses. The Committee did not dispute the difficulty of planning but felt that without some kind of corporate consideration of where it stood a university was in danger of drifting and in danger of wasting resources.

In the British public sector, a study just completed shows that eight case study institutions reacted to the period of constraint centred around the NAB 1984/85 planning exercise in like ways (Pratt and Gill, 1986). There were widely differing responses between institutions, because of the different circumstances in which they were placed at the beginning of the exercise. The establishment of a uniform, centrally administered instrument to allocate resources and student numbers did not result in a uniform outcome. Institutions which had a history of cuts before the NAB planning exercise, for example, had already learned lessons on how to cope with sudden changes in financial circumstances and developed flexible institutional strategies. Other institutions were still coping with the effects of recent mergers or other local circumstances which limited their freedom of manoeuvre in response to financial constraint.

Common features in the pattern of policies adopted by institutions included a tendency to preserve academic profiles despite reduced resources — to do as much of the same as possible at lower cost — and hence to emphasize the 'efficiency option'. There was also a tendency to reorganize academic structures and to improve procedures for allocating and controlling resources and for monitoring and evaluating courses.

These studies suggest that when faced with cuts higher education institutions tend to react as other organizations — conservatively — by cutting costs rather than radically reappraising their products, functions or services (Pfeffer, 1977). There are numerous behavioural explanations of this, in terms of the stress placed upon administrators which deflects them from more creative activities toward anxiety reducing responses, and as the penalty for making a wrong decision is usually higher in a time of constraint than in prosperity they may use decision-making strategies that reduce risk.

The studies show that the changing 'rules of the game' nationally and, in the case of the universities, the absence of information about these — and institutional managers' perceptions of national priorities — had a clear impact on responses. There was a tendency to crisis management directly related to the limited planning horizons caused by shifts in government policy and uncertainties about their future financial situation. Institutions facing large cuts could do little else than get spending within acceptable levels. And since time scales were short, there was little time for detailed planning in these circumstances.

Woodhall and Towse (n.d.) argue that although cuts in government funding in both sectors of higher education were intended to lead to greater efficiency and cost-effectiveness, they have in some cases had the opposite effect. Much of the reduction in spending in institutions was 'random and uncontrolled' (p. 69); universities shed staff they wanted to keep and retained staff they would have preferred to lose; low cost polytechnics were sometimes penalized and high cost ones rewarded. Moreover, the changes in the ways in which funds are allocated meant that they tended to favour one kind of institution or one type of activity rather than another on different occasions, though institutions could not be sure of exactly how until close to the beginning of the financial year. The Jarratt Committee (CVCP, 1985) and Pratt and Gill (1986) both argue institutions need a clear indication from the government of the broad objectives of the system so that they can operate with reasonable foresight.

Resource Allocation and Control

Similarly, the elaborate budgeting methods and processes once beloved of economists of education (as in Husain, 1976) and students of educational management are rarely operated in institutions in determining their overall strategies under stress. Few institutions in the circumstances of limited planning horizons, unpredictable cuts and overall declining resources are able to use, if they ever wished to, the procedures of systems like PPBS. Jarratt recorded that because of the lack of strategic planning in universities there was little relationship between long-term objectives and the allocation of resources (CVCP, 1985). Incrementalism was the dominant approach and resources were often allocated on a historic share basis and quality was, with some notable exceptions, not normally considered. The allocation process in most universities was fragmented and there were instances of lack of coordination between committees dealing with different areas of spending and some cases where no single body oversaw the whole allocation pattern. Alterations in patterns of allocation were often unnecessarily restricted.

In the public sector some of this criticism also applies, but the findings of Pratt and Gill (1986) suggest that their case study institutions were better able to cope with constraint because of their familiarity at an institutional level with the process of preparation and approval of estimates deriving from their local authority relationship. Unlike some of the universities reported in Shattock and Rigby (1983) most of their case study institutions did not have to resort to special committees or change structures for planning and resource allocation to cope with constraint. They used, with only one exception, existing structures of governance and executive responsibility.

In terms of more detailed procedures, however, the public sector institutions showed greater variety. Several found that they had to develop new systems for allocating and controlling resources. Much of the literature on responses to constraint is concerned with the extent to which such systems should or must inevitably be centralized. Shattock and Rigby found not that some of their institutions chose to avoid such centralization of decision making but argued that those which did centralize may not have dealt so successfully with cuts as those which did not. In the public sector, Pratt and Gill found cases where the intention and effect was to heighten control of resources and to centralize control. Even when a system used the participative procedures of academic governance members of the Directorate became identified as the key figures determining staffing and often seemed pleased to be so regarded.

The crunch question for institutions has generally been one of deciding whether or not cuts were sufficient to require more than adjustment to budgets, usually by across-the-board reduction, or more serious reassessment. Research reveals that response depends on a number of factors, particularly the size of the cut, the institution's previous history and the period over which it has experienced constraint, and sometimes the personal characteristics of an institutional leader. Institutions facing constraint have to seriously scrutinize all aspects of their spending. One inclination is to cut the areas that can most easily be cut without immediate damage. Most institutions examine spending on non-teaching activities before the heart of their academic activities. The Jarratt Committee noted a tendency to reduce spending on maintenance and buildings in universities (CVCP, 1985), a finding also by Pratt and Gill (1986) in the public sector. This can be only a temporary expedient, and Jarratt warned of the long-term dangers. Kenny (in Lockwood and Davies, 1985), however, argues convincingly that economies can be made by effective utilization of space and accommodation. Institutions facing large cuts have to take more drastic steps. For some, a major cut in staffing is a prerequisite of survival, as in one polytechnic in the study by Pratt and Gill. In others, as at Aston

University, major staff losses were precipitated by cuts and the need to improve the quality of the university's courses as measured by such indicators as 'A' level scores. In the celebrated case of Salford University, cuts were compensated for by major initiatives to generate new sources of income from industry, with the creation of several innovative organizations within the university to foster these links (Ashworth, 1985). As a result the quality of entrants has also improved. Other institutions, like the University of Warwick, have taken a judicious middle path, meeting reductions in the UGC grant partly by economies including staff losses and partly by increasing other sources of income. Pratt and Gill (1986) found that public sector institutions have ambivalent views towards entrepreneurialism. Most responded to constraint by seeking increased external funds, but others found that financial stringency reduced their inclination to such innovative policies, and some institutions expressed the view that they were inimical to their educational aims. Interestingly, Jarratt does not refer to the topic.

Institutions have had to face declining resources at the same time as maintaining or increasing student numbers, though funding agencies in both sectors now show an inclination to halt the decline in the 'unit of resource' in order to maintain quality. The imperative of funding mechanisms in both sectors is widely seen as to increase efficiency, and this has generated a felt need in institutions to increase control over their resources and to develop and use performance indicators for their allocation and evaluation.

Performance Indicators

Again institutions can draw on a considerable quantity of literature on performance indicators and cost analyses. Sizer (1982) presented a comprehensive account of the issues and problems of performance evaluation, though fell short of offering specific indicators. Batten and Trafford (in Lockwood and Davies, 1985) discuss a wide range of evaluation techniques. A substantial literature is also produced by the National Center for Higher Education Management Systems in the USA (for example, Ewell, 1984; Brinkman and Krakower, 1983).

Delany (1979) and Bottomley *et al* (1971) argued that the determinants of costs are found in the process of education, in terms of the amounts of time spent by students and staff in class contact and class sizes. Delany has related these variables in a now familiar formula:

$$\text{SSR} = \frac{\text{Average class size (ACS)} \times \text{Average lecturer hours (ALH)}}{\text{Average student hours (ASH)}}$$

Wagner (1981) summarized much research in this area, which tends to suggest that costs per student fall as numbers increase and that distance learning methods offer low cost alternatives to conventional teaching (as in Wagner, 1977) though there is considerable dispute still in this area on both economic (Mace, 1978) and educational grounds (Pratt, 1971), and a paper in Squires (1983) suggests that costs of approaches based on new technology will initially be greater than what they replace. Bowen and Douglass (1971) in a study of the cost consequences of different instructional models suggested that (in the USA) independent study has the lowest costs per output.

The use of performance indicators such as SSRs, ALH, ACS and ASH has been advocated for some years nationally, and in the public sector they are used in the Pooling Committee's annual monitoring survey, which incidentally is one of the few data sources with information on performance of non-advanced courses. They have been incorporated into the FEMIS system of management information and used by the Audit Commission in its scrutiny of further education (both advanced and non-advanced [Audit Commission 1985a; see also Birch and Latcham, 1985a]) whilst in the university sector an extremely detailed data analysis has been developed by Taylor and used to interesting effect in analyzing responses to constraint in Shattock and Rigby (1983).

Most institutions now make use of relatively simple indicators such as student/staff ratios in allocating resources — as do the funding agencies — although Jarratt (CVCP, 1985) noted that whilst universities collected 'plenty of information' they often did not properly use it and did not effectively analyze it.

The issue has become something of a vexed question particularly in the public sector. Here, the problem arises from the unit funding mechanism used by NAB. This has relied since 1984/85 on the use of weightings for students in different subject areas, based on so-called 'best practice' SSRs derived from an HMI planning exercise undertaken at NAB's request. Institutions' allocations are thus broadly (though not wholly because of other factors in the methodology) based on these SSR weightings. Most institutions have felt compelled to use the weightings in their internal allocations (Pratt and Gill, 1986), notwithstanding that the allocation is a lump sum. The matter is further complicated because allocations were based on 'normalized cost factors' derived from the relativities of non-academic spending in the various subject areas nationally. Again institutions are seeking to establish whether or not they conform to these 'norms'. Whilst similar issues arise in universities the problems are less acute and institutional practice varies (Shattock and Rigby, 1983) partly because the precise 'units of resource' used by the UGC — or even if they are used at all — remain unknown.

The dilemma arises again from the weighting factors used in calculating student FTE numbers. The issue is more acute in the public sector with its varied modes of study. The weightings used by NAB have been widely criticized as underrating the costs of part-time education; institutions again are faced with a dilemma of conforming to the NAB figures or making their allocations on their own weightings. Again conformity seems to be becoming the norm. In universities, however, there appears to be greater variety (Lockwook and Davies, 1985) in weightings; and the relativities of post-graduate and undergraduate students are also more of an issue. Whatever decision on all these issues that institutions take, there are drawbacks. If they conform to the norms, they are allowing their internal policies to become externally determined and resource led; national norms may not suit local circumstances or an institution's educational mission (Pratt and Gill, 1986). If they use their own weightings they are vulnerable to pressure from those within the institution deprived by comparison with the norms.

The consequence of defining efficiency in terms of such standard indicators as SSRs, however, appears to not always be understood by either institutions or funding agencies.

In responding to constraint institutions can improve their efficiency insofar as this is measured by SSRs only by increasing class size or lecturer hours and/or reducing student hours. The scope for increasing lecturer hours is usually limited because of contractual agreements on contact hours, (notwithstanding that the Audit Commission (1985a) believed it found considerable scope in further education as a whole); most institutions have sought and achieved considerable increase in SSRs by increasing average class size. Pratt and Gill found that in the public sector these changes often involved a polarization of teaching group sizes, with large lectures compensating for small group work or tutorials and resulted in changes in teaching methods and course structures.

Another problem with standard indicators, based as they often are on national calculations, is that they are unable to take account of actual differences between institutions, subject areas, etc. As a result, institutions or courses which do not conform to the 'national' pattern for whatever reason, can be penalized. In the public sector, for example, innovative courses structured on a multidisciplinary or modular basis suffered from the categorization of courses into NAB's strict programme areas. Courses which by their nature required small group teaching, such as practical 'hands-on' training with expensive equipment, in-service education requiring intensive visiting, clinical work or fieldwork were all threatened by higher SSRs. The weighting system adopted by the DES for part-time work was seen to threaten its viability in some institutions.

Conclusion: The Vexed Question of Output

This chapter has discussed developments in the economics of education and the way that changes in national policy related to them have affected institutions. It has shown that in managing constraint, institutions face major problems, particularly concerned with the assessment of their 'efficiency'. It is in this area that the relationship for institutions between economics and education is most evident, yet it remains one of the most problematic.

The major problem of measuring efficiency in post-compulsory education, however, is the long standing and vexed question of assessing output (see Lockwood and Davies, 1985; Pace, 1979; Craven *et al*, 1983). Most attempts by economists and governments to do so have led to their resorting instead to inputs (or in one famous phrase — 'intermediate outputs' which were inputs just the same [DES, 1970a]). Student/staff ratios and unit costs and the host of other performance indicators are useless not only in that they relate only inputs to one another, but that they do not of their nature take account of the qualitative change that the student undergoes, or of the quality of other outputs of the system such as research.

This problem arises from the tendency of economists to concentrate on the quantitative, notwithstanding Lord Robbins' (1935) dictum which describes economics as 'a relationship between ends and scarce means'. In education the ends are qualitative as well as quantitative. It is possible only to consider what qualitative changes can be achieved for what quantitative cost.

The failure to tackle these questions lies partly with economists but equally with educators; the education service has not evolved many ways in which the quality of its output can be assessed. Existing examinations and assessment procedures are of little value;

there is considerable doubt whether they measure anything at all (Beard, 1970). Assessment is often tautologous: the examination is set and prepared for and the success of the preparation judged. Even external validating bodies like the CNAA have failed so far in this respect. The CNAA is responsible for ensuring that its courses are comparable with university degrees, but has validated not output but input — the entry qualifications of students, the time taken on the course, the qualifications and experience of staff — the colleges' facilities and so on.

But the failure does not invalidate the need. It is a necessary task for those in education to begin to assert what they actually attempt to achieve. One way of doing this has been suggested by my colleagues and me (Pratt, Travers and Burgess, 1978) in terms of 'educational value added'.

Some interesting, though rather mechanistic, developments have been undertaken in the USA on this subject, relying mainly, alas, on test scores at various stages of a student's progress (Astin, 1982). Northeast Missouri State University (1984) reports one scheme. Bogue (1982) reports a study in the USA where funding was related to performance/quality indicators.

For institutions and funding agencies this is the crux. Decisions about resource allocation and efficiency are at heart judgmental (see Browne, 1984). They cannot be isolated from educational issues such as the ways and extent to which educational aims are achieved and the judgment between different kinds of educational aims. As Popper (1945) argued, facts and decisions are independent; decisions cannot be derived from facts though they may be useful in examining the consequences of alternatives. In the end, the question of resource allocation, both to institutions and within them, is not just economic, it is political in the sense that Crick (1964) describes politics as a means for dealing with conflicting interests without violence, and this points to the need for research not only into the economics of education but also into ways of establishing open, and accountable institutional arrangements at all levels of the post-compulsory sector.

Economics and the Management of Schools

Tim Simkins

Introduction

In a review of the current state of the economics of education, Gareth Williams (1982) suggests that there appears to be an increasing convergence between the concerns of educationists and those of economists of education. The latter

> who have previously concentrated on inputs and outputs, treating the educational process in between as a 'black box', are beginning to realize that it is not possible to tell a convincing story about the relationship between inputs and outputs without understanding the processes by which inputs are converted into outputs. (*ibid*, p. 105)

In essence, Williams, is arguing that the economics of education, for so long dominated by such 'macro' concerns as the relationship between education and economic growth or the choice of appropriate economic tools to underpin national educational planning, must now switch its attention to 'micro' questions of resource deployment and management at the level of the institution. This chapter attempts to address this switch in emphasis by exploring the contribution of economics to an understanding of management at the school level. It begins by examining traditional production function approaches which do, on the whole, take a 'black box' view of the educational process in general and schools in particular. It then proceeds to consider the limitations of such approaches and to examine other types of studies which are perhaps more closely concerned with issues of direct interest to those who manage schools. The discussion is inevitably selective; the topics examined have been chosen in the light of their potential for suggesting ways forward in the study of the economics of schools.

Production Function Approaches

Although studies of educational finance and the economics of education have been concerned with issues of efficiency, equity and freedom over recent years (Guthrie, 1980), there is no doubt that studies by economists of resource allocation in education have been dominated by the concept of efficiency, and hence with the functional relationship between inputs into the educational process and the outputs resulting from it. Over the last twenty-five years or so studies deriving from this perspective have centred around the concept of the production function, but within this broad area studies have focussed at two distinct levels: on the one hand schools and school systems; and, on the other, classrooms.

Macro-level Studies: Schools and School Systems

The first, and more dominant, perspective has involved the specification of a functional relationship between school-level educational outcomes and various inputs classified under such headings as school-related variables, home and other variables relating to the students' background, peer group variables and students' innate endowments. In terms of policy, especially in the area of resource allocation, an important aim of such studies has been to identify those school-related inputs with the highest marginal productivities. This, it was assumed, would enable policies to be developed concerning the allocation of resources which would lead to specified outputs being maximized. A number of excellent reviews of this work have been written (for example, Cohn, 1979, chapter 8; Hanushek, 1979) and no attempt will be made here to duplicate these. One review summarizes the main conclusions to be drawn from such studies as follows:

> In terms of consistent findings, differences in family socio-economic background without question lead to significant achievement differences. Socio-economic status is interpreted as a proxy for quality of the home learning environment . . .

Second, there is conclusive evidence that differences among schools and teachers are important in achievement. Schools simply do not have homogeneous impacts on students. Yet the identification and measurement of specific teacher or school attributes which are important is much less certain . . .

Third there is quite conclusive evidence that schools are economically inefficient; that is they do not employ the best mixes of inputs, given input prices and their apparent effectiveness . . .

Fourth, there are significant differences in production functions by race, and, perhaps, by family background; that is, school resources interact importantly with the background characteristics of individuals'. (Hanushek, 1979, pp. 376–8)

Such results are interesting and this kind of research has generated a good deal of controversy. However, there can be little doubt that its value to the administrator or educational manager responsible for the allocation of educational resources has been quite limited. One reason for this is that such studies, although producing conclusions about statistical relationships between resource and other inputs and student performance, typically express these relationships at a macro- rather than a micro-level. This means that even when clear conclusions for resource allocation emerge, the policy implications are far from clear, not least because, in Monk's words:

Until we understand more about the way resources are actually distributed among students within educational systems, our ability to devise policies with the potential of improving educational efficiency will be severely constrained. (Monk, 1982b, p. 167)

It is such considerations that led to the development of research into resource allocation within classrooms.

Micro-level Studies: Classrooms

In this 'second generation' work on educational effects (Dreeben and Thomas, 1980b) the basic model used is a generalized production function, similar to that used in macro-level studies but operating primarily at the level of the classroom. These studies criticize traditional production function approaches because they have been preoccupied with stocks of resources and do not address explicitly their allocation and utilization. Resource measures such as teacher numbers, qualifications, and experience, expenditure on books and materials and student characteristics merely tell us what is available for deployment, not how it is used, and such measures of availability can only be related to schools as units or, at the limit, to classrooms, not to individual learners. This is clearly inadequate and has led to

> the second generational emphasis ... on resource flows to students, the behaviour of teachers rather than their demographic characteristics, and microlevel processes. Furthermore, second generational studies are almost unanimous in regarding students' time as an important variable in schooling. (*Ibid*, p. 8)

When we consider the distribution of student time within the classroom issues arise concerning both the allocation of time among various kinds of learning activities, which is mainly controlled by the teacher, and the use of time for active learning, over which the student has a good deal of control (Harnischfeger and Wiley, 1978 and 1980; Thomas, 1980a).

Perhaps the most interesting element in classroom-level models concerns the transformation of inputs into outputs, and in particular the concept of student efficiency. This concept represents the relationship between inputs of time and other resources and increments of performance for individual students. Monk argues that this concept is a crucial element in the model because variations in it can affect: (i) the marginal productivity of inputs made available to students (either neutrally or differentially among different input types); (ii) the opportunity cost of students' time (if this is defined in terms of learning foregone); and (iii) the degree to which student performance is sensitive to changes in the balance of resources made available to students (Monk, 1982b). Operationalization of student efficiency is problematic, but this approach emphasizes the role of actors outside schools in contributing to the education production function. For if student efficiency in class is an important concept, then it is likely to be determined at least in part by the previous contribution of resources to the students' education by the home as well as the school (Benson *et al*, 1980).

For our purposes perhaps the most significant point made by some of the authors under review with respect to the classroom production function concerns the preferences of the actors involved. Virtually all production function studies couched at a macro level assume that the definition (if not the detailed specification) of outcomes is relatively unproblematic. Some classroom studies do this also. Others, however, take a more complex position, concerning the resource allocation choices that different participants will make, given certain assumptions about their respective objective functions (Brown and Saks, 1980; Monk, 1982a). For example, Monk's (1982a) discussion considers the perspectives of administrators, teachers, students and parents, although his main concern is with the resource allocation behaviour of teachers. When considering this behaviour, reference is made to Brown and Saks' (1975) distinction between 'levellers' who prefer smaller dispersions of student performance and 'elitists' who are willing to accept wider dispersions for the sake of higher mean levels of performance. Using this distinction Monk argued that 'levellers' will shift resources from more to less efficient students and 'elitists' will do the opposite, assuming that students' relative efficiency is neutral as between inputs. If this assumption is removed, and if other variables are considered, a variety of more complex predictions can be made (Monk, 1982b).

The key point about such analyses is that they use essentially economic concepts to attempt to explain and predict intra-classroom differences in the allocation of resources. Empirical work in this area has so far been limited but has included studies of differences in the time allocated by teachers among different curricular areas, among different modes of instruction (Thomas, 1980a), and among different students (Monk, 1982a and 1982b). Monk's studies suggest that significant variations exist at classroom level in terms of the specific flows of resources that students receive, and that these differences seem to be related to differences in student characteristics such as test score performance and father's occupations.

Such studies provide an important complement to and extension of macro-level studies. Their focus on the classroom clearly provides an important dimension in our understanding of the economics of schools (Drake, 1979). Nevertheless, production function studies, at whatever level they are couched, have serious limitations when viewed from a management perspective. We will consider these limitations now.

A Focus on Schools as Organizations

One criticism of both macro- and micro-level production function studies is that neither addresses in any depth questions of resource allocation at the level of the school itself. It is at this level that the resources at the school's disposal are distributed for use by teachers and students to pursue educational and other purposes. This is an area where economics has to date contributed very little to our understanding. Indeed, to this writer's knowledge, only one work, albeit a significant one, explores in any depth the idea of the school as an economic system (Thomas, 1971). And yet in policy and management terms this level is surely crucial. As Levin argues in this critique of the production function approach to the economics of education:

> It would seem that a more productive approach to future research in this area would be to attempt to ascertain a behavioural theory of schools that describes what schools are producing and how they are doing it. Such studies would investigate the internal processes of educational enterprises as well as the various types of outcomes that they produce. They would also study the interface between schools and their external environment in order to determine the types of political sanctions and other characteristics that create the existing operations of the schools. (Levin, 1976, p. 174)

Implicit in all of the economic studies examined above, is the assumption that the school represents a production unit, much like a firm, which attempts to produce defined outputs at least cost. However, for an organization to seek to operate at least cost a number of conditions need to be fulfilled. First, there must be a clear system of goals or preferences against which alternative patterns of resource allocation may be judged. Second, adequate information should be available to predict the consequences of particular patterns of resource allocation in terms of the preferred outcomes. This implies an understanding of the technology of the processes being managed (the relation between inputs and outputs), and a knowledge of the relative costs of inputs. Third, the managers in the organization must have sufficient discretion over the way resources are allocated to enable the most appropriate pattern of resource utilization to be chosen. And finally, there must be some incentive for the managers concerned to seek to employ the resources available in the most appropriate way. If these conditions are fulfilled it is likely that the distribution of resources and levels of cost which result will represent an optimal allocation in terms of the organization's objectives and priorities.

Problems arise with respect to education in general and to schools in particular in all these areas (*ibid*). Goals are often too diffuse and controversial in schools to enable them to be specified to the degree that would be necessary to provide a basis for resource allocation. Input prices tend to be administered and, in any case, managers at institutional level are not normally offered the possibility of purchasing most educational resources — especially staff — in the market. And the educational production function is still largely a mystery so that 'educational managers at all levels lack knowledge of the production set for obtaining particular outcomes' (*ibid*, p. 157).

Such difficulties, it is often argued, make many of the conclusions drawn from production function studies inherently suspect, and they give rise to a real need to consider the nature of schools as organizations (Miles, 1981; Thomas, in this volume). Yet, despite the fact that references can be found to the idea of schools as optimizing or sub-optimizing resource allocation systems (for example, Cohn, 1971), most economic studies do not address this issue. Yet there a number of ways in which it could be addressed. An attempt will now be made to identify three such approaches which seem to offer potential for further development.

Objectives and Outcomes

While sometimes paying lip-service to problems of objective-specification, most economic studies adopt the essentially reductionist approach of assuming that the preferences of decision-makers can be expressed simply in terms of desired learning outcomes commonly proxied by test scores or examination results. The use of such output measures clearly reflects the circumstances of the societies within which the studies are undertaken. Thus, in the United States standardized achievement tests scores have been the prime measures of output used, while in the United Kingdom, despite the increasing use of testing programmes by local education authorities (Gipps *et al*, 1983) and the work of the Assessment of Performance Unit (Gipps and Goldstein, 1983), examination results have been the main area of interest. The importance that such results still hold in the national consciousness is reflected in the provision in the 1980 Education Act for such examination results to be published, and in the developing literature on the value and limitations of examination results as measures of school performance (Plewis *et al*, 1981; Ouston and Maughan, 1985). However, few studies as yet give serious consideration to other measures (Rutter *et al*, 1979, is an exception here). Yet if we are concerned with understanding schools as economic systems we need to consider much more carefully both what they actually produce and what the individuals within them perceive themselves as trying to achieve. Thus in reviewing Lord's (1984) work on the effectiveness of LEA expenditure, Jesson *et al* (1984) argue that:

> The most obvious weakness in the assumptions he was prepared to make was that all local authorities are equally committed to maximizing examination success and that the vast bulk of expenditure is devoted to this single aim.

Clearly this is unlikely to be so, not least because only a half or fewer of an authority's pupils can be expected to achieve success in these terms. Hence it is necessary to know how such an 'academic' objective relates to other objectives within the school system as a whole and how objectives differ for different client groups. Very little work has been done in this area to date. A number of ideas are suggestive, however. Brown and Saks' (1975) distinction, referred to earlier, between 'elitists' and 'levellers', while expressed in relation to the values of individual teachers, clearly has implications at an organizational level in terms of the relative priority given to the achievements of different sub-groups of pupils. In contrast, Rutter *et al*'s (1979) concept of 'academic emphasis' relates to priority among types of school outcome rather than their distribution among pupils. Rutter *et al* operationalized academic emphasis in terms of a number of indicators including emphasis on homework, total time devoted to teaching, expectations of success in examinations and use of the school library. It is hardly surprising that such disparate indicators were weakly intercorrelated; but nevertheless Rutter *et al* (1979) concluded that:

> The findings as a whole suggest that children tended to make better progress both behaviourally and academically in schools which placed an appropriate emphasis on academic matters. This emphasis might be reflected in a well planned curriculum, in the kinds of expectations teachers had of the children they taught, and in the setting and marking of homework. (p. 114)

The purpose here is not to overemphasize the significance of conclusions of this kind, but rather to draw attention to the need for studies of the economics of schools to be much more concerned with what such organizations perceive themselves to be doing. This is not without its difficulties of course. Statements about values within educational organizations have enormous micropolitical and symbolic significance which means that they need to be treated with caution, whether obtained from formal policy documents or from informal discussions. Nevertheless they provide a starting point for analysis. Beyond this we need to examine the economics of areas of provision whose objectives are relatively non-problematic; or alternatively to explore preferences through the patterns of resource allocation in which they result. We will consider some of these possibilities now.

Cost-effectiveness Approaches

One possible economic approach is to view the school as an organization whose prime concern is with the provision of courses of study for pupils, and to examine in particular those courses which have clearly defined learning objectives and a clearly defined pupil clientele. The focus on courses of study in this way immediately raises the question of whether some patterns of resource provision are more cost-effective in achieving course objectives than others. One way of approaching this question is to consider the contribution of particular resources to pupil performance. This is the emphasis underlying studies of teacher effectiveness (Hanushek, 1981, pp. 202–7; Murnane and Philips, 1981) and of the effects of class size on pupil performance (Burstall, 1979; Glass *et al*, 1982). While such studies clearly have important potential for policy-making — for example in relation to questions of teacher appraisal — most of the studies in these areas have been inconclusive in their results. Furthermore from an economic perspective their rationale is defective. As Cullen (1979) put it in discussing class-size studies, the economist

> will not expect to gain much useful knowledge by observing the effect of varying one input — for example, one type of labour — in isolation. If the quantity of other inputs were not held constant in such a study, he would not know whether to attribute higher output to the labour, or to

uncontrolled variations in other inputs. And if the quantity of other input *were* held constant, he would still not know whether an increase in output resulting from an increase in labour could be achieved at lower cost by increasing other inputs instead of labour. (p. 32)

This suggests that there is room for more comprehensive cost-effectiveness studies which are clearly focussed at the programme level. Such studies are still relatively underrepresented in the literature on the economics of education. Nevertheless, there are now a number of excellent references on the methodology of cost-effectiveness analysis (Levin, 1975 and 1983) and reviews of research findings are also beginning to appear (Geske, 1979; Drake, 1982).

Two recent pieces of work illustrate the possibilities. One was the study conducted by Henry Levin and his associates which examined the relative cost-effectiveness in improving mathematics and reading test scores in US elementary schools of four educational interventions: increasing instructional time, reducing class size, computer-assisted instruction and cross-age tutoring using adults and peers (Levin *et al*, 1984). This study found that cross-age tutoring was clearly the most cost-effective method of improving mathematics scores, and also, together with CAI, the most cost-effective method of improving reading scores. Further, the rank order of cost-effectiveness of the interventions differed between the two areas and differed from the rank order when costs alone were considered. As the authors themselves note, the study was subject to certain limitations in its design. Nevertheless, it demonstrated that a cost-effectiveness approach of this type facilitates a rigorous examination of the implications of possible alternative educational technologies at school level, in ways in which more traditional studies, such as those of a production function type do not.

A second rather different example of cost-effectiveness analysis was Thomas's (1981) pilot study of the relative cost-effectiveness of 'A' level economics teaching in four schools and colleges of further education. This study compares the institutions in terms of their relative cost-effectiveness in 'producing' 'A' level scores and also in terms of the relative value added which emerges when 'A' level performance is related to earlier 'O' level performance of students. As in Levin's study the rank order of institutions differs when different performance measures are used but unfortunately the paper is unable to relate value added scores to costs to produce a real cost-effectiveness ratio. This approach has been developed in work by the Audit Commission (Reeson, in this volume).

Cost-effectiveness studies such as those by Levin and Thomas are important in that they force managers and administrators to think beyond traditional assumptions concerning class sizes, time frames and resource combinations. Furthermore they lead to a detailed examination of the cost structures of particular technologies. Thus, for example, one spin-off of the Levin study was a thought-provoking examination of the cost implications of different means of implementing computer-aided instruction (Levin and Woo, 1981). Perhaps most important for the manager and policy-maker, cost-effectiveness analysis provides a clear analytical framework for examining alternative ways of making educational provision.

A major limitation of such cost-effectiveness studies, of course, is the need to specify effectiveness in an appropriate way. The studies described above are based on the assumption that this is relatively unproblematic. Thus Levin focusses on programmes specifically designed to improve defined skills in reading and mathematics; and Thomas and Reeson look at courses where most would agree the main objective is to maximize examination performance. As has been seen, the definition of outputs for many educational programmes will be much more problematic than this; and it must be accepted that true cost-effectiveness studies are likely to have their greatest value in areas of the curriculum where programmes of study can be defined which have clearly specified and measurable outcomes. Within compulsory education such areas will of necessity be limited. Nevertheless, it can be strongly argued that cost-effectiveness analysis has the potential to be used much more widely and more rigorously in the schools sector than it has been to date.

Patterns of Resource Deployment

If we are interested in the economics of schools viewed as total organizations, whose outputs are multiple, complex and controversial, then cost-effectiveness analysis is likely to be of limited use. A more fertile approach would seem to be to examine patterns of resource allocation in order to enhance our understanding of the cost structures of schooling and to explore the preferences which are embodied in curricular and other choices. If this is to be the focus it virtually goes without saying that time is the central variable. As Thomas (1971) puts it:

> It may be stated as a general principle that the lower one is in the organizational hierarchy, the more his decisions will involve allocating time rather than money. (pp. 40–1)

To illuminate some of the issues here it may be useful to employ Harnischfeger and Wiley's (1980) distinction between '*extensity*' and '*intensity*' in resource allocation patterns. The extensity of an educational activity refers to its duration, while intensity refers to the quantity and quality of resources provided during a particular time period. Using these concepts, patterns of expenditure can be examined at a number of levels. At the level of the school as a whole, despite the heavy constraints of the law, considerable variations can exist in the 'extensity' of the formal timetable. As long ago as 1970, the NFER study of comprehensive schools found differences in school weeks equivalent to a difference in provision of seven weeks a year or one year's schooling over a six year course. Longer days were found to occur more frequently in Welsh schools, ex-grammar schools and schools with 'more able' pupils (Bates, 1970).

When we turn to questions of 'intensity' of resource provision within the curriculum as a whole, questions of staff deployment are probably more important than any other. Clearly given a particular staffing level there is a direct trade-off between the amount of teacher time put into the curriculum (usually measured in teacher-periods) and the proportion of the timetabled week during which teachers are allocated to classes (measured by the contact ratio). A number of studies have reported considerable variations around the mean contact ratio both nationally and locally, particularly at secondary level (DES, 1979; Crispin and Perkins, 1980). Such variations in patterns of staff deployment are likely to become an increasing source of attention. Indeed, questions of teacher deployment strike at the heart of many of the major policy questions facing schools today. Government policies, aimed at achieving 'breadth', 'balance', 'relevance', and 'differentiation' (DES, 1985a, chapter 2) have implications within both primary and secondary schools for the ways in which pupils are grouped and teachers are deployed, as do new policy initiatives in such areas as examinations and records of achievement, the development of new vocationally-oriented courses, provision for pupils with special needs and teacher in-service training and staff development. Thus a recent DES study (1984c) suggested that if additional staffing resources were to be provided to support the kinds of initiatives enumerated above they would need to be used to reduce contact ratios (or time with the teacher's regular class in the case of primary schools) or to provide additional support from outside the school rather than to reduce class sizes which had been the main effect of improved staffing ratios over recent years.

The central economic question raised by such discussions concerns the effects of changes in the availability of resources on their deployment at the margin. The choices that are made here are likely to provide important clues to the values held by decision-makers within schools and outside them. And this does not just apply of course to questions of extensity and intensity of resource provision to the curriculum as a whole. It applies with even greater power to the more detailed and complex issues of how resources are to be distributed within the formal curriculum itself.

Of the various resources over which the school has control, that of teacher time has tended to receive by far the most attention. This is hardly surprising. Given the dominance of the teacher resource in terms of overall expenditure on schools, the opportunity costs implied by particular patterns of teacher deployment inevitably become of central concern. The development of staff deployment or curriculum analysis has helped considerably in the examination of this area in recent years, particularly in the secondary sector. Based on Davies' (1969) pioneering work, we now have a much greater understanding of the complexities of choice involved in staffing the secondary school curriculum, and Her Majesty's Inspectorate now use such analysis as a matter of course in their work and, through COSMOS courses, have encouraged most secondary schools to do so. A number of studies have appeared which examine staff deployment in some detail (DES, 1979; Butterworth, 1983), and here again substantial differences in patterns of staff deployment have been found among schools.

Much work remains to be done in analyzing staff deployment within the curriculum; yet other areas of resource allocation have received much less attention. Some studies are available, for example, concerning the use of non-timetabled as well as timetabled time by teachers (Hilsum and Cane, 1971; Hilsum and Strong, 1978), and the distribution of Burnham points among different areas of responsibility (Smith, 1975a and 1975b; Gray, 1983). Other areas, however, such as the allocation of teachers with particular qualities and qualifications among pupil groups and curriculum areas, the utilization of space, or patterns of expenditure of capitation and other kinds of finance are almost entirely uncharted. So too is the use of students' time both in and out of the classroom, despite the fact that in economic terms the purchased resources provided by the school represent only some of the inputs to the learning process. This is an issue recognized by the importance attached to homework in the Hargreaves Report (ILEA, 1984) and the White Paper on *Better Schools* (DES, 1985a), but in research terms it is a relatively neglected area.

Useful as studies of the distribution of particular resources are, we need ultimately to examine the combined impact of separate resource allocation decisions on the costs of the curriculum that schools provide. In order to do so, however, the question immediately arises: what is the 'budgetary structure' of the curriculum? In other words, what is the most meaningful framework for analyzing resource allocation within the school. An output budgeting perspective would lead us back to the problems, discussed earlier, associated with objective specification in the school. Yet some kind of framework is essential. Three dimensions of analysis seem to make sense in a school context. The first concerns curriculum areas. Such areas might be defined in terms of traditional subjects, in terms of 'areas of experience' (DES, 1978) or in terms of the time devoted to the learning of particular kinds of skills. The appropriate framework would undoubtedly vary depending on the nature of the school being considered. The second dimension concerns pupils with particular characteristics. Hence the distribution of resources might be examined among pupils of differing levels of ability or between boys and girls; or we might look at the allocation of resources to provision for pupils with particular educational needs such as those with defined handicaps or for whom English is a second language. Finally, and bringing the first two dimensions together to a degree, consideration might be given to the expenditure of resources on particular, definable courses of study.

Curriculum costing studies of these kinds are relatively rare. Most major studies (for example, Hough, 1981) are concerned primarily with the costs of schools as a whole, and cost differences between schools with different characteristics. The most important study of in-school costs, which still stands out for its range and depth of analysis, is Cumming's (1971) work. Many methodological problems arise in such analyses, both in terms of obtaining school level data and of allocating joint costs among curriculum areas and pupil groups, and hence it is not surprising that no studies using this methodology have been published since. Nevertheless, further such studies are necessary if greater understanding is to be obtained of the factors which affect resource allocation decisions in schools and the impact of these decisions on curriculum provision and pupils' access to educational resources.

Conclusion

Studies of educational outcomes, of the cost-effectiveness of particular programmes, and of resource deployment patterns within schools inevitably lead to questions concerning the processes through which resource allocations are determined within schools: Who is involved in resource allocation decisions? How do they perceive the choice opportunities open to them? And what criteria do they use? Such questions lead in turn to a consideration both of the constraints which are imposed on decision-makers and of the kinds of freedom which they are permitted and which they exercise. There is no doubt that choices concerning the use of resources in schools are heavily constrained by legal and financial regulations. For example, the law strictly limits choices concerning the amount of time children spend in the classroom during the compulsory years; and most local education authorities resource schools in ways which limit the possibilities of significant substitution between expenditure on teachers, on non-teaching staff and on equipment and consumables. Nevertheless, within these constraints, a wide range of choice still exists and is exercised. Indeed, there can be little doubt that schools are becoming much more self conscious about their resource management procedures than they have in the past. There are, perhaps, two major related reasons for this.

One arises from the current pressures created by falling rolls and financial stringency. These trends are not affecting all schools equally. The falling rolls problem has now largely passed its peak in the primary sector while its impact is still increasing on secondary schools; and some local education authorities are succeeding in insulating their schools from financial constraints to a much greater degree than are others. And some areas of provision, such as TVEI schemes, have access to levels of resourcing which are extremely generous compared to those which are available to the schools sector as a whole. Nevertheless, these trends are bringing questions of priorities to the fore in a way which is quite new for managers within schools. In particular, they are giving rise to important questions about choices at the margin. Such issues were first explored in depth in Briault and Smith's (1980) study of falling rolls and have been explored further by Walsh *et al* (1984) and in HMI reports on the effects of expenditure policies (DES, 1986). Their relevance from our point of view concerns the possibilities they provide for examining in some detail the resource allocation process in schools. For while the broad national picture appears to be fairly clear in terms of those parts of the curriculum that are under greatest threat as rolls fall and resources become scarcer, there are undoubtedly differences among schools in the sacrifices they choose to make at the margin. Detailed examination of the reasons for these differences may change considerably our understanding of the nature of schools as organizations.

The second reason for schools greater self-awareness about resource management issues can be traced to the present government's concern for improving efficiency throughout the public sector. Policy initiatives reflecting this concern can be traced at many levels (Thomas, 1983). At local government level it can be seen in the creation of the Audit Commission and the latter's increasing involvement in detailed comparative studies of institutional resource management, particularly its controversial study of further education (1985a). Although the Commission's report on non-teaching costs in secondary schools (1984a) raised questions that might be considered marginal to the central issue of curriculum delivery, this will certainly not be the case with the study it is currently undertaking of teaching costs in secondary schools. One result of the Audit Commission's work has been its recommendation that schemes for increasing the degree of financial autonomy granted to schools, which have been introduced on a pilot basis in a number of local authorities, be extended more widely (Audit Commission, 1984a). This call has been taken up by the Government (DES, 1985a, paragraph 246), and insofar as it is implemented school managers will be faced with a whole series of new challenges. There is clearly considerable potential for the development of case studies of the ways in which schools respond to these. The Audit Commission's primary concern is that such autonomy schemes will facilitate more effective and efficient management. Such a concern is reflected in those evaluations of existing autonomy schemes that have been published (Humphrey and Thomas, 1983a and 1983b; Hinds, 1984); but as more schemes are introduced, and schools develop more experience in managing them, questions clearly arise as to whether schools will choose to use their resources in ways which are significantly different from those which they have developed under earlier regimes of tight control and limited virement.

These major issues — the pressures of contraction and the movement towards greater financial autonomy for schools — reinforce Williams' arguments, stated at the beginning of this chapter, for a greater economic concern with schools as organizations. They provide a backcloth against which the micro-economics of schools needs to be developed in order to contribute more directly to educational management and policy-making. Despite the very considerable literature on the economics of education, it is surprising how little we know at present about the processes through which schools allocate resources internally and how these processes relate to educational outcomes. An attempt has been made in this chapter to identify some of the main directions in which these issues have been or might be addressed by economists.

Part Three

Education and the Economy: A View from the MSC[1]

Judith Marquand

Introduction

The need is urgent to redraw the conceptual map for much of the policy area with which the MSC is concerned; the textbook concepts of economic theory and policy which underlie most policy-making are far too narrow to handle the urgent problems of growth and distribution which we see around us. More particularly, much conventional economic analysis is largely irrelevant for evaluating the contribution which education makes to society or for judging priorities in the development of vocational education and training. A shift in perspective appears to bring great gains in the relevance of economics to current educational concerns.

One area of development in economics which has clear relevance to education and training policy is new work on technological development, innovation diffusion and the learning process. In this chapter I shall attempt speculatively to point to some of its implications.

A New Techno-Economic Paradigm?

Over the last quarter of a century, mainstream economics in Britain has tended to neglect the whole area of economic development in industrial society, concentrating instead on the problems of inflation and stagflation. I hope that this may start to change as interest in evolutionary or neo-Schumpeterian growth theory revives (for example, Nelson and Winter, 1982; Freeman and Soete, 1986, Gibbons and Metcalfe, 1986). This emphasizes questions of technological development, innovation diffusion and economic growth and leads directly to a view of societal development where the extent of participation in world-wide economic growth (and with it, the possibility of increased well-being for all sectors of society) depends crucially on the ability of societies and individuals within them to adapt. The adaptability of institutional stuctures (including educational institutions) raises a host of fascinating questions on the boundaries of political science, sociology and economics (Rogers, 1982). I do not intend to pursue them here, but rather to point to the connection between the learning process, the individual and the adaptability required to reap the benefits of technological change.

I make no apology for emphasizing technological change in this way. We live in an era of major technological upheaval, where by far the most important technological changes are those associated with the development and application of the cluster of new information technologies. Information technology has several remarkable characteristics: it is at once capital-saving and labour-saving (in the production of a unit of output); information is a component of every transformation process, so that in principle it can affect every economic activity in society; it has the potential to generate a wide range of new products of which, so far, we have seen only the first (Bessant *et al*, 1985; Van der Werf, 1985).

Current academic debate as to the nature of Kondratieff long waves is unhelpful. For our present purposes, it does not matter whether demand factors influence the rate of innovation, or *vice versa*. What is relevant is that the rate of development of new information technologies has already set the scene for a sustained economic upswing for those countries who are poised to take advantage of it. The question is rather that of what are the conditions to be able to do so (Freeman and Soete, 1985).

The wave of innovations associated with information technology is *not* unprecedented in the order of magnitude of the changes which it can facilitate. Energy and information are the twin inputs to all transformation processes and there have been major changes throughout history to the technologies available for each of these: the development of language, of writing, of printing, of telegraphy and telephone; the Neolithic Revolution, the first Industrial Revolution (steam power), the development of electricity and electrical networks. But it is on this scale that the new information technologies need to be viewed. A crucial characteristic of such innovations is that their social implications greatly outweigh their immediate technological and economic ones.

Thus the new information technologies are characterized by a greatly enhanced facility of machines to receive, store, analyze and transmit information, with the capacity to communicate both with human beings and with other machines. The convergence of information and communication technologies allows the messages to be conveyed rapidly and cheaply irrespective of distance. Hence the ways in which they can affect employment are far-reaching, through changed processes and products, changed organization structures to produce them, changed boundaries between organizations, changed skills and changed combinations of skills.

Yet, whilst most attention so far has been paid to the impact of information technologies on manufacturing and producer services, their potential to affect consumer activities and services is in principle just as far-reaching. As well as the application of what are now well-tried fourth-generation technologies to aspects of transport, distribution, public administration, education, health and various leisure activities, the development of intelligent knowledge-based systems offers enormous potential for change in almost all areas dependent on professional expertise. Education, health, legal services, aspects of public administration are all candidates for major change, as well as various professional activities in support of manufacturing or extractive industry (Bessant *et al*, 1985; Burgess, 1986). And the impact of the convergence of information and communication technologies, whether on producers or on consumers, is only just starting to be considered.

Whilst the technological feasibility of all these changes is no longer in doubt, the shape of the social changes which will accompany them is far more dimly perceived (Van der Werf, 1985; Bessant *et al*, 1985). It is the interplay of individual, institutional and political responses which will determine which of them come about. Moreover, it is the ability to adapt and the speed of adaptation of society — institutions and individuals — which will determine how far and how fast they take place.

Training for Successful Adaptation

Thus, competitive success by an economy depends on the facility for rapid adaptation by its individuals and institutions as well as on the particular skills directly relevant to the competitive products and all the intermediate goods and services which enter into their production. In this chapter I shall not discuss institutional adaptation, despite its crucial importance. I shall consider only the implications for vocational education and training of assigning a central role to adaptability in the pursuit of economic development.

Successful adaptation to take advantage of the developments in information technology does not only (and perhaps does not even) require competitive skills at the leading edge; it depends on the rapid and effective diffusion of innovative products and processes throughout those exporting or import-competing sectors which are to become competitive, including the many sectors on which they draw for inputs of goods or services. Detailed studies of the impact of information technology on the firm are finding again and again that the difficulties in adaptation lie in the need for fundamental re-examination of the firm's conversion processes which is precipitated by the new technology; failures are time and again related to the narrow horizons and competences which go with the lamentably low levels of education and training of most of our managers and workforce (for example, Cross and Mitchell, 1986).

It is now widely held that the ability of an individual to adapt, to learn new patterns of behaviour, is closely related to his/her ability to make higher level 'plans', to perceive a problem in its wider environment and to make relatively general 'plans' for dealing with it, capable of flexibility in execution because of the wide range of more detailed 'plans' which each one can embrace (for example, Miller, Galanter and Pribram 1960). Such adaptability can be taught; one of the main functions of education (or of training in broadly conceived competences) already is to try to foster it.

If this view of learning behaviour is correct, the dichotomy between the economic and social objectives of education and training policy is largely a false one. If the most important part of the training process is to enhance the ability to analyze that wider environment and to make 'plans' accordingly, this ability is likely to include a large element of 'transferable skills', which apply whether the individual is learning a technical trade, to run a small business, or simply to manage his or her own life better in circumstances of infrequent paid employment. Of course, there are particular specialized skills to be learnt, but this is only a small part of enhancing people's capacity to 'plan' successfully to cope with changing situations.

I cannot speak for the education sector, but this view certainly has implications for training policy. If adaptability can be taught and if we are to compete successfully, then first and foremost we need to look to the quality of training, of whatever type. In many cases, the attainment of more appropriate skills may entail *more* training too.

Secondly, as is well known from all the evidence of skill shortages (MSC, 1986a), CBI/MSC, 1985 and 1986), we need more people with those higher level skills directly appropriate to the development and adoption of new technology. The direct effect of the adoption of new technologies is almost always to increase the numbers required with skills at technician level or higher, while tending to reduce the numbers needed with lower level skills. Furthermore, the nature of many lower level jobs is changed by the new technology (Burgess, 1986, and references therein). Many of the lower level skills affected are office skills or service sector skills (often in jobs held mainly by women). For such jobs, greatly increased interpersonal skills in dealing with customers are required (MSC, 1985; Swann, 1986). Increased interpersonal skills are indeed needed at all levels, as IT reduces the need for technical manipulation and increases the importance of relating well to the wider environment of suppliers, users within the organization and customers outside it. Managers need increased interpersonal skills in order to be able to manage the introduction of change.

After the changed skills directly associated with the introduction of new technology come the changed numbers of skilled people needed in those sectors which will expand if efforts to compete meet with any success. Any sector can compete successfully; which sectors become competitive in any given economy depends on their speed of adaptation to meet or create the changing pattern of demand. Technical, managerial, marketing and customer-service skills are all important (MSC, 1986b).

Whichever sectors expand, there will be a demand for the investment goods appropriate to those sectors. In the scenario of successful adaptation which we are positing, this will, of course, include the information technology industries. It will also certainly include the construction industry and indeed industries of all kinds (including education and training) which provide the infrastructure for economic development. Leontief and Duchin (1984) show that, for the United States, the biggest employment effects from the successful expansion of the IT-using industries will be felt in the investment industries. Similar input-output based studies for this country would almost certainly show similar results, with the biggest employment expansion of all accruing to the construction industry.

As competition succeeds and the country becomes richer, increased purchasing power is generated. Where it accrues and on what it is spent depends on which are the competitive sectors (including those competing successfully within the home market) and on how increased earnings from successful competition are divided between wages, profits and taxes (and on how the taxes in turn are divided between a reduced PSBR and an increased level of public spending).

We can also point to some demographic factors and attitudinal factors suggesting that increased spending on (and increased employment in) health services and community social services of all kinds are likely. Repairing the damaged social structure of the inner cities could absorb substantial numbers of people in social, educational and economic development work of all kinds. Increased investment in infrastructure could likewise put many people to work. It is the extent of the political will to redistribute resources in this way and the extent of success in ensuring the acquiescence of those who may not wish to pay which will determine how far this redistribution takes place; the broad social consensus to allow it to be done would appear to exist (Heath *et al*, 1985). But these are matters outside the scope of this chapter; what is relevant here is that, although changed policies would take time to have any substantial impact on employment, there are training implications now if such redirection of resources is to be possible at all.

In the transitional period before any improved competitive position is achieved and before the wave of new products and services generated by the new technologies is upon us, what is the appropriate training policy for those who remain unemployed? One part of the answer must be training for self-employment, but the other part must surely be training to help them to cope better with unemployment, or with occasional employment, or with part-time employment, or with voluntary employment. Fortunately, training appropriate for these appears scarcely to differ from training appropriate for full-time work — improved ability to 'plan', improved interpersonal skills and other core skills, increased self-confidence.

Suppose now that we discover or decide that we are unlikely to be able to compete successfully. How does the appropriate training differ from that already described? For the vast majority of the population, in fact it appears that there will be little difference. Training appropriate to a poor society is training in all activities which do not require expensive or extremely sophisticated capital equipment and that do not require rich customers (except perhaps foreign tourists). Now, one of the most exciting aspects of the new information technologies is their apparent capacity for transfer to developing countries (Freeman and Soete, 1985), provided there are sufficient user and maintenance skills in the workforce. Thus all the training except some of that at the leading edge of the new technologies will continue to be relevant, but the problems of financing it will loom large.

Conclusions: Implications for Economics, Education and Training

If the view presented here is accepted, of learning processes and their central role in economic development, then the implications for the education and training systems, for the perception of the role of education and training in economic analysis, for the perception of their role in economic policy, and for the perception of an irreconcilable dichotomy between economic and social welfare policies are far-reaching.

Firstly, there are implications for the institutional structure of education and training. The distinction between them is already starting to blur; there appears to be no good reason why it should remain at all. This has implications for access criteria — matters such as assessment, certification and credit transfer — and for questions of funding, where like should be treated likewise across institutional boundaries.

Secondly, to the extent that economic analysis concerns itself with the conditions for the attainment of economic growth, subject to constraints, rather than the satisfaction of equilibrium conditions in which growth plays at most a secondary role, then work on technological change and its diffusion assumes a central importance. In particular, the use of simple (or not so simple) aggregate production functions becomes unsuitable. A vintage approach to modelling capital and investment has to be adopted, where moreover the flexibility is limited to vary the quality of labour input associated with a given vintage of equipment. Skills and technologies become inseparable, with broad-based educational attainment an essential concomitant of skill. The more that skills and technologies are intertwined, the more difficult it becomes to determine the *macro-economic* benefit from a marginal increment of education or skill; what becomes relevant is the macro-economic benefit from adoption of a new technology combined with the skills required to implement it successfully. Especially in times of major technological change, this benefit is likely to be by far the greater. None of our existing macro-economic models is equipped to handle technological change and skills in this way; there must be a presumption that they all understate the economic importance of education and training. Pioneer work by Soete and Freeman (1984) and Clark at SPRU (Clark, 1986) attempts to start to redress the balance, but there is a long way to go before production functions which realistically reflect the adoption of new technologies are adequately incorporated into economic theory, let alone overcoming the data deficiencies which would need to be remedied if their large-scale application were to become possible.

Fortunately, we do not need to wait for full-scale economic modelling before adjusting the stance of economic policy. The third implication is that policies for education and training — and I emphasize both — assume a central economic importance. Whilst acknowledgement is often made of the importance of one part or another of the education and training system for economic development, the impression is not usually given that the centrality of the whole learning process, at all levels of skill and in all parts of the economy, is widely appreciated.

Finally, the learning process is central to the well-being of society. It is central to many of the aspects of society with which economics is concerned. If economists, followed by politicians and administrators who act on the myths which economists generate, can come to integrate this recognition into their mental models, many conflicts between apparent economic imperatives and the demands of other social needs may become easier to resolve. Economics stands out among the late-twentieth century social sciences by operating with a nineteenth-century view of man. We shall all benefit if it can be updated.

Notes

1 The views expressed here must not be taken to represent an official MSC view; whilst they have developed within the context of working in the MSC, they represent the author's personal views only.

The Cost Disease and Educational Finance: The Adverse Effects of Cash Limits[1]

Paul Ryan

Introduction

The last decade has witnessed a dramatic reversal in policy towards the finance and provision of schooling in the public sector. Since the period of budgetary expansion ground to a halt in the mid-1970s, cash limits have been used to control, and even reduce, public spending. The operating methods of educational institutions have come under scrutiny as part of a concern for increased efficiency in the public sector.

The fiscal difficulties faced by public education are part of those of the public services as a whole (table 1). After growing markedly more rapidly (in terms of employment) than the private services during the years 1960–75, the public services ground to a halt in the second half of the 1970s, while in the 1980s they have contracted — at a rate faster than the growth of private services in the 1960s. The reversal has been particularly marked in education, fed by the decline since 1976 in the number of school age children.

This chapter discusses a crucial deficiency in the new regime under which public education has been financed during the last decade. It has long been recognized that the intrinsic potential of formal education for productivity growth is low, with the result that the costs of providing it will, under plausible assumptions, tend to increase steadily over time. However, budgetary policy has simply ignored the problem, with adverse implications for the quality of public education in particular.

The next section discusses the effects of differentially low productivity growth when fiscal controls take the form of level funding.

'able 1: Annual Rates of Growth of Employment and Real Expenditure in Services

	1960–70	1970–75	1975–79	1979–83
Employment				
Private services	0.5%	1.0%	1.75%	1.0%
Public services	2.5	3.5	0.25	−0.75
Education staff[1]	7.4	4.7	1.1	−1.0
Real Recurrent Expenditure[1,2]				
on Education	6.1	8.0	−0.2	0.2

Sources: HM Treasury (1984) *Economic Progress Report*, February; Dept of Education and Science *Education Statistics for the UK*, (1970b, table 4) and (1984 table 4).

Notes: 1. All public educational institutions.
2. On financial year basis; excluding related expenditure; deflated by implicit GDP deflator.

Objections to the notion of a cost disease in education are considered in the following section. A further section provides an assessment of the severity of the financial constraint upon public education during the last decade, and is followed by a concluding section.

The Implications of Unbalanced Growth

A cost disease will characterize any sector in which the rate of increase in productivity is significantly less than that in the rest of the economy. In a two-sector model of unbalanced growth, the low growth of productivity in the 'stagnant' sector results in secular growth in the unit cost, and therefore the price, of its output relative to those of its 'progressive' counterpart (Baumol, 1967). For example, if trend annual productivity growth is 3 per cent in the progressive sector but only 1 per cent in the stagnant one, then, under simplifying assumptions, the price of output in the stagnant sector will increase secularly by 2 per cent per annum relative to that in its progressive counterpart.[2] The stagnant sector has traditionally been identified with the services, the progressive one with manufacturing.

The implications of rising relative prices for employment and output depend then upon the price and income elasticities of demand for services. The share of services in total output (at current prices) will rise as long as the share of services in final demand (at constant prices) does not fall faster than the rise in relative price. This outcome will fail to materialize only if the price elasticity of demand is high, the income elasticity of demand low and/or the rate of growth of national income low — in which case the share of services in output (at current prices) will decline as a result of rising relative costs. Evidence from the US suggests the reverse: low price elasticity and moderate income elasticity of demand for services, resulting in secular increase in their share of output at current prices.[3]

The source of the cost disease is taken to be the underlying technical difficulty of raising productivity in many services, particularly the personal services, where the low standardization of the product militates against mass production; where product quality is important to the customer; and where the quality of the product depends heavily upon inputs of time and skill from individuals. The mainstream methods of raising productivity in industry, viz., mechanization and sub-division of labour, can then increase the volume of output in services only at the expense of unacceptable reductions in quality.

Education typically joins artistic performance and health care as the leading presumptive examples of the cost disease of the services.[4] The technical rationale is taken to be the centrality for student learning of personal interaction with a teacher. The scope for raising productivity is not taken to be negligible. Various innovations can reduce the quality losses associated with cuts in teacher inputs. However, the postulated irreducible requirement for personal and interactive teaching experiences still implies low technical scope for productivity growth, in contrast to the regularity of improvements in both process and product in industry (Baumol, 1985).[5]

To the extent that the Baumol model applies to education, both the relative price of educational services and their share in the value of national output (at current prices) must rise over time. The speed of the increase depends upon the size of the gap in productivity growth.

If we interpret level funding as a policy of holding constant both the real unit cost of, and total real expenditures on, public education (so that total money costs vary only with overall price inflation) then its implications are clear.[6] As level funding ignores the underlying forces for secular growth in the real unit cost of educational services, it must lead to cuts in output, either in quantity (for example, student years) or quality (for example, amount of learning), or both.

Objections and Qualifications

The relevance of the cost disease to education in contemporary Britain is however less than self-evident. Objections arise to the propositions that the real unit cost of education must rise over time and that the share of national income devoted to education must rise if public demand is to be satisfied.

Taking first real unit costs, a leading source of difficulty involves the scope for productivity growth in education. If educational output is defined narrowly as cognitive development, the technical options for raising productivity appear numerous, including programmed learning materials, teaching machines (computers audio and video tapes), distance learning via telecommunications and self-instruction.[7] In some cases, such as typing and language skills, machine-led learning may prove superior to traditional methods.[8] Moreover, even if interaction between students and teachers remains important for high levels of quality in parts of education, technical progress in related areas may make a big difference to the productivity of teacher time. Thus, even though the Open University still uses personal instruction, the importance of distance learning in its operations allows it to claim a resource cost per undergraduate degree less than one-half that in a conventional university, while the quality of its teaching materials is often superior (Open University, 1984; Gershuny, 1983). Moreover, the Baumol model, by assuming labour homogeneity, fails to allow for increases in productivity as a result of improvement in the quality of the education of teachers themselves. Finally, the importance of education outside formal schooling (adult education, self instruction, etc.) has grown rapidly and productivity growth may be more rapid there.

The upshot is that the rate of productivity growth in education is non-negligible, not that it has been (or can be) raised to the levels prevailing in other sectors. In particular, the use of new learning technology has yet to displace the role of the teacher in either normal or best educational practice (Rossmiller, 1982).

The difficulty of assessing the scope for productivity growth results in part from the multidimensionality and intangibility of educational output. In addition to cognitive learning, the output of the formal education system includes affective learning; the degree of inequality in each type of learning; and the custody of children (Bowles and Gintis, 1976). Even were it possible for cognitive development to proceed with limited loss of quality in a mechanized and depersonalized learning environment, acquisition of the desired social skills and personality traits (notably response to authority) would be seriously affected. Few would want the custody of children to be performed in large groups by warders rather than in small groups by teachers, even though it would be less costly to do so. Indeed, it may be these social and affective functions of education, rather than the cognitive ones, which are the least conducive to productivity enhancement and which constitute the principal source of the cost disease. In any event, the problem of measuring output makes it intrinsically difficult to assess the existence or severity of the cost disease in education.

Some would argue further that, even if productivity growth in education is low, this reflects constraints which are not so much technical as organizational and social (see chapter 13 in this volume). There is the control of methods of production in the universities by academics, with our adherence to such traditional but dysfunctional educational methods as wholesale lecturing. Similarly, the limited nature of competition between public educational institutions weakens a major incentive for efficiency in resource usage in schools.[9] As long as the institutions remain unaltered, such organizational factors join the technical ones in limiting productivity growth in education.

However, public policy has recently attempted to deal with organizational inefficiency in the public sector (Forte and Peacock, 1985). Allocation of marginal funding to more efficient institutions, improved accounting and control procedures in educational bodies, alteration of the terms of employment of teachers, the closure of small schools — these and related measures have been implemented at least partly to improve resource utilization in education (see chapters 5, 13 and 20 in this volume). Were such organizational changes capable of raising the growth of productivity in education towards economy-wide levels, then the adverse effects of level funding could be averted.

The prospect of raising productivity by such policies is far from assured, given the lack of good measures of output and the severity and arbitrariness of many recent interventions (see chapter 12 in this volume). However, even were productivity to increase, the cost disease would still recur, as any gains are largely 'one off.' As long

as the underlying technology of public education remains unchanged, the discrepancy between productivity growth *rates* in
education and the rest of the economy will endure and 'level funding' will eventually, if not rapidly, force reductions in output.[10]

The operation of the cost disease may be held in abeyance by
another influence: sector-specific cuts in factor prices. If we relax
the assumption that factors of production, and particularly labour,
are paid at constant relative rates in all sectors, then the productivity
penalty upon a stagnant sector can be offset by the advantage of
paying lower factor prices. If the two opposing forces are equally
powerful, then relative unit costs and prices will not alter over
time.[11] Such developments are clearly relevant in the case of education, the costs of which are dominated by teacher salaries.[12] The
non-pecuniary rewards associated with professional service might
permit cuts in relative teacher pay. Again, however, little relief for
the cost disease will remain if pay cuts impair morale and teaching
quality; while any such relief is itself intrinsically short-term, as
it would take a continuing reduction in the relative pay of educational staff to prevent level funding from affecting educational output. Such an outcome is clearly unattainable, not to mention its
undesirability.

The central prediction of the Baumol model, rising unit costs in
education, is actually consistent with most of the limited evidence
available.[13] The relative price of educational services has generally
risen secularly. Changes between 1963 and 1970/73 in real educational outlays per student proved positive in fifteen advanced capitalist economies, averaging nearly 20 per cent (OECD, 1976, table
8). Similarly, during the last decade the real price of private education in Britain has increased by more than 3 per cent per annum.[14]
As long as educational quality was not increasing still more rapidly
in each of these instances, the presence of a cost disease can be
inferred.[15]

Even if the real unit costs of formal education can thus be
expected to rise over time, aggregate real spending on education may
be restrained by customer resistance to price increases. The analysis
is complicated in the case of education, as opposed to say hair-
dressing, by the dominance of public over private provision and
finance. In the public sector the main constraint upon service consumption, were the government to seek to emulate market outcomes, would be not the price to the individual customer (as in a
market allocation) but rather the effect of public spending upon
individuals' tax liabilities. The more diffuse nature of the fiscal than

of the market constraint — education being only one among many categories of public expenditure and increases in educational spending falling upon all taxpayers, not just those with school-age children — might lead one to expect a weaker reaction to the increasing cost of education in the case of public than of private finance, resulting in more rapid growth in the share of national resources devoted to education than were finance to be privately based.

The experience of the last ten years has belied such prediction. Not only has low growth in national income dampened the forces promoting educational expansion; the fiscal constraint has also proved tighter than might have been expected of its market equivalent. To some extent this may reflect the greater diffuseness of the benefits (and not just the costs) of public as opposed to private finance. However, as there is nothing new here, benefit diffuseness can hardly account for the change in the fiscal climate.

Alternatively, a policy of restricted funding might be interpreted as the manifestation in the public sector of a high price elasticity and a low income elasticity of demand for education. People may not want to purchase as much education as the state had previously provided on their behalf. Political controversy over public spending provides the medium for the registration of such preferences in the case of a public service (Gramlich, 1985). Certainly the present government, in an attempt to justify its policies in terms of individual preferences, has invoked a popular unwillingness to foot a rising bill for public services.

Public resistance to increased tax bills is undoubtedly a factor, encouraged by lack of understanding of the cost disease. But it does not provide a full answer. Instead of general public relief at the savings effected in the education budget, public concern about the condition of the education services has by now become a major source of government unpopularity. There is also the evidence of strong customer willingness to pay for education in the private sector. Enrolments at private schools are growing strongly at present, despite fee increases markedly in excess of inflation.[16]

The fiscal constraint upon education at present derives instead primarily from the search for politically palatable responses to the increased difficulty of macroeconomic management and intensified distributional conflict which followed the oil and productivity shocks of the mid-1970s. Many economists and politicians found a convenient villain in the size of the public sector (Bacon and Eltis, 1978). Monetarism subsequently turned fiscal restraint into a crusade against public spending. Thus, although rising real incomes have continued to permit an increasing share of national income to be devoted to education, the argument that we can no longer afford to do so has proved politically persuasive, its economic flimsiness notwithstanding.

We therefore affirm the likelihood that the cost disease implies secular increase in both the unit cost, and the share, of national resources devoted to education if the output of the sector is not to fall over time. The magnitude of these trends cannot easily be established, particularly in the absence of detailed enquiry. However, there is good reason to hold that level funding violates the requirements of technology and organization in education, as well as public preferences for adequate levels of educational provision.

Public Outlays and Educational Quality

Level funding has indeed proven a prominent component of both broad fiscal politics and detailed cash limits in the 1980s (Likierman, 1983). However, as rhetoric and reality may have diverged, we examine now the degree to which level funding has prevailed *ex post*, in terms of both real unit and real total educational expenditures.

The funding of public education is analyzed separately for primary schools, secondary schools and universities (table 2).[17] The quantity of educational output is proxied by 'student years.' No adjustment for changes in quality is attempted, the intention being to assess the likely implications for quality of any discontinuity in the growth of real expenditure. The years 1966–83 for which data is available are broken into four groups in order to produce two periods before the fiscal constraint began to bite (1966/69 and 1970/74), followed by two of increasing severity (1975/78 and 1979/83).

Level funding emerges only unevenly in the expenditure record. Real total expenditures certainly declined after 1975/78 in primary and secondary schools and failed to grow markedly in universities. However, as the population of school age also declined after 1975 for primary, and 1978 for secondary, education, per capita expenditures provide a superior indicator. Here the years since 1974 have seen marked growth for primary schools, stagnation for secondary schools and substantial decline for universities. It is also helpful to abstract from capital outlays in view of the declining need for net investment when school rolls are falling. The pattern of change in real recurrent expenditure per student proves similar in all cate-

Table 2: Indices of Real Public Expenditures, Relative Pay Levels and Student Teacher Ratios by Category of Institution and Period (1970–74 = 100)

	1966–69	*1970–74*	*1975–78*	*1979–83*
Real Total				
Public Expenditure[1]				
Primary	75.0	100.0	109.6	101.6
Secondary	72.5	100.0	117.0	113.3
University	87.2	100.0	102.7	104.3
Real Total				
Expenditure per Student[2]				
Primary	81.1	100.0	114.3	124.6
Secondary	86.1	100.0	100.8	98.3
University	110.1	100.0	87.9	82.0
Real Recurrent				
Expenditure per Student				
Primary	82.5	100.0	125.2	141.2
Secondary	88.4	100.0	110.4	113.4
University	95.1	100.0	96.0	93.1
Relative Teacher Pay[3]				
Primary (female)	na	100.0	100.8	95.1
Secondary (male)	na	100.0	107.6	99.1
Student/Teacher Ratios				
Primary	109.4	100.0	91.8	86.7
Secondary	102.9	100.0	96.5	94.2
University	98.8	100.0	109.5	114.6

Sources: Department of Education and Science, *Education Statistics for the U.K.*, annual; Department of Employment, *New Earnings Survey*, annual; UGC (1984), annex G, table 9.

Notes: 1. All expenditure figures on financial year basis and deflated by implied GDP deflator at market prices.
2. Part time and OU students counted at half full-time equivalent.
3. Average gross weekly earnings of full-time teachers whose pay was unaffected by absence as ratio of those of all full-time employees of same sex; figures for 1970–74 refer to 1973–74 only. Data incomplete for universities.

gories, again rising strongly for primary schools; rising, but at a rapidly declining rate, for secondary schools; and sagging steadily for universities.[18]

Level funding was thus approximated in total expenditures for primary schools; in per capita expenditures for secondary schools; and in none of the categories for universities, consistent with the explicit cuts in real funding since 1979. At the same time, it is clear that the fiscal regime has tightened significantly since the mid-1970s in all three categories. The growth of real recurrent expenditure per student fell steadily across sub-periods for secondary schools; between the first and last sub-periods for the primary schools; while it proved negative after the second sub-period for the universities. It is here that we find evidence suggestive of a collision between the cost disease and fiscal restriction in the recent history of public education.

The situation in the school system is complicated by changes in both staffing rates and teacher pay, as well as by the substitution of current for capital outlays (table 2). Average class sizes fell throughout the period (most notably in primary schools through 1975/78), thereby offsetting pressures to reduce recurrent costs per student and even potentially raising quality. The pay factor had similar short-term effects. The relative earnings of teaching staff have fluctuated considerably since 1970 and, in the case of female primary teachers, stood no lower relative to all females in the early 1980s than they had in the early 1970s (table 2). However, despite the Clegg awards of 1980/81, teachers in secondary schools stood in 1979/83 more than 8 per cent below their relative earnings position in 1975/78; while for primary teachers the loss was nearer to 5 per cent. Such reductions made possible some reduction in spending growth without directly cutting quality. However, the increasing shortages of teachers in science subjects and the industrial warfare of the mid-1980s have made it clear that any relief from the consequences of the cost disease has been strictly temporary.

A further factor cushioning the impact of overall expenditure controls upon recurrent educational spending has been the concentration of cuts upon capital outlays. A marked bias towards capital account can be inferred in table 2 from the lower rate of growth of total than of recurrent outlays. Indeed, gross investment in public education declined by 60 per cent between 1970 and 1982. Priority has been given to protecting current expenditures, and in particular teacher employment, within a shrinking overall budget.

The upshot is a prospectively uneven effect upon quality. Fiscal retrenchment has since 1975 cut either the growth (for primary schools) or the level (for secondary schools and universities) of real outlays per student. In the presence of underlying constraints upon productivity growth, adverse effects are to be expected. Given that student-teacher ratios in schools have been not only protected but have fallen further, difficulties have been concentrated upon other areas. Quality has been damaged not just by overall fiscal restriction but also by the bias in resource allocation towards teacher hours, away from such vital complementary inputs as facilities, materials, development spending and, above all, teacher morale, motivation and qualification.

Such a conclusion is supported by the findings of the Schools Inspectorate. While making due reference to the importance of improved utilization of resources, their reports have criticized with increasing force the underlying inadequacy of funding. 'It is difficult to see how on present funding the education service can prevent further decline let alone reverse the situation ... overall the school sector is stretched for money and resources ... many schools are finding it increasingly difficult to replace old books, equipment and furniture; to implement curricular change; and to respond to planned changes in assessment and examination procedures ... the damaging effects of all this on pupil performance and teacher morale are showing themselves clearly' (DES, 1986, pp. 10–12).

More serious effects upon quality might be anticipated for higher education, subject as it has been to falling real funding. Part of the adjustment has been completed through cuts in the volume of output, with the 5 per cent cut in home student numbers after 1981. Quality has suffered as well. Obsolescence and disrepair of equipment and facilities have become serious problems. Student-teacher ratios rose by more than one-fifth between 1972 and 1982. The 'research capability of the universities has been seriously eroded' (UGC, 1984), with adverse effects upon teaching as a likely side-effect. The damage to quality is hard to assess and has undoubtedly been mitigated by improvements in efficiency. But there can be little doubt of its significance. Even the efficiency-oriented Jarratt Committee could find no scope for further expenditure cuts which would not affect the quality of teaching or research (CVCP, 1985).

Conclusions

A critique of the defects of cash limits and level funding as operated in recent years is not an argument for leaving the technology and organization of education untouched. Detailed assessment of the scope for raising productivity becomes particularly important when fiscal curbs are on the agenda. Some such evaluations have been undertaken, with public scrutiny of educational organization and methods increasing after 1979 through the work of the Audit Commission and the University Grants Committee, *inter alia*. However, the detailed implementation of the cuts has been governed by the political urgency and arms-length methods of the monetarist attack upon public expenditure. Although the relevance of the cost disease has been widely recognized during the last twenty years, its implications have been ignored by budgetary policy.

An example is provided by the treatment of the Open University. The gap between its unit cost and that of conventional higher education temporarily offset the cost disease in higher education during the rapid expansion in its enrolments during 1965–75. Yet, when it came to the allocation of cuts after 1979, not only did the Open University receive no less than 'its share,' but also no public assessment was made of the case for using its distinctive technology to maintain output in the face of fiscal cuts. Distance learning may in fact be able to make little further contribution to higher education; but an analysis of such structural issues should precede any attempt to rationalize the education system.

On the budgetary front, the central task for public policy is to devise a fiscal regime which simultaneously recognizes both the considerable scope for increasing efficiency and the limited scope for raising productivity growth in public education. Neglect of this vital distinction, long recognized in the literature[19], represents a central element in the policy failure of the years since 1975. The current trend towards greater budgetary autonomy for public educational institutions (UGC, 1984; and see chapter 19 in this volume) would, if combined with a more liberal and forward-looking determination of cash limits, go some way towards recognizing each requirement in educational finance.

Notes

1   This chapter represents part of a wider research project, *The Information Sector: Unbalanced Growth and Its Implications*, currently being undertaken by Lars Osberg, William Baumol, Edward Wolff and the present author. We acknowledge gratefully the financial support of the Institute for Research on Public Policy (Canada). The author thanks Lars Osberg, Edward Wolff and the participants in the Birmingham

seminar of April 1986, particularly Hywel Thomas and Keith Drake, for comments on earlier drafts of this chapter.

2   The productivity measure in question is generally taken to be labour productivity, consistent with interest in employment rather than output; but the same analysis can be applied to total factor productivity when other inputs, notably physical capital and labour quality, are considered as well.

3   The share of services in output in the US, measured at constant prices, remained broadly unchanged between 1929 and 1965. As the relative price of services rose, the service share in output measured at current prices therefore increased at the same rate (FUCHS, 1968).

4   'Education, like the arts, affords little opportunity for systematic and cumulative increases in productivity' (BAUMOL and BOWEN, 1966, p. 171).

5   The two sector model has been extended to consider a hybrid category, the asymptotically stagnant, whose output depends upon a combination of progressive (for example, computing hardware) and stagnant (for example, software) components, with the cost disease applying to the whole only in the longer term, as the progressive components extinguish their contribution to cost reduction (BAUMOL and WOLFF, 1983; BAUMOL, BLACKMAN and WOLFF, 1985). Some technical advances in education, such as distance learning based upon broadcasting, may be analyzable in such terms.

6   We abstract here from the complications associated with economies of scale in the production of education services, with their potentially important consequences for unit costs in the presence of fluctuations in the size of the student body (THOMAS, 1984).

7   In recent work BAUMOL (1985) accepts that there may be significant scope for raising productivity through such combinations of mechanisation and self-service (termed 'model shift' by GERSHUNY, 1983).

8   I am grateful to Lars Osberg for this suggestion, derived from personal experience.

9   Widespread preoccupation with price-based forms of competition (for example, through privatization or voucher systems) typically means little recognition of the extent to which non-price competition for pupils (in terms of numbers, ability and social class) reduces inefficiency in public education.

10   In economic terminology, even if the rate at which the production frontier shifts outward is intrinsically low, moves toward the frontier from positions within it will indeed increase productivity growth, but only temporarily.

11   The importance of factor price changes was accepted in the early application of the two-sector model to the performing arts, where relative salaries were not only low but also open to decline as higher real incomes made the non-pecuniary benefits of working in the arts increasingly attainable (BAUMOL and BOWEN, 1966, pp. 168–71).

12   In 1981–82, wages and salaries of education staff and employees accounted for 77 per cent of all outlays on public education (DES, 1985c, table 5).

13 National accounts are of no help in this respect. By assessing educational outputs wholly through labour inputs, they assume zero growth in labour productivity, thereby imposing a growth in unit costs greater than is likely to prevail in practice (CSO, 1985, p. 26).

14 The average annual increase between 1978 and 1986 in fees for day pupils at private schools affiliated to the Headmasters' Conference was 12.5 per cent, as compared to 9.2 per cent in the Retail Price Index (ISIS, 1983, table 4; ISIS, 1986, table 3).

15 A further difficulty is posed by estimates that educational productivity actually declined during the postwar period, as output grew less rapidly than inputs (WOODHALL and BLAUG, 1965 and 1968). Were such estimates close to the mark, the intensity of the cost disease would be all the greater. In fact, the inference of declining productivity is (as the authors accept) tenuous, based as it is upon only the academic and labour market dimensions of educational quality. Consideration of the quality of student life in schools and universities might soften or reverse the conclusion.

16 Between 1984 and 1986 pupil numbers in private schools affiliated to ISIS rose by 2.6 per cent despite an increase in real fees charged of 3.8 per cent, a 1.2 per cent decline in the number of schools covered by the survey and the continuing shrinkage of the school age population (ISIS, 1984, 1986).

17 Other categories (nursery, further education, etc.) were excluded because of the importance of part-time attendance, which makes cost comparisons more difficult.

18 Recurrent costs are used as a guide to total costs in the absence of data on inputs of physical capital services (as opposed to gross investment).

19 'The fact remains, however, that efficiency and productivity are distinct concepts that must be judged by different criteria. Even if we showed that the productivity of universities has not increased in the recent past, we would still be far from the conclusion that they could be more efficient' (BLAUG, 1969, p. 316).

A Model of Education Expenditure Change in English Local Authorities[1]

John Gibson and Peter Watt

Introduction

In this chapter we describe a model of education expenditure change which we have estimated for English local authorities for the years 1982/83 to 1984/85 — a period of increasing tension in central-local relations. Our estimations of the model's parameters show the influence of the rate support grant (RSG) system and local politics upon expenditure during these years.

The chapter contains two parts. First, we provide the background context of local government finance and explain the objectives of the new grant system — the block grant — introduced in 1981, and the expenditure targets and grant penalties which were then rapidly added and grew in severity each year. Second, we describe a measure of the 'fiscal pressure' that this complex grant system exerted on different local authorities, and present the model of education expenditure.

The Block Grant and the Crisis in Central-Local Relations

The Conservative government, which took office in May 1979, was committed to a substantial reduction in public spending and taxation. In fact, apart from in the field of law and order, it hoped to see larger reductions in local government spending than in other areas. It believed that the structure of the existing grant system — which funded over 60 per cent of net expenditure in 1980/81 — encouraged many local authorities to maintain or increase high levels of spending. High spending authorities were also perceived to get an unfair share of available grant at the expense of low spending authorities.

The grant system of the late 1970s had attempted by means of two separate general grants — the needs element and the resources element — to compensate fully for differences between local authorities in their needs and resources. Local authorities' needs, or rather the cost of providing similar standards of services, were measured by means of a complex statistical exercise relating assessed needs to observed associations between differences in local authorities' past spending and various social and physical indicators. Resources were measured by rateable values per head and all local authorities had their tax bases supplemented by an amount sufficient to bring their effective tax base up to a national standard rateable value — set at £178 per head in 1980/81.

The result was a system in which, for most authorities, the local tax rate (the rate poundage) was a standard function of spending per head in relation to their assessed spending needs. In London, however, where rateable values were higher and a few inner boroughs had very large non-domestic rateable values, a combination of 'clawback' on needs element and a within-London resource redistribution left all authorities on lower, and thus more generous, rate poundage functions.

Both elements were felt to give incentives to high spending. The use of past spending as the basis for needs assessment was felt to give undue weight to those indicators prevalent in high spending authorities, such as single parent families, and was thought to create a 'feedback' effect where the higher level of grant received encouraged such authorities to increase their spending still further. The resources element gave a constant rate of grant support (at a rate which depended upon the level of local resource deficiency) on expenditure no matter how high that expenditure was in relation to assessed needs.

The new grant system planned for 1981/82 involved three major changes:

(i) The block grant, replacing both needs and resources elements, would have a 'taper' on the rate of grant support given to any local authority which spent above threshold, itself to be set at some margin above 'needs'. This is shown by the increase in slope of the rate poundage function in Figure 1.

(ii) A new measure of needs, called grant related expenditure

Figure 1: The Rate Poundage and Local Authority Spending.

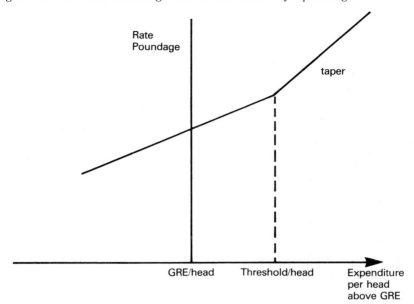

(GRE), based on the average unit costs of providing for identifiable client groups, such as school children, and the numbers of such clients within each local authority. The use of regression based on past expenditure was to be minimized.

(iii)   For the first time measures of each local authority's needs were to be made explicit by publication.

It was hoped that all three changes would encourage local authorities to decrease their spending. In presenting the RSG settlement for 1981/82 the Secretary of State for the Environment laid great stress on the importance of local government restricting its expenditure to the levels planned by the government:

> The new system I have announced today ... is fairer, more visible and more comprehensible ... The new block grant system does not of course guarantee delivery of any given aggregate volume of expenditure, since it is primarily concerned with the fair distribution of grant and leaves local authorities free to reach their own spending and rating decisions. This means, however, that the Government must look

to local authorities to deliver, as they have done in the past, the reductions in the volume of expenditure prescribed in our expenditure plans. At this stage I do not propose to issue formally a guideline for each authority but I am seeking urgently the views of the local authority associations about what steps need to be taken to secure the delivery of the national target.[2]

Some further features of the GREs are important both to the general issue of 'overspending' and to education spending in particular. First, the sum of GREs initially[3] was set equal to the planned provision for English local government. This meant that if plans were to be met, spending above GRE by existing high spending authorities had to be balanced by equal amounts of spending below GRE by other authorities. However, the toughness of the government's requests for cuts can be gauged from the fact that the 1981/82 provision for 'total expenditure' was only 1 per cent above the 1980/81 first budgets of English local authorities at a time when inflation between the two years was anticipated to exceed 10 per cent. Where were the underspenders to come from?

Second, GREs were, unlike assessed spending needs, service-based and thus gave rise to hopes amongst those concerned with low levels of education provision in some areas that they would encourage some increase in provision — although we can see that, given the overall severity of the government's spending plans, greater uniformity was a more feasible hope. Service GREs provided a possible instrument of influence within the framework of a general grant system where the freedom of local authorities to ignore the wishes of education ministers to spend upon specific programmes — such as in-service training — had emerged as an issue in the later 1970s.

Of course, it must be remembered that the service base of GREs was a major point of criticism of the new system by many in local government who were concerned to preserve local freedom with respect to service priorities.

As events turned out any concern for increasing provision by low spenders was overridden by the government's first priority of reducing expenditure. The government decided that it needed real cuts in expenditure by all authorities rather than just from the 'overspenders' and for this purpose introduced expenditure targets and grant penalties for spending above target. This concern with the expenditure of individual authorities was a dramatic departure from previous practice — a departure not even hinted at by the government when the block grant proposals were proceeding through Parliament during 1980. In fact, the grant penalties had to be given legality retrospectively through the Local Government Finance Act of 1982.

The years from 1981/82 to 1985/86 saw grant penalties increase in severity each year, but despite this local government overspending persisted both on its aggregate current expenditure and education current expenditure as we show in table 1. Also as table 2 shows the government had consistently revised upwards its plans for spending in order to make its plans appear more attainable. Local government actually increased its current expenditure in 1982/83 and 1983/84 — this second successive increase being regarded by the government as the final straw, and they finally decided to introduce the Rates Bill in 1984 enabling them to set limits on the rate levels of selected authorities.

Table 1: Current Expenditure, English Local Government (£m. cash)

	Provision			Budgets			Overspend	
Year	Aggr. Crrnt Expd.	Educ. Crrnt Expd.	2/1 %	Aggr. Crrnt Expd.	Educ. Crrnt Expd.	5/4 %	Aggr. 4on1 %	Educ. 5on2 %
	1	2	3	4	5	6	7	8
81/82	16180	8333	51.50	17534	8862	50.54	8.37	6.35
82/83	18000	9190	51.06	19260	9601	49.85	7.00	4.47
83/84	19692	9882	50.18	20550	10331	50.27	4.36	4.54
84/85	20389	10123	49.65	21439	10489	48.92	5.15	3.62

Source: Extracted from Association of County Councils: Rate Support Grant various years.

Table 2: Revisions to Government Plans for Local Government Current Expenditure, England (£m. 1983/84 Prices)

White Paper	1981/82	1982/83	1983/84	1984/85
Cmnd 8175 (Mar 81)	18226	17852	17700	
Cmnd 8494 (Mar 82)		18902	18720	18558
Cmnd 8789 (Feb 83)			19620	19142
Cmnd 9143 (Feb 84)				19543

Real spending on primary education fell throughout the period and was more or less static for secondary education. This is shown in table 3. However, this disguised large differences between authorities in spending changes. Travers (1986) has calculated, using 1983/84 prices, that real spending on primary schools fell by 19.6 per cent in South Tyneside between 1979/80 and 1984/85 and by 18.4 per cent in Leeds and 16.4 per cent in Trafford, whereas Hounslow spent 12.1 per cent more, Nottinghamshire 5.9 per cent more and Waltham Forest 5.2 per cent. In secondary education Richmond reduced spending by 23.4 per cent, Bromley by 17 per cent, and Harrow by 15.4 per cent; increases took place in Leeds (9.2 per cent), Wigan (7.6 per cent) and Bradford (7.3 per cent).

Table 3: Real Current Expenditure: Primary and Secondary Education (£m. 1984/85 costs)

	1979/80	1980/81	1981/82	1982/83	1983/84	1984/85
Primary	2751	2702	2615	2548	2518	2535
Secondary	3796	3824	3827	3844	3876	3880

However, the most disturbing feature of events during these years for those concerned with levels of education provision was that targets tended to be lowest for those authorities already spending at the lowest levels relative to GRE. Table 4 gives the data for 1983/84 which shows how much more severe targets were for the low spending shire counties.

Table 4: Comparison of 1983/84 Targets and GREs

Class of Authority	Sum of Targets (£m)	Sum of GREs (£m)	Excess of Sum of Targets over Sum of GREs (%)	No. of authorities with Target: Below GRE	At or above GRE
London Precepting	1,673	1,343	24.6	—	3
Inner London Boroughs	898	695	29.2	1	12
Outer London Boroughs	1,719	1,615	6.4	2	18
Metropolitan Counties	1,104	928	19.0	—	6
Metropolitan Districts	4,057	3,891	4.3	11	25
Non-Met Counties	9,237	9,287	−0.5	23	16
Non-Met Districts	1,446	1,471	−1.7	199	98
ENGLAND	20,134	19,230	4.7		

The reason for this feature, which given the expected effects of grant penalties would tend to increase spending disparities, was twofold: (i) targets were related to previous budgets; and (ii) the higher spending authorities included a number who ignored grant penalties or were not subject to them — such as ILEA[4] whereas the low spending counties tended to respond to the restraint of targets.

We now turn to considering education expenditure modelling for local authorities.

Existing Work in Education Expenditure Modelling

There have been a number of papers published seeking to explain the level of local authority spending on education.

Dawson (1976) constructed models of education expenditure determination which explained 48 per cent of the variation of expenditure per primary school pupil for all local education authorities in England and Wales, and 59 per cent of the variation in expenditure per secondary school pupil. Her study considered primary and secondary education separately. It sought to explain expenditure per school pupil. The most important variables in the study of primary education were an index indicating the extent to which small schools featured in an authority's service, and the percentage of teachers employed to meet special educational needs. For secondary schools the most important variables were those indicating the mix of school type, and the course of study followed by older pupils. For all the regressions a dummy variable, set to one if the authority was in Greater London and zero otherwise, indicated a significant positive effect on expenditure.

Using a broadly similar approach Foster, Jackman and Perlman (1980, p. 270) reported the following results for the (then) county boroughs:

$$\text{XPRI} = 107.50 - 0.24\text{PROPO} + 0.008\text{Y} + 0.11\text{PRI}$$
$$(0.09) \qquad (0.003) \qquad (0.5)$$

$$- 2.28\text{CON} + 36.68\text{ILLEG} + 3.29\text{LAB} \qquad \text{RSQ } 0.24$$
$$(2.47) \qquad (24.58) \qquad (3.25)$$

and

$$\text{XSEC} = 222.94 - 0.59\text{PROPO} + 0.022\text{Y} - 7.05\text{CON}$$
$$(0.25) \qquad (0.009) \qquad (5.31)$$

$$+ 67.27\text{ILLEG} + 1.30\text{DEC} - 10.65\text{HIGHD} - 0.90\text{NEDGR}$$
$$(66.34) \qquad (0.78) \qquad (7.28) \qquad (0.63)$$
$$\text{RSQ } 0.15$$

where PROPO measured the proportion of owner-occupiers, Y measured household income regionally, CON and LAB measured the proportion of councillors in the Conservative and Labour parties, PRI was the number of primary school children in the authority, DEC was the rate of decline of population, HIGHD the proportion of the population in densely populated wards and parishes, ILLEG measured the proportion of illegitimate births, and NEDGR the receipt of needs grant per head of population.

Jackman and Papadachi (1981) estimated a model to explain education expenditure for the 104 education authorities in England and Wales for 1978/79. They found more success in explaining primary education expenditure than secondary education expenditure with multiple correlation coefficients of 0.74 and 0.60 respectively. They classified their explanatory variables as representing three factors: a cost factor, a preference factor (percentage Labour or other left councillors) and budgetary factors, such as the share or marginal expenditure met by domestic rates, the level of lump sum grants per schoolchild and a measure of regional income.

Most recently Jesson *et al* (1985) have estimated a model which explains 71.3 per cent of expenditure per secondary school pupil in the ninety-six English LEAs in 1981/82. They report the following regression:

$$EXP = £1.305 + 2.24BA - 4.73CH - 6.11OS + 3.35GRADS$$
$$(2.8) \qquad (-3.9) \qquad (-4.2) \qquad (2.9)$$
$$+ 9.5AS -- 7.23CONTACT$$
$$(2.1) \qquad (-2.0)$$

where BA measures the percentage of children born outside the UK, Ireland, USA and the old Commonwealth or in households whose head was similarly born, CH measures the percentage change in numbers of 11–16 year old pupils on the LEA roll over the five years preceding 1982, OS measures the proportion of oversize classes, GRADS measures the percentage of graduate teachers employed, AS measures the percentage of 'additional' teaching staff employed other than on the permanent staff, and CONTACT measures the class-contact ratio (the proportion of school staff actually teaching at any given time).

Lastly, we make mention of, but cannot do justice to in discussion here, the enormous continuous annual undertaking which is the education expenditure modelling element of the construction of GREs.

The Effect of the Fiscal Environment

The model of education expenditure developed in this chapter differs from all the models discussed above in taking as its focus of interest incremental change in education budgets. We attempt to model year-on-year changes in education expenditure firstly because of the intrinsic interest of such an approach, secondly because one of our major objectives was to investigate how far expenditure responded to the guidelines implicit in GREs, and thirdly because the government itself focusses on expenditure changes in policy debate.

In modelling the determinants of change of education expenditure a major effect to take account of is that of the grant system. The amount of grant paid to a local authority determines the level of local rates which must be set for any given level of expenditure and has always been considered a major determinant of local authorities' expenditure by economists. Empirical studies have confirmed these expectations.

The grant system of recent years has presented novel difficulties for those wishing to model the role of grant as a determinant of expenditure. Economists distinguish two categories of grant — lump sum grants, which do not vary with expenditure, and matching grants, where the amount of grant increases with expenditure, usually at a constant rate. The introduction of the basic block grant brought a new complexity to the grant system by generating two rates of matching — one on expenditure below threshold and one on expenditure above threshold. A further consequence of its introduction was the occurrence of negative matching grants, that is grants which fall as expenditure rises, for those authorities with larger rateable values per head.

Onto this already complex structure were added grant penalties for spending above targets which made the system yet again more complicated, greatly increasing the negative matching effect[5] and creating as many as six different branches to the rate poundage function, often within a very narrow range of expenditure. In modelling expenditure change we were concerned to include in our explanation some measure of recent change in the generosity/ severity of the grant environment in which a local authority operates. Within such a system it is very misleading simply to use the amount of grant received by each authority as a measure of its treatment under the grant system, because the amount received is so dependent upon the expenditure of the authority.

We required an objective measure of the severity of grant changes, that is one which was invariant with respect to the expenditure behaviour of individual authorities. For this purpose we used a measure developed in Gibson and Smith (1985) called 'fiscal pressure' which is the rate poundage change required for maintaining a constant, or given, volume of expenditure. The fiscal pressure variables derived there answer the question: 'If all authorities increased their expenditure by x per cent, what would be the consequent rise (fall) in rates for each authority?'

A Model of Local Authority Education Expenditure Change

The estimation of education expenditure change developed in this chapter is based on the following hypothesized model:

(1) $\quad$ CHEDB = f[ALIGN, CEDGR, $-$CRPb,
$\qquad\qquad -$(CRPb $-$ CRPa), PCT, PCG, $-$C, $-$N]

For the regressions explaining the change in education budgets from 1982/83 to 1983/84 the definitions of the variables are given below. The definitions of the variables for the regressions explaining the change in education budgets from 1982/83 to 1983/84 may be deduced by simply moving all years in the definitions one year forward.

CHEDB — the percentage year-on-year change in the education budget 1982/83 to 1983/84.

ALIGN — the change in education budget that would make education's share of the local authority budget in 1983/84 the same as education GRE's share of total GRE in 1982/83.

CEDGR — the percentage change in education GRE between 1982/83 and 1983/84.

CRPb — the change in rate poundage for a 5 per cent cash increase in 1983/84 (and for a 3 per cent cash increase in 1984/85) — given zero use of balances and zero provision for clawback.

CRPa — the change in rate poundage for a 3 per cent cash increase in 1983/84 (and for a 0 per cent cash increase in 1984/85) — given zero use of balances and zero provision for clawback.

CRPb-CRPa — the increase in the change in rate poundage for the increase in the change in expenditure used to define the CRPs (see above).

PCT — the percentage change: 1983/84 target compared to 1982/83 budget.

PCG — the percentage change: 1983/84 GRE compared to 1982/83 budget.

CON — equal to 1 when majority of seats held by Conservative party mid-1982 (mid-1983 for 83/84 to 84/85 regressions).

NOC — equal to 1 when no party holding a majority of seats (or where majority of seats held by Liberal party) mid-1982 (mid-1983 for 83/84 to 84/85 regressions).

Fiscal pressure is measured by the variables CRPb and (CRPb − CRPa). The first is a measure of the average fiscal pressure facing the authority — the expected rate rise if expenditure were raised by a hypothetical 5 per cent by every authority in 1983/84, and, for the second of our two time periods studied, the expected rate rise if expenditure were raised by a hypothetical 3 per cent by every authority in 1984/85.

The second variable is a measure of marginal fiscal pressure. This variable indicates the extent of the change in rate rise on moving from a low hypothesized across-the-board expenditure increase (CRPa as defined above) to a higher hypothesized expenditure increase.

Both the average measure of fiscal pressure and the marginal measure of fiscal pressure are expected to be negatively related to increases in authorities' total expenditure and hence they are expected to be also negatively related to changes in what is usually the major part of total expenditure: education expenditure.

Four more variables are included because of their likely effect on the overall budget and hence, indirectly, on the education budget: firstly two guideline variables: PCT — the percentage change in target compared to previous budget and PCG — the percentage change in GRE compared to previous budget. These two variables — the grant/fiscal effects of which are already embodied in the fiscal pressure variables — are expected to be positively related to increases in education budget to the extent that authorities treat them as guidelines. Secondly political influence is measured by CON — a dummy variable representing Conservative control of a local authority, and NOC a dummy variable indicating where an authority is subject to no overall political control.

Two variables are used to measure education-specific effects: ALIGN and CEDGR. The variable ALIGN is included to test for the presence of convergence/divergence between local authority education budgets and education GREs. Education GREs attempt to be the best objective measure of the costs of providing education services to a similar standard in different local authorities. The derivation of the variable is as follows. Consider a local authority for which the education budget represents 45 per cent of the total local authority budget, but for which education GRE represents 50 per cent of the total GRE for the authority. For this authority there is a substantial divergence between education's share of the budget and education's share of GRE. Suppose now we consider the possibility that a local authority might use GRE as a guideline and might wish to remove this divergence next year.

If a local authority wished to adjust its spending to remove entirely the last observed divergence between education's share of their GRE and education's share of their budget, then it would need to raise its education budget in the next year to the level at which it represents 50 per cent of the total local authority budget. Of course spending on other budgets may change, but for simplicity let us assume that other budgets remain constant. The question then is, by what percentage must spending on education rise so that education budget share equals education GRE share? Let this percentage rise in education budget be denoted by the variable ALIGN, then algebraically we can write:

$$(2) \quad \frac{EDGRE1}{TGRE1} = \frac{EDB1 + [(ALIGN/100).EDB1]}{TB1}$$

where EDGRE1 is education GRE in year 1, TGRE1 is total GRE in year 1, EDB1 is education budget in year 1 and TB1 is total budget in year 1. Rearranging (2) above we obtain:

$$(3) \quad ALIGN = 100. [(EDGRE1/TGRE1)/(EDB1/TB1) - 1]$$

In practice we expect such adjustment, where it occurs, to be both less than complete and not accomplished entirely in one year. The coefficient on this variable is expected to be positive but considerably below the figure of unity that full adjustment would entail.

The variable CHEDGR — the percentage change in education GRE for the two years considered — is included to test whether changes in education GRE are reflected in changes in education expenditure.

The Results

The task of modelling expenditure changes is more ambitious than that of modelling expenditure levels because one would expect to see greater randomness in year-on-year changes if only because of data measurement errors. However, our results from testing the model are pleasing in terms of their overall explanatory power.

Table 5 gives the regression results of the model used to explain the increase in education budgets for 1983/84 over 1982/83 for Metropolitan Districts, non-Metropolitan Counties and outer-London Boroughs. Table 6 gives the corresponding regression results for increases in education budgets for 1984/85 over 1983/84. Overall the explanatory power of the regressions is pleasing given that the estimation is for year-on-year changes and for a cross

Table 5: Regression Results for 1982/83 to 1983/84, Dependent Variable CHEDB

	Met Districts		Non-Met Counties		Outer-London	
	Coeff	t	Coeff	t	Coeff	t
ALIGN	.158b	1.759	.267a	2.521	.106	.530
CEDGR	−.125	−.459	−.099	−.297	−.398d	−.766
CRPb	.013	.293	−.059d	−.947	−.180	−1.052
CRPb−CRPa	−.325d	−.923	.141	.257	−.056	−.054
PCT	−.290	−.482	.233	.220	.211	.150
PCG	−.107d	−1.129	.188d	1.026	−.024	−.102
CON	−1.520c	−1.692	−1.839b	−2.088	−3.987d	−1.285
NOC	.259	.266	−1.039d	−1.067	−.701	−.245
CONST	9.074b	2.010	5.924d	.803	13.154d	.980
RSQUARED	.494		.322		.254	
RBARSQUARED	.344		.142		−.288	
No of Obs	36		39		20	
SSR	71.031		97.259		131.772	

a, b, c and d denote regression coefficients significantly different from zero in a one-tailed test at the .01, .05, .10 and .25 levels respectively.

Table 6: Regression Results for 1983/4 to 1984/5, Dependent Variable CHEDB

	Met Districts		Non-Met Counties		Outer-London	
	Coeff	t	Coeff	t	Coeff	t
ALIGN	.322b	2.349	.143d	1.065	.388a	3.241
CEDGR	−.139	−.408	−.072	−.224	1.853a	2.927
CRPb	−.051d	−.752	.738d	.827	.038	.332
CRPb−CRPa	.075	.451	.572	.219	1.304a	3.727
PCT	.059	.081	.069	.047	4.264a	3.950
PCG	.058	.583	.189d	.851	.466a	3.440
CON	−.809d	−.701	1.497d	1.103	−6.188b	−2.134
NOC	−.050	−.044	1.587d	1.165	−1.873d	−.786
CONST	4.189d	1.214	1.766	.331	−11.822c	−1.584
RSQUARED	.233		.145		.819	
RBARSQUARED	.006		−.083		.687	
No of Obs	36		39		20	
SSR	120.088		110.718		52.107	

a, b, c and d denote regression coefficients significantly different from zero in a one-tailed test at the .01, .05, .10 and .25 levels respectively.

section study. ALIGN has the expected sign in all six regressions and is usually significantly different from zero. CEDGR is less successful, usually not being significantly different from zero, though it does carry the correct sign in the one case where its significance is firmly established: in outer-London Boroughs for 1983/84 on 1984/85. The regression as a whole in this case stands out from the rest in having by far the highest value for R squared and all the coefficients significant except average fiscal pressure and with their expected signs. Generally the average and marginal fiscal pressure variables are not very successful, usually not being significant, the exception being marginal fiscal pressure for outer-London Boroughs in the second time period. This story is repeated for target to budget and GRE to budget, which generally show up poorly except for outer-London Boroughs in the second time period. The political variables CON and to a lesser extent NOC are usually significant with generally the expected negative signs, except in the case of non-Metropolitan Counties in 1983/84 to 1984/85 where the effect is quite strongly in the direction opposite to that expected.

Conclusions

The model described above is directed at the difficult task of explaining not levels of education budgets but what is at once more difficult but more interesting in a policy context — year-on-year change in education budgets. It is therefore pleasing that the levels of explanation obtained are quite high. ALIGN is a variable that in general works well. Overall its coefficients suggest that when budget share for education is out of line with GRE share, budget changes are made in the following year that on average remove about one-third of the discrepancy.

The effect of change in education GRE (CEDGR) is less well established with all coefficients carrying the 'wrong' signs though insignificantly different from zero except for outer-London Boroughs in 1983/84 to 1984/85. Fiscal pressure measures are not very successful in these models. The chain of causation with these variables is indirect in that they were included because of their likely effect on the total budget and hence by implication a partial effect on the education budget. In results reported elsewhere where we have tried to explain changes in overall local authority budgets the fiscal pressure variables are far more successful (Gibson and Watt 1986). Changes in overall GRE and target also have limited explanatory power except for the regressions for outer-London Boroughs in 1983/84 to 1984/85 where they are very successful.

In fact the regressions for outer-London Boroughs in 1983/84 to 1984/85 perform outstandingly well for reasons that are not entirely clear. Lastly, the effect of politics is generally well-established in these models with Conservative, or no overall control, having a negative effect on changes in education budgets.

Notes

1 This chapter results from work carried out on a DES-financed research project on the Effect of GREs on Education Expenditure and Budgetary Decision-Making by Local Authorities. Any views expressed in this chapter do not necessarily reflect those of the DES. Crown copyright 1986. This chapter is reproduced with the permission of the controller of Her Majesty's Stationary Office.

2 Statement by the Secretary of State for the Environment to the Consultative Council on Local Government Finance on 16 December 1980.

3 In the third year of the new system, 1983/84, it was decided to create a gap of £904m between what the government saw as a desirable level of

provision, equal to the national aggregate of targets, in order to make targets more attainable. This practice continued until 1986/87 when the system of targets and penalties was abandoned.

4   The ILEA was spending so far above its GRE that, because it lost grant as it increased spending, it had zero block grant entitlement, and, therefore, could not be subject to any effective grant penalty.

5   To give one example of the relative severity of penalties compared to the basic block grant taper: an extra £1 of spending by Manchester in 1985/86 cost local ratepayers £1.12 below threshold, £1.40 above threshold, but £3.08 for spending over 2 per cent above target. The target related grant penalty was £1.68 compared to the taper of 28p. For the data on other authorities see CIPFA (1985).

Labour Market Signals and Graduate Output: A Case Study of the University Sector

Andrew Gurney

Introduction

The 1985 Green Paper on the development of higher education into the 1990s put a special emphasis on the subject balance of graduates, and in particular expressed concern that the British higher education system was producing insufficient graduates with science and technology skills. This chapter considers the factors that determine the output of graduates by subject, using empirical evidence to suggest that shortages are best tackled by assessing and responding to changes in labour market signals. The case study concentrates on the university sector because of the greater availability of data. It is anticipated that the results will apply equally well to other parts of the higher education spectrum.

The Demand for University Places: A Theoretical Framework

There is an ample literature on the determinants of the demand for higher education (for example Blaug, 1970). However empirical studies such as Dolphin (1981) and Pissarides (1981 and 1982) have generally looked at overall trends without differentiating by subject. Recent work by Bosworth and Ford (1985) suggests that students in different subjects may react differently to economic signals. This chapter considers this in greater detail.

Economic models of the demand for higher education tend to split education demand into consumption and investment components, the distinction between the two being that the consumption component is a demand for education as a good in its own right, while the investment component is a demand for education because of further benefits it may yield, most notably in terms of improved career prospects. This analysis may be readily transferred to the subject demand of prospective students. It may be expected that the consumption element of demand is something that is given for individuals in the sense that their preferences for studying a particular subject *per se* are unaffected by external economic factors. In contrast the investment element of demand may respond to changing economic signals, and in particular to changes in the labour market demand for graduates of different disciplines. Hence economic theory suggests that labour market signals are likely to be an important influence on the future supply of graduates, provided that the investment component of education demand is strong. The theory can be tested by looking at how closely labour market signals have affected the pattern of student demand.

Empirical Evidence

The Demand for Graduates

Reliable indicators of employers' demand for graduates of different disciplines are not easy to find. The General Household Survey provides information on graduate earnings by subject group, but it is difficult to separate out how much of earnings differentials are attributable to specific discipline skills and how much are attributable to factors such as ability or experience. In addition it is not clear that the earnings differential of a 40-year-old graduate engineer will in any way represent the expected differential of a current engineering student, on account of changes in the supply of, and demand for, engineering skills. In this respect graduate starting salaries are more reliable indicators, although these can still be misleading (for example low starting salaries for lawyers, doctors and accountants do not represent poor career prospects). An additional problem is that graduate starting salary data is disappointingly sparse. The careers service at the University of Leeds has obtained and published such information for their graduates since the 1960s, and some other careers services have recently followed suit, but the data remains too narrowly based for meaningful analysis.

One other indicator of labour market demand for graduates is the unemployment data from UGC first destination statistics. These record the number of graduates unemployed at 31 December following graduation, and hence are primarily a flow measure of unemployment indicating how quickly graduates are absorbed into the labour market. The data has been analyzed in some detail by Tarsh (1985a and 1985b). An analysis of the data between 1970 and 1983 shows that graduate unemployment varied substantially by subject group, and also tended to vary according to the state of the economy, as measured by overall adult unemployment, although the degree of responsiveness to the general economic climate varied across disciplines. Unemployment rates were consistently lower than average for graduates in the health, education, professional and technology subject groups, and within the science and social studies groups for graduates in mathematics, business studies and law. But graduate unemployment rates do not of themselves indicate the relative economic worth of graduates of different disciplines. Much of the graduate labour market is more interested in the general skills and personal characteristics of graduates than in their degree subject. Variations in graduate unemployment should therefore be at least partly attributed to such general characteristics. In practice this cannot be adequately quantified, although the average 'A' level points score of course entrants provides some indication of academic calibre, albeit imperfect. UCCA statistics on the qualifications of course entrants reveal some correlation between the 'A' level grades of university entrants by subject and subsequent graduate unemployment rates. Two interesting exceptions to this finding are education and technology, where entrants were generally less well qualified than average, but where graduate unemployment was nonetheless low.

While in principle one might interpret the graduate unemployment rates themselves as evidence of graduate shortages or surpluses, in practice one should take account of the circumstances of each sector of the graduate labour market. For example while low unemployment rates for graduates in law and accountancy are evidence of the buoyant demand for such graduates, they do not indicate a shortage of graduates in either profession, since graduates can be readily recruited from other disciplines. Similarly low unemployment rates in education and in medicine occur because of the close control over the supply of such graduates, and do not necessarily indicate a shortage. The area of greatest concern in recent years has been of a shortage of engineering and technology graduates. Such a shortage could be met to some extent by the recruitment of graduates in other scientific disciplines (principally physics and mathematics), but the scope for substituting skills is much more limited than in accountancy and law. The empirical evidence shows that unemployment rates amongst graduates in civil and mechanical engineering were low in the 1970s, but have since risen, suggesting that any shortage of such graduates may have been alleviated (although some of the increase may be due to the effects of the recent recession which was especially severe for manufacturing industry). Graduate unemployment remains low for electrical engineering.

The Supply of Graduates

Movements in the pattern of prospective students' demand for university courses are revealed by UCCA applications statistics. The data is not strictly comprehensive as it only includes those candidates that make use of UCCA's applications procedure, but as this is the vast majority of home candidates the figures are assumed to be a reasonable indicator of all candidates' demand.[1]

The relationship between labour market signals and students' demand for courses was tested using regression analysis. The UCCA applications data for eight subject groups were first standardized, and then changes in the level of course applications were regressed on changes in subject unemployment rates, and on changes in the overall graduate unemployment rate (which acted as a proxy for unemployment in other subjects).[2] It was anticipated that the relationship might differ across subject groups, and subject dummy variables were included to allow for this. The regression also included trend variables to allow for factors such as changes in the number of places available, and for the increasing participation of women in higher education. Over the period 1971–83 a coherent regression was obtained that explained 52 per cent of the changes in applications by subject groups. An interesting feature was the different responses to the unemployment signals across subject groups. In arts and social studies the change in applications increased by 0.1 per cent for each 1 per cent fall in the level of subject unemployment, compared to an increase of 0.3 per cent for science and engineering subjects, while a 1 per cent increase in overall graduate unemployment resulted in a 0.1 per cent increase for arts and social studies compared to 0.4 per cent for engineering and science subjects. These results indicate that students' demand for courses is indeed responsive to signals about the demand for graduates, and that the response is especially sensitive in the science and engineering areas. However the regression coefficients proved to be unstable when re-run over the sub-periods 1971–77 and 1978–83, which could be attributable to the change in the university regime in the 1980s. The severe cuts in certain disciplines could have had an independent influence on demand as students switched their preferences towards those areas that were relatively unscathed. As yet though there is insufficient data to test this adequately.

The supply of graduates is, of course, not only determined by the pattern of students' demand for courses, but also by whether sufficient course places are available to satisfy that demand. There are many factors that can influence the supply of places, including financial opportunities and constraints, physical facilities, and the enthusiasm and influence of departmental staff, as well as the pattern of student demand. Data on the number of candidates admitted to universities is available from UCCA annual reports, and it was hoped that it would prove possible to analyze the relationship between changes in the demand for and supply of university places using regression analysis. Unfortunately it proved difficult to quantify some of the other determinants of supply, which meant that no satisfactory regression could be obtained. The relationship was, however, investigated using alternative means. One such method looked at the correlations between changes in applications and changes in admissions. This revealed strong positive correlations for science and engineering subjects, but not for arts and social studies, but since the strongest correlations were for concurrent rather than lagged changes in applications, the evidence suggests that the supply and demand for places may be determined jointly rather than supply patterns following demand. This could occur if students switch their demand towards subject areas that are offering more places, at the same time as universities are switching their supply towards those areas where student demand is growing.

Another method of looking at the relationship is to construct an 'excess demand index' from the applications and admissions data, by expressing applications as a percentage of admissions. Strictly speaking the admissions data is not consistent with the applications data, since it applies to all home candidates, while the applications data applies only to home candidates applying through UCCA. However, since most home candidates do apply through UCCA, the index should be reasonably sound. The results showed that with the exception of medicine, professional subjects, and to a lesser extent agriculture, the subject indices have remained fairly constant, indicating that changes in the demand and supply of places have tended to move together at the subject group level, although the index proved more volatile at the individual subject level, especially among subjects in the social studies group.

The disadvantage of the excess demand index is that it contains no information on the quality of applicants. This may be remedied by looking at UCCA statistics showing the relative academic standards of entrants by subject. Average entry standards have risen sharply in the 1980s as a result of the cutback in available places combined with a continued buoyancy in applications. However relative entry standards have been fairly constant, with law and medicine having had high standards throughout the period, while science and social studies have been close to average. Relative entry standards have however declined in education, languages and to some extent arts, and have recently risen in engineering. Interestingly, standards for technology were not very high in the early-mid 1970s, and hence the 1970s problem of a shortage of good graduates in engineering appears to have been due to an inability to get sufficient good school-leavers to study the subject rather than to under-provision of places by the university sector.

Conclusion

This chapter has considered the determinants of graduate supply by subject, both in theory and in practice, over the last fifteen years. The theory predicted that labour market signals should be an influential determinant of graduate supply, and the empirical evidence suggested that they do indeed influence students' demand for courses. On the other hand it is acknowledged that the pattern of students' demand can be frustrated by the pattern of university supply, and hence there is a need for the national planning bodies to monitor and where necessary to seek to influence the supply of student places in order to ensure the system works effectively. An important corollary of the analysis is that it is likely to prove difficult to induce a subject switch through supply-side measures alone, in the absence of strong supporting signals from the labour market. This point is reinforced by considering the evidence of the 1970s where there was little evidence of excess student demand for undergraduate courses in engineering, suggesting that the shortage of graduates resulted from a failure to provide sufficient incentives for students to study in this area. The evidence from the 1980s suggests that student demand for engineering has since picked up, which should lead to an improvement in both the quality and quantity of graduate engineers. It is hoped that current government initatives will combine with appropriate labour markets signals to assist this development.

Acknowledgements

This chapter was written whilst I was at the DES. I would like to acknowledge the advice and encouragement of my colleagues there, especially Bernard Cullen, Kevin Sear and Tom O'Brien. The views expressed here are those of the author and are not necessarily shared by the DES.

Notes

1   UCCA statistics identify nine subject groups, but data for the education group was distorted by the incorporation of colleges of education into the university sector during the 1970s. Because of this, the education group has not been included in the subsequent analysis.
2   The eight subject groups were medicine, technology, agriculture, science, social studies, professional subjects, languages and humanities. The data was standardized by scaling each subject's applications to equal 100 in 1976. A more detailed description of the regression procedure was included in an appendix to the original paper. This may be obtained from Economics Division, Department of Education and Science, Elizabeth House, York Road, London SE1.

Higher Education and the Labour Market: A View of the Debate[1]

Jason Tarsh

Introduction

This chapter is concerned with two broad issues. How well does higher education (HE)[2] meet the needs of the economy for highly qualified manpower? And second, what are the implications of labour market signals for HE? That these matters are the subject of a long-running debate I hope would be generally agreed. The debate has the disconcerting characteristics of many issues where economics links with public policy. The same issues and disagreements continually reappear seemingly without any resolution. And yet against this background there is a whole series of firm declarations and actions which, as it were, build on these uncertain foundations. As immediate practical examples I would quote the beliefs that polytechnics are the vocational sector of HE, that sandwich courses are a good thing and that we need more engineers. My aim in this chapter is first to suggest that we are relatively well-informed about the graduate labour market. In particular the annual survey of first destinations of new graduates provides a good basis for assessing this market and for making some sharp policy recommendations. In the final part of this chapter I have outlined how the survey — and related information — could be used to manage HE. The middle part of the chapter attempts to sort through some particular parts of the debate.

The seminar on economics and education management was certainly timely as far as HE was concerned. The sector was facing a time of decision with the imminent decline of its traditional major client group, 18-year-old school-leavers. This raises the policy option of a substantial transfer of resources out of HE. As for the application of economics we now seem to be entering the third of three distinct phases of analysis of the post-Robbins system. In phase 1, in the early 1970s, the background was an expectation of continued economic growth, continued expansion of HE and a belief that HE would contribute to that growth. Concern then was with rational planning of that expansion and concepts such as manpower planning and rates of return were fashionable. I would date phase 2 from the late 1970s to the early 1980s. High points here would be the Leverhulme Enquiry, the Report on HE by the Select Committee on Education, Science and Arts and the UGC cuts. Indeed July 1981 might mark the end of this particular era. One view of the early 1970s is that the appeal to economics was in part a way of rationalizing a lobby for extra resources for HE. It was 'obvious' that more graduates meant more prosperity. By the time of the late 1970s it was realized that this argument was no longer a runner and indeed economic analysis could be used to give a distinctly cool appraisal of the expanded HE system. Discussion of HE at that time consisted of an attempt to re-state the traditional case for the existing system while being uneasily aware that part of that case — HE's contribution to economic welfare — could be undermined.[3] I would suggest that phase 3 represents an imposed solution to the problems of understanding the graduate labour market. The implication that HE has not properly responded to the needs of the economy has laid the way open to greater control of HE and the need to justify public expenditure. The emphasis is on managing HE and using explicit management techniques such as performance indicators. What at present is not clear is whether this new approach will make full use of economic analysis and whether current methods and information are sufficient for the purpose.

Monitoring the System: The First Destinations Survey

It is my view that this survey is an essential starting point for any debate on the graduate labour market. It is also likely to form a major part of any assessment of HE. The details of the survey, very briefly, are as follows. It is directed at all new graduates each year soon after they graduate. The Careers Advisory Service at each institution sends out a short postal questionnaire which seeks details of graduates' first firm destination after graduation. The response rate is about 60–70 per cent and this is supplemented by information from course tutors, friends etc to give information on between 80 and 90 per cent of each year's new graduates. Destinations fall broadly into employment, unemployment, further study and other training. Graduates who report that they have entered UK employment are also asked for details of their occupation and sector of the economy (industry). All results are available for men and women, seventy-six subjects and for each individual institution. Indeed, results are available in principle for every course, although published results only show whether graduates were from a university, polytechnic or college.

If it is accepted that it is reasonable to assess the demand for graduates by such a survey and that the new graduate unemployment rate is a measure of demand then a number of important results emerge. First, the survey shows that there are sharp differences in demand for graduates according to their degree discipline and graduating institution. These differences have persisted over time and where they have changed it is possible to explain this in terms of wider economic factors. The subject differences cut across academic boundaries and, for example, it is not the case that all science and engineering subjects are equally employable. As a group biological sciences have had the highest unemployment rate of any set of subjects and this covers arts, languages and non-economic social sciences. A second finding is that there have been some sharp adverse structural changes in the demand for graduates. Most notable of these have been the fall in the proportions of new graduates entering employment in central and local government and sharper falls in the proportions of graduates entering teacher training and other academic study. These changes have occurred at a time when the number of new graduates each year has increased at a much faster rate than growth in national output and employment. All this has also coincided with a trend increase in the new graduate unemployment rate over the 1970s and a trend fall in the relative pay of new or recent graduates. (The pay data are not particularly strong although all sources point in the same direction on the graduate relativity).

A third finding is that a large minority of new graduates find first employment in work where there is either no apparent link with their degree subject or where they are competing for jobs with graduates from a wide variety of subjects. It is also notable that, as a generalization, graduate employment tends to be more dispersed for subjects where new graduate unemployment is also high.

Fourth and finally, student demand to enter HE has adjusted in line with these signals from the graduate labour market. The fastest growth for university entrance has been in those subjects where demand for graduates has been strongest on conventional evidence of unemployment and pay. Examples of such subjects are law, accountancy, business studies, computer science and certain branches of engineering. By contrast, subjects such as arts, languages, non-economic social sciences (such as sociology) have grown more slowly or else demand has been fuelled by the general expansion in female participation in HE. Even here though girls' subject choices have reflected the observed switch to the more employable subjects.

Just this brief run through the first destinations survey is sufficient to challenge a fair number of beliefs about the graduate labour market. The trend increase in new graduate unemployment and fall in relative pay argue against the view that the economy could or should absorb ever increasing numbers of graduates or that the absorption can take place costlessly. The clear subject patterns in unemployment again argue against the view that employers' views of the graduate they are seeking are an incoherent mess. Rather all employers, after the event, do have clear revealed preferences. The subject patterns also show that while a large number of jobs are open *in principle* to graduates of any discipline this is certainly no panacea for graduate employment. The 40 per cent plus unemployment rates in zoology, history, geography and polytechnic pure science contradict that view.

The first destinations also offer some salutary evidence on institutional differences in the graduate labour market. The idea that polytechnics in general are the vocational sector of HE is very clearly knocked on the head if 'vocational' is proxied by employer demand. Subject for subject and overall university graduates have consistently had lower unemployment rates than polytechnics. Furthermore changes in the subject balance of polytechnic output over the 1970s have meant that the polytechnics have moved towards the university pattern and have reduced the proportion of their graduates with degrees in engineering and business studies. The universities by contrast have moved their subject balance to the more employable subjects. More recently, and perhaps in the light of such evidence, there has emerged the view that polytechnic graduates are as if damned in the labour market. On this view employers are free to indulge a prejudice for university graduates and since in any case they are really just seeking trained minds the specific subject knowledge and vocational intent of polytechnic courses suffer a heavy discount. The first destinations survey shows that this view is clearly false as a general description.[4] In subjects where employer demand for university graduates is high polytechnics also do well. Thus while unemployment amongst poly graduates in computer science, accountancy or electrical engineering is a little higher than for university graduates in these subjects it is well below the unemployment rate of university graduates in arts or biological sciences.

The first destinations survey has many limitations even as a record of new graduates' entry to the labour market. The survey would therefore benefit from extension and validation. But its strengths are that it does measure meaningful economic variables. Results from the survey are consistent internally and with the wider economy. Conclusions from the survey are also plausible. The first destinations survey cannot measure shortages of graduates but other survey evidence that shortages are highly concentrated in electronics and that demand is strong in computer science and accountancy is well consistent with first destinations. Similarly the survey cannot show the extent to which graduates filter down in the labour market and take jobs that are also open to people with lower qualifications. But it does at least show that there is a positive association between graduate unemployment and the likelihood that graduates will find employment in secretarial, clerical or manual jobs.

Some Debates

This section of the chapter assesses some of the main areas of debate on HE and the labour market.

The Student Demand Model

'Student demand' still seems to be the predominant model of how the HE system should operate. There is therefore embedded in it a view of HE and the labour market. The model seems to run as follows. There is a right to enter HE as dictated by the Robbins Principle. HE institutions have considerable autonomy but are almost entirely state funded as are students. Meeting the needs of the labour market is one aim of HE but it is not closely defined nor given a priority and other aims of HE might explicitly conflict with it. The main policy aim is to expand access to HE, in principle within a budget constraint. Allocation of resources across courses and institutions is broadly determined by the pattern of student demand but extra incentives to study particular subjects and some control over subject balance is allowed. Student demand should be informed by whatever market signals are available although the normal sub-text is that these signals are pretty poorly defined and contradictory. There should be no attempt at manpower planning.

The prime feature of this system is that it gives maximum discretion to HE and, by extension, to the schools if they gear themselves to providing future undergraduates. Further the total size of the system is totally uncontrolled. If demand by young people falls then institutions have the right to supplement this with other sources: overseas students, mature entrants etc.

A system along these lines can respond to the economy's need for trained manpower and indeed the broad evidence is that it has. There is no history of persistent shortages of graduates that the system has failed to react to. It is one goal of HE to respond to the labour market and this in turn does provide incentives and constraints for particular types of study. Some academics will use their freedom to do their best to meet employer demands. However while such a system can be responsive it is much less clear that it is cost-effectively so.

First, the Robbins Principle is likely to be an impediment to economic efficiency for it imposes a quite arbitrary rule on the allocation of public resources. Education is uniquely favoured compared with other forms of public expenditure and within the whole area of education and training it is HE that is uniquely favoured. Indeed one interpretation of Robbins is that it is an attempt to take HE outside of the scope of economic assessment. HE is assumed never to run into diminishing returns and not to be substitutable with other forms of education and training. One defence of Robbins is that it takes HE out of the political domain while allowing for some objective control over total resources through the operation of student demand. But this is surely fallacious. Student demand to enter HE is not objective and given. It is a function of young people's perceptions of the net rewards from taking a degree compared with the alternatives. Demand therefore stems in part from the level of the maintenance grant, support for lower level forms of education and training and from the rewards to different qualifications. A graduate earnings tax or subsidy would affect demand to enter HE. Robbins is silent on all this. But the reality is that while the principle of open access remains in practice resources have been moved out of HE. Indeed it has been suggested that the quality of provision has deteriorated as a result of recent efforts to cram more students into the polytechnics. Robbins therefore implies a rigid trade-off between numbers in HE and the quality of education on offer.

It surely should also be said that Robbins has no moral force whatsoever. It is not clear why, of all the calls on public expenditure, HE alone should be protected. The economic assumption must be that HE provides a unique contribution to the general welfare where also the gains always exceed the costs of supply.

A second weakness with the student demand model is that while there are incentives to respond to student demand which reflects market signals there is no explicit incentive to cut back elsewhere if student demand can be sustained. Expansion is therefore never achieved by savings elsewhere and there is an in-built tendency to growing expenditure on HE. Third, and related to this, the present system of undiscriminating grants for degree study and much less generous benefits for other training means that there is a strong incentive for young people (a) to choose degrees rather than alternative qualifications; (b) to discount the employment benefits of different types of study and subjects. The standard consumer benefits of HE have the same effect.

A fourth feature of the model is that employers do not bear the costs of potential graduate employees' training. There is therefore an incentive to hire graduates for jobs which use only a part or indeed none of their degree training. Indeed the present system gives employers an incentive to transfer training costs from themselves to the HE system. The moves in many occupations from 'A' level to graduate entry are consistent with this although they do not of themselves prove that this has happened. It is generally accepted that one function of HE is to screen potential employees by allowing them to display personal and intellectual attributes in an objective way. And incidentally screening of itself does not invalidate any of the standard arguments for public support for HE. It is reasonable in theory to regard screening as an investment which yields a return. However, just as the present system encourages employers to transfer training costs to HE, so it could prompt them to use HE as a screen because it is costless. Indeed it has been argued that employers and potential recruits can find themselves locked into a screening process which is in neither party's interest. Thus, beyond a certain level of graduate output, HE moves from being a means of identifying an elite to a means of excluding the less able. At the margin then there is a strong incentive to compete for entry by people who could benefit more from a lower level course. Indeed, a development of this view is that the generally favourable resourcing for HE acts to compete away student and employer demand for lower level courses which then just dwindle away. Furthermore, one consequence of opening access to HE for people with qualifications other than 'A' levels could be to engulf these altogether. Making BTEC a readily acceptable qualification for entry to an engineering degree course could therefore reduce the flexibility and diversity of the whole training system for engineers.

But a fifth and final weakness of the standard model is that it fails to address the implications of the considerable autonomy that HE institutions enjoy. The main economic argument for autonomy seems to be linked to the case for having publicly funded HE at all. Public funding is necessary where there are significant external benefits and where socially useful training would not otherwise occur. The case for public funding is weakest where HE courses are most closely tailored to the needs of individual employers and where they could in principle make a profit by financing provision directly. Autonomy then allows institutions to resist the pressure for very specific courses and to concentrate on training where externalities are greatest.

There are, however, many practical adverse consequences of autonomy. For if HE institutions can resist the improper blandishments of employers equally they can also fend off any role in providing trained manpower or they can impose additional costs on this. Autonomy also allows HE institutions to form themselves into an interest group with common goals and defence against outside influences. Yet if training organizations are to perform effectively it must be readily possible to trade them off one against another and shift resources across and out of the system. Finally the lobbying function of HE is one major source of the obscurities about the graduate labour market that were noted in the introduction. For where institutions have a vested interest in any assessment of their efficiency they are likely to use information about their activities selectively and to seek to control its use by outsiders. The informed student demand required for the standard model to work can thus be undermined by institutional autonomy and self-interest.

The Role of Employers

Employer dissatisfaction with HE is one of the perennial complaints made against the system. Yet as frequently there is the counter-attack that employers do not know what they want or else give views that are contradictory or which have no value as practical guidance. Frequently employers are accused of being unwilling to cooperate with HE institutions or to say what they want.

One answer to the 'inconsistent view' hypothesis is that this is based on naive (or else rather cunning) reasoning. For the view seems typically to draw on the public pronouncements of individual captains of industry or specific groups of employers. The fallacy here is simply that there is no such thing as a representative employer. The graduate labour market can only be judged *en masse* and, as suggested earlier, evidence of this sort does show well-defined patterns of demand for graduates. But a second defence against inconsistency is that it is HE itself that offers inconsistent or paradoxical choices. If indeed Oxbridge classicists are recruited in preference to polytechnic electronic engineers for the same job then it may simply be that great ability outweighs subject knowledge. Similarly if large accountancy firms recruit arts graduates in preference to those from accountancy degrees then this may reflect differences in ability, an awareness that much that is taught on accountancy courses is redundant or that learning on the job is as efficient as a full-time degree course.

If the standard externalities model of publicly-funded HE is accepted then of course some employer dissatisfaction with HE is necessary and desirable. For HE should be providing general training and employers should not expect to recruit new graduates and employ them at full productivity right away. Similarly, the complaint that new graduates lack industrial experience is surely a statement of obvious wishful thinking. Clearly an employer would like new graduate recruits to be fully conversant with their way of doing things from day 1. In theory there is a clear balance to be struck in HE's relations with employers. General training still should be useful and there is a case for publicly financed provision of industrial experience such as through sandwich courses. But in practice it is hard to see where the line should be drawn. Some courses will be too academic but others will be too applied to warrant public funding. This uncertainty does have important practical consequences. For it is not clear that, under the existing rules, employers should be expected to contribute to an expansion of courses just because they are in subjects in demand. It is surely also legitimate to argue that expansion should be financed by cutting courses that employers do not value.

There is a further caution about interpreting employers' views especially when these are expressed in some corporate form. For while employers might suffer from the effects of over-expansion of HE and the diversion from more appropriate courses they also gain from this. It can be in employers' interests to recruit someone who has been expensively educated and then use them on a trifling job simply because the individual employer does not bear the costs of providing that training. Indeed if the distribution of public expenditure is seen as in part the result of the weight of lobbying then it may well be in employers' interests to lobby for HE. In this case employers' views are neither the same nor necessarily consistent with the needs of the economy and it is necessary for a central authority to take a view.

On employers' refusal to get involved in HE, surely the answer is that employers do this when it suits them. The evidence from our work on graduate shortages showed that when employers feared that they might be unable to recruit the graduates they needed they did stir themselves and did seek to develop extensive contacts with HE. Trends in sponsorship show that this has reflected general patterns in demand for graduates in science and engineering. Where employer indifference is in evidence this might simply reflect a lack of urgency or of any real unsatisfied demand for graduates. It is perhaps for this reason that some employers simply ignore the polytechnics as a source of graduate recruits in their annual recruitment rounds.

The Engineering Dimension

No commentary on the graduate labour market would be complete without an assessment of the engineering case. Indeed it frequently appears that this is the main critique of HE. The case in outline seems to run as follows. Engineers are a vital contributor to economic prosperity. The aim should be to achieve a growing long-term share of engineers in total employment. Engineers are needed for jobs using their specific skills but an engineer in any job is an advantage. Further, current demand is misleading as an indicator of real demand (or 'need') for engineers. This is because (a) more engineers would generate a demand for their services by untapping new enterprise, extra investment etc; (b) employers are short-sighted about the number of engineers they ought to employ. They do not pay their existing engineers sufficiently or accord them suitable status. There are variants of the engineering case. One view is to stress that the need is not so much for more engineers but for a higher quality. Interestingly quality usually seems to refer to personal attributes rather than to technical ability. The long-term view of the role of engineers tends to discount current shortages. Rather the aim is to seek ways of predicting future demands and meeting these. An alternative view is to give shortages the main weight and seek ways of avoiding these. The engineering market is seen as very cyclical and the solution is a mixture of general expansion and the establishment, by some means, of buffer stocks of engineers.

It is ironic that although the engineering case is always presented as a hard-headed, economic critique of HE it is as much removed from reliance on economic principles as the most traditional defence of the current system. One major problem is that the case ignores the evidence from successive investigations by economists that there are no general shortages of engineers — on conventional criteria of shortage. The references in the engineering case to employers needing to value engineers more are an implicit acknowledgement of this. But such exhortations miss the larger point that it is necessary to show how such market failure occurs at all. The notion of a latent need for engineers fails to show how this can be measured. It also fails to show how this can be addressed. How are buffer stocks of engineers to be achieved, who is to employ these engineers until they are needed and what is to stop their skills from decaying while they are in store?

The idea of engineering as a general qualification fails to take account of the relatively high cost of training engineers. Further, if it is predicated on the view that if it is alright to use arts graduates in generalist jobs then this also holds for engineers then the simple answer is to deny that over-supply of any type of graduate is acceptable. And while it may be the case that in West Germany and the USA senior managers are likely to have engineering qualifications it is still necessary to see whether there is any causal connection with those countries greater prosperity and to see whether it is sensible and practical to transplant this to the UK. Certainly it is possible to think of instances where foreign experience could be quite misleading. Thus it might be that other countries can give greater weight to engineering because their costs, design and marketing are efficient. If these are weak areas in the UK then giving power to people with engineering qualifications might only reinforce our disadvantages. It is surely also fair to point out that one of the biggest recent industrial failures was in Rolls-Royce — a company that was stuffed with engineers in positions of authority.

But the engineer as good generalist is surely just naive. Engineering at degree level is much more akin to a branch of applied mathematics. It is not teaching people to be practical or to get things done. The case for engineers as new renaissance men also ignores the tendency in all subjects to refinement and specialization of knowledge. There seems no reason in principle why mastery of such material should give engineers any more advantage over physicists, econometricians or Sanskrit graduates.

The Way Ahead

In the light of the first part of this chapter my view is that it is reasonable to remove resources from HE. The economic case for this is the persistent signs of over-supply of graduates, the lack of evidence of shortages except in very specific areas and the increasing movement of graduates into areas of general and lower level employment. Coupled with this evidence, there is a clear incentive to over-supply from the present system of graduate support and employers' minimal direct contribution to this. The reduction of resources should be highly specific to particular courses (rather than broad steers) and should be coupled with other means of improving the flexibility of HE to meet market demands and of deriving general indicators for withdrawal and re-allocation of resources.

If there is a precedent for such a policy it is the 1981 UGC cuts — yet the way in which these were presented and interpreted illustrates all the weaknesses of the present HE system and public understanding of this. The UGC cuts made sharp distinctions between subjects in their advice. They did distinguish biological sciences (for cuts) from other sciences (for selective expansion). Yet the public face of the cuts was of an arbitrary attack on technology. The general argument that the cuts attacked subjects in demand is simply wrong although part of the public misunderstanding of this is presumably because of the mistaken equation that demand equals science and engineering. But what of the distribution of cuts by institutions? The UGC has never given a clear single statement of their reasoning but it is possible to deduce the main factors from the debate. These seem to have been: 'A' level entry scores, unit costs of courses, extent of research support, overall view of quality of courses, presence of similar courses in the locality. Thus if the cuts redistributed science and engineering resources from certain technological universities this was perhaps because these universities had low entry standards, were close to alternative sources of provision and had high unit costs (the colleges of advanced technology (CATs) specialize in sandwich courses).

My own view is that from the point of view of the practical use of economics these were the appropriate criteria to use in conjunction with the first destinations[5] as a means of reallocating resources.

It is, of course, possible to make interesting speculation about why the UGC's case appeared so unfavourable in the public debate. One view is that the UGC were making clear choices in a system that survives and thrives on ambiguity. But two general features of the cuts do deserve criticism. Cuts and reallocation of resources should have been made explicitly across the whole HE system. University courses should have been compared with polytechnics and colleges. But the cuts should have been made against a background of flexibility of resource transfer within HE and of transfer out to lower level training and from employers and students. In very summary terms flexibility and transfer do imply an end to tenure, variable salaries, student loans and direct employer finance. Lower level training could include two-year courses and more general courses and could also mean the creation of new institutions or at least the conversion into an explicit two-tier system instead of the shadowy version of this which the poly/college and university split implies. Putting all this in a different and optimistic way I would suggest that real diversity and experimentation in HE can only be achieved when it is realized that at the margin HE's output is not crucial to the economy. Resources are spare and can be used to better effect than simply extending and duplicating what is there already.

Notes

1 JASON TARSH was formerly with the Department of Employment and is now with the DES. This chapter reflects the personal view of the author and does not represent an official view of the either the DES or the Department of Employment.

2 Throughout this chapter HE is used to refer to degree level education only.

3 As an example of this see Lindley's overview of the debate on HE and the labour market in LINDLEY (1981). Having accepted that the economic benefits no longer provide a case for expanding HE the impression is that it is for economics to rescue HE from the implications. The question is not what can HE do for the economy but what can the economy do for HE. See also the Select Committee's visible

shrinking from any notion even of broad steering of HE to improve its links with the labour market.

4 The recent Brunel University 'Expectations of Higher Education' research has sometimes been interpreted along these lines.

5 The UGC appears to have looked at current patterns of first destinations and also consulted about likely future patterns of demand for subjects. Whither manpower planning now?!

The Role of Selectivity in Alternative Patterns of Financial Support for Students

Maureen Woodhall

Introduction

One of the central questions in considering the effects of alternative financial mechanisms on education is the degree of selectivity in the distribution of subsidies for education. Debates about selective versus universal subsidies are often couched in ideological terms, but as Blaug (1970) points out, 'the polar extremes of selectivity and universalism ... fail to do justice to all the subtleties of the debate. Within both camps, there is so to speak a "right" and "left" wing' (p. 287).

This is certainly true when we look at debates about financial support to students, particularly the question of loans versus grants, and the role of fees in financing higher and further education. Both issues have attracted controversy in recent years, not only in the UK but also world-wide. This is an area where the economics of education can make a significant contribution, since the choice between alternative financial mechanisms and the degree of selectivity of financial support for students raises both efficiency and equity issues.

This chapter will examine some of the effects of alternative ways of financing student support, looking in particular at:

(i) changes in support for overseas students in Britain, since the introduction of full-cost fees in 1980;

(ii) the pattern of financial support for home students, and the loans versus grants debate.

Questions about the level of fees and financial support for overseas students, the level of grants for home students and whether these should be replaced or supplemented by loans, are usually debated quite separately in the UK, but the issue of selectivity is crucial to both. Some of the changes in student aid policy that have taken place or been proposed involve a clear shift towards greater selectivity, while other changes mean less, rather than more, selective support for students. There are differences and inconsistencies in the extent to which different categories of student receive selective subsidies in Britain. This can be seen not only in the distinctions drawn between home and overseas students, but also in the different treatment of full-time and part-time students, or those studying at different levels.

Financing Support for Overseas Students

The introduction of full-cost fees for overseas students in Britain in 1980 was followed, after a period of intense criticism at home and abroad, and a reexamination of the benefits, as well as the costs, of overseas students (Williams, P. 1981 and 1982) by the announcement, in 1983, of a new programme of support for overseas students, the 'Pym Package', which meant an additional £46 million over three years. This included:

(i)   an increase in the Technical Cooperation Training Programme (TCTP);

(ii) additional awards under the Commonwealth Scholarship and Fellowship Plan (CSFP);

(iii) country/territory support schemes for particular countries, including Hong Kong, Cyprus and Malaysia;

(iv) a new FCO Scholarships and Awards Scheme, involving scholarships to students in over 100 countries, which are intended to bring to the UK potential 'leaders, decision makers and formers of opinion', in the belief that this will be in the long-term diplomatic, cultural and commercial interest of the country.

In addition to these targeted awards, there are other types of support for particular categories of overseas students. When the policy of full-cost fees was introduced it was agreed that students from European Community (EC) countries should pay the same fees as home students, which in 1984–85 meant that 6800 students from EC countries paid home student fees. The government also introduced the Overseas Research Students Award Scheme

(ORSAS) for high ability research students. In 1984–85 total expenditure on British government-funded award schemes was £72.5m, which financed awards to 17,400 overseas students, as shown in table 1. The most recent additions to the range of support schemes for overseas students include the introduction of an ODA Shared Scholarship Scheme, intended for 'bright but poor' Commonwealth students, to be funded jointly by the ODA and receiving institutions, and new scholarship schemes for black South African postgraduates and for students from China, announced in 1985.

The new policy towards overseas students in Britain represents a major change in the financial mechanisms used to support both institutions and students. Gareth Williams, in his chapter, touches on some of the implications for institutions. Equally far-reaching are the implications for methods of student support. In the first place, the introduction of full-cost fees, followed, somewhat belatedly, by targeted awards, represents a shift towards subsidies for individuals, rather than institutions. The Robbins Committee recommended such a shift, on the grounds that it is better 'up to a point' to subsidize individuals rather than institutions. The arguments for such a shift are (i) that the size of the subsidy to individual students can be more clearly identified, and open subsidies are preferable to hidden subsidies; (ii) that it would give greater power to the consumers of higher education and could therefore act as a spur to competition and greater efficiency in institutions; and (iii) that it would allow a shift towards more selective distribution of subsidies, which has clearly happened in the case of overseas student support.

Recent government statements on overseas student policy seem to suggest that the change from indiscriminate subsidies for all overseas students to a programme of targeted awards represented a deliberate and carefully thought out policy. For example, in a recent speech Timothy Renton, Parliamentary Under-Secretary at the FCO, said: 'In place of the previous indiscriminate subsidy we changed to a targeted policy of help ... which is more cost-effective than a policy of haphazard and indiscriminate subsidies, which were not being directed to serve the aims of British policy at all closely' (Renton, 1985). This conveniently ignores the gap of three years between the introduction of full-cost fees and the announcement of the main targeted award schemes.

Nevertheless, the new policy does represent a major change, and it is important to try to assess its effects. One of the most obvious is that it has focussed attention on the criteria for selective assistance. The Pym Package was intended to reflect a number of

Table 1: British Government Funded Award Schemes 1984/85

Scheme	Expenditure £m	Number of Awards (including renewals)
Technical Cooperation Training Programme (TCTP)	48.9	10,323
FCO Scholarships and Awards Scheme (SAS)	3.0	620
Country/Territory Support Schemes (Malaysia, Hong Kong, Cyprus and Dependent Territories)	4.7	2,850
Commonwealth Scholarship and Fellowship Plan (CSFP)	7.5	1,245
British Council Fellowships	3.3	480
Overseas Research Students Awards Scheme (ORSAS)	4.1	1,760
Marshall Aid Commemoration Scholarships	0.74	72
Fulbright Commission Scholarships	0.26 (DES — one-third of budget)	50
ODA Shared Scholarship Scheme (ODASSS)	0	0 (up to 100 new awards annually over 5 years from 1986/87)
Total	72.5	17,400

Source: Inter-Departmental Group of Officials (IDG) (1985) *Internal Review of the British Government and British Council Funded Award Schemes*, December.

different aspects of British policy, including aid, trade and foreign policy. Subsidies are now targeted on particular countries or groups, particularly the EC and the Commonwealth, or students whose presence is believed to serve British interests, such as high ability research students. An Internal Review of British Government Funded award schemes, in December 1985 (IDG, 1985) identified three main groups of awards, intended to serve different policy objectives:

(i) schemes introduced for developmental reasons, such as the ODA's technical cooperation training programmes;

(ii) the ORSAS scheme, intended to boost and maintain the research capacity of British universities;

(iii) schemes which 'are intended to help Britain to win friends and influence people abroad', including the various FCO programmes and the British Council's Fellowship Programme.

Thus, different criteria are emphasized in various schemes, but there is always the danger of either overlap or conflict. For example, the distribution of awards would be quite different if trade-related benefits of overseas students were given greater priority than aid. As it is, the review showed that in 1984–85 nearly 70 per cent of awards went to students from Commonwealth countries, over 40 per cent of award holders were studying science or engineering, and the majority were postgraduates rather than undergraduates. Awards were also heavily concentrated on particular countries: Cyprus, Hong Kong and Malaysia, in the case of the FCO schemes; and India, Pakistan, Kenya and Nigeria, in the case of TCTP.

Research recently carried out in DEAPSIE[1], which involved a survey of 1760 overseas students in universities, polytechnics and colleges, showed that 55 per cent of the students studying in universities or polytechnics had some form of award in 1985, compared with 46 per cent in a similar survey in 1980. Nearly a quarter of the students had an award from British funds, but considerably more overseas students (33 per cent) had an award from overseas. Students who receive a British award are rather more likely to come from families of lower occupational status (for example, farmers or craftsmen) than non-award holders (who were more likely to be children of businessmen or private company employees). British award holders were also more likely to come from poor countries, and to be studying at the postgraduate level.

This suggests that the policy of targeted support is having some success in concentrating resources on particular groups, such as low-income students, and on developing countries. The concentration of subsidy on a smaller group of students also means that the students who do receive an award are relatively generously treated. The median income, *after* payment of fees, of students on a British Council administered award[2] was £2900, which was lower than that of students with a foreign award, but higher than the median income of privately financed students. Our survey also showed that 70 per cent of British award holders would not have come to Britain to study if they had not received an award, and in the case of students from the poorest countries, the percentage was over 80 per cent. Selective subsidies therefore clearly succeed in bringing students to Britain who would not otherwise be able to afford full-cost fees.

On the other hand, it is striking that the number of students from developing countries has fallen far more sharply since the introduction of full-cost fees than the number from richer countries. Between 1979 and 1984 the total number of overseas students in publicly-funded higher or further education fell from 88,000 to 56,000, a 36 per cent reduction, but the numbers from developing countries fell by 43 per cent, while the number from EC countries slightly increased. Since 1983, when the Pym Package was introduced, the number of students from the poorest fifty countries has begun to increase, and the number of EC students has also increased, while numbers from other countries have continued to decline. One effect of the shift to selective subsidies for overseas students has clearly been a change in the balance between different sending countries.

Changes in Financial Support for Home Students

Whereas there has been a clear shift from general to selective subsidies for overseas students, the trend in support for British students is less clear-cut. On the one hand, the means-testing of mandatory grants for maintenance has become more severe: the thresholds for parental contributions have increased, and the minimum grant, previously paid to all students regardless of income, has been abolished. The proposal to charge tuition fees to students from wealthy families, announced in November 1984, would have meant a marked shift towards selectivity, but this proposal was withdrawn after fierce opposition.

However, other changes have meant a move in the opposite

direction. The change in arrangements for travel grants means that students with high travel expenses (i.e. those who live far from their place of study) are no longer reimbursed, but the value of the mandatory award has been increased to include a notional figure for travel. The government admitted that this would involve a measure of 'rough justice'.

Similar criticisms were levelled at the proposal to reduce students' eligibility for social security benefits. The long-term aim of the government is to remove students from the social security system, on the grounds that it is wasteful to channel support for students through two different systems. The White Paper on social security reform proposed to remove students' eligibility for supplementary and unemployment benefit in the short vacations and limit entitlement to housing benefit. In total this would reduce student entitlement by £45m. In compensation, those students who receive a mandatory grant will receive an extra £36 a year. This would mean that some students, who do not currently claim housing benefit, will gain, while many other students will lose. The NUS complained that this was a cost-cutting exercise which would operate indiscriminately and to the detriment of many students, and critics in the House of Commons claimed that the proposals 'switched some of the specifically targeted benefit saving to indiscriminate flat rate subsidies' (Hansard, 18 June 1986, col. 1043). The complaint that it is 'indiscriminate' rests on the fact that an addition of £36 a year to the student grant takes no account of a student's specific needs, although since grants are means-tested the amount students actually receive will depend on the level of parental income.

This illustrates the fact that the notion of selectivity inevitably raises the question of what criteria are used. The NUS complains that students' actual needs will not be reflected in the new arrangements, and so claims that they are 'indiscriminate'. On the other hand, since student grants are means-tested, they are selective in terms of *parental* income, though less so in terms of *student* income, since it is well known that many parents do not pay the assumed parental contribution.

The present system of student support is also selective in terms of level and mode of study. Part-time students and those not on 'designated' courses do not qualify for mandatory grants. Nor do those who have previously received an award and withdrawn from their course, or who want to change their field of study. Such students are dependent on discretionary, rather than mandatory awards, and these are increasingly difficult to obtain in many LEAs. Here is an example of selectivity which discriminates against certain categories of students who in many other countries receive financial support.

In the US or in Sweden part-time as well as full-time students are entitled to support, but a large part of the support is in the form of loans, rather than grants. There have been many proposals to introduce loans or a mixed system of loans and grants in Britain and the government is, once again, considering introducing a loan element into the student support system.

Loans and Grants as a Means of Student Support

Experience in other countries shows that students loans are feasible, flexible and can be fairer than a system of grants which transfers income from taxpayers with average and lower-than-average earnings to students with higher-than-average earnings expectations. Loans or a combination of loans and grants are widely used in Europe, North America, Japan, Hong Kong and in a number of developing countries, particularly in South America and the Caribbean, as a means of financial support for students, either for living expenses alone, as in Sweden or Germany, or for tuition fees as well as living expenses, as in the USA or Japan. Foreign experience shows that loan schemes can and do work, and I have argued in previous publications (Woodhall, 1970, 1978, 1982a, 1982b and 1983) that a combination of loans and grants would enable more students to receive support than the present system of mandatory grants for the fortunate who qualify, and a steadily diminishing chance of a discretionary grant or nothing at all for those who wish to study part-time, change courses or fail to meet residence requirements. On the other hand, the National Union of Students (NUS, 1985) has concluded that 'none of the systems observed meet the needs of students, education or the country concerned' (p. 6).

The deep-rooted opposition of the NUS to student loans is not surprising. Most people would prefer a gift rather than a loan which has to be repaid. The NUS argues that the present system of grants is 'miserable, miserly, ... inegalitarian, cumbersome ... and does not meet its objectives' (*ibid*), but nevertheless believes that any introduction of loans, even if combined with grants, would be a retrograde step, which could herald the dismantling of the grants system, a substantial shift of the costs of higher education on to students, rather than the taxpayer, and a reduction in access particularly for the working class.

On the other hand, advocates of loans in Britain believe that the introduction of a loan element would be more equitable than the present system of grants which quite clearly does not ensure equality of opportunity (see, for example, Blaug, 1970). Those who now do not qualify for a grant have no recourse to any alternative, which discriminates against certain categories of student far more effectively than a loan system. The fear that working class students or women would be discouraged from borrowing is not borne out by the experience of the USA, or Sweden. In the USA in 1984–85 over 4 million students financed their higher education by means of loans and the existence of a highly subsidized loan programme for low-income students (the National Direct Student Loan Program or NDSLP) means that low income, as well as middle-income students are willing to borrow. Opponents of loans point to high rates of default in the USA, but a recent review (Hauptman, 1983) showed that default rates have been falling in the USA since 1980.

The American experience with both loans and grants brings us squarely back to the issue of selectivity. In the USA there are three different loan programmes: the highly subsidized NDSLP for low-income students, the Guaranteed Student Loan Program (GSLP) for middle income students, and an almost unsubsidized programme for parents, to enable them to finance their children's higher education (Parents Loans for Undergraduate Study — PLUS) or for students, mainly postgraduates, who do not qualify for subsidized loans (Auxilliary Loans to Assist Students — ALAS). Thus, loan subsidies are distributed selectively, but some sort of loan, backed by a state government guarantee agency, is available to everyone who wants one. Grants (known as Pell Grants) are available to low-income students as well as subsidized work-opportunities (College Work Study); these are also distributed selectively, on the basis of financial need.

The trend in the USA is towards greater use of loans, and a relative decline in grants and other forms of aid. Some commentators note this trend with alarm, but a study for the National Commission on Student Financial Assistance in 1983 concluded that loans were the most cost-effective system of aid because 'for every one dollar of federal funds invested, the GSL program generates approximately two dollars of student assistance' (Miller, 1985, p. 9). The notion of 'self-help', either through loans or work-study, is central to the American system of higher education. A recent comparison of the way the burden of financing higher education is shared between students, parents and taxpayers in the US, UK, France, Germany and Sweden (Johnstone, 1987) showed that the share of total costs borne by the student is lower in Britain than in any of the other countries, and highest in Sweden and the USA, which rely extensively on loans.

The question of how the costs of education should be shared raises issues of both equity and efficiency, and it is not a simple matter of 'right' or 'left' wing ideology. For example, recent World Bank publications (for example, Psacharopoulos and Woodhall 1985; Mingat and Tan, 1986; Jimenez, 1986) show that the present pattern of subsidies for higher education in many developing countries favours the most wealthy, rather than the poorest sections of the community and in its most recent policy paper on financing education the World Bank (1986) argues strongly that a shift towards higher fees and loans, rather than scholarships or grants, for students in higher education is justified on both efficiency and equity grounds. Hansen and Weisbrod (1969) reached a similar conclusion for California many years ago, and more recently Hansen suggested that the large expansion of federal aid in the USA in the 1970s really benefitted middle-income, rather than low-income students (Hansen, 1984).

A mixed system of grants and loans, with flexible repayment terms and interest subsidies for those with low incomes, would seem to offer the best way of targeting student support where it is most needed, while ensuring access and choice for as many students as possible. If such a system of student support were introduced in Britain, it could widen, rather than reduce access, by enabling those who do not qualify for any support at present to borrow to finance their own higher education. Interest subsidies for the low paid, combined with grants for the most needy students, would ensure that no one need be deterred from higher education by the prospect of massive debt. However, such a system would not produce significant savings in the short run, and would certainly face strong opposition, particularly from the NUS.

Conclusions

The way in which subsidies are distributed to both institutions and individuals has important implications. This chapter has attempted to sketch out some of the implications of alternative ways of providing financial aid for students, and suggested that more detailed research is needed on the effects of different patterns of student support, and changes in the degree of selectivity.

One important issue is what should be the criteria for selectivity. For example, should subsidies for overseas students be concentrated on particular countries or on particular individuals? What should be the basis of selection? In some countries grants or interest subsidies for student loans are means-tested on the basis of *parental* income, whereas in others interest subsidies go to those who have low incomes *after* graduation. Several countries use interest subsidies to provide incentives; for example, in Germany those who complete their degrees in minimum time have part of their loans converted into grants, and in other countries interest subsidies are used to influence career choice.

Although there has been some research on the effects of different types of student support on student behaviour, many questions remain unresolved, as well as many questions about the use of fees as a financing mechanism. The concept of selectivity is crucial to both, and even a preliminary examination of some of the effects of recent changes and proposals for change in the way students receive financial support in Britain reveals this to be a fertile area for further research. It is to be hoped that the review of student support, recently announced by Kenneth Baker, will tackle this issue.

Notes

1 Department of Administrative and Policy Studies in Education, University of London Institute of Education. This research project, funded by the DES, forms part of a programme of research on overseas students commissioned by the Overseas Students Trust (see WILLIAMS, WOODHALL and O'BRIEN, forthcoming).
2 This includes awards funded by the ODA and FCO as well as the British Council's own fellowship scheme.

The Management of Institutions of Higher Education into the 1990s

John Sizer

In Chapter 1 of its recent Green Paper, *The Development of Higher Education into the 1990s* (DES, 1985b) the government sets out its main concerns, including:

> It is vital for our higher education to contribute more effectively to the improvement of the performance of the economy. (para. 1.2)

> Universities in particular need to develop greater ability to adapt to change. (para. 1.5)

> The need to increase the effectiveness of the money spent in universities, polytechnics and other institutions on research. (para. 1.11)

In a subsequent chapter concerned with institutions and their management, it states:

> The establishment of specific objectives for whole institutions and for their separate faculties and departments, and the monitoring and evaluation of their achievement, are demanding management tasks. The executive head of each institution of whatever type is responsible far more than anyone else for standards of efficiency and effectiveness. (para. 7.4)

It goes on to argue the need to develop and use measurements of performance, and welcomes the Jarratt Report's (CVCP, 1985) suggestions for developing reliable and consistent performance indicators designed for use both within individual universities and for making comparisons between them (para. 7.5).

Higher education will need, as the Green Paper emphasizes, to be responsive to the changing needs of a post-industrial, advanced information and manufacturing technology society. The major institutional management challenge is, and will continue to be, how to maintain the vitality, responsiveness and creativity of faculty when many of the pressures are working in the opposite direction, i.e. ageing faculty, diminished career prospects, declining real salaries, and little new blood. Despite the adverse conditions, the government considers the challenge is to manage not for survival, but for excellence. Improving upon the effective and efficient use of resources, and responding to the changing needs of society will necessitate the application of management expertise, including the employment of relevant economic concepts and techniques. This chapter, written by an accountant, suggests ways in which economists might assist institutional managers in the areas of planning, resource allocation and performance assessment, as well as assisting economists in formulating a research agenda.

All the signs indicate that pressure on institutions of higher education to justify their activities and account for their use of resources and their performance in terms of their responsiveness, effectiveness, and efficiency is likely to be sustained. Within institutions further consideration will have to be given to the relevance, effectiveness and efficiency of the various academic and service departments, and there will be a continuing need to make difficult decisions relating to the allocation and reallocation of a diminishing resources cake. Managements will need a sound basis upon which to arrive at and justify such decisions to internal constituencies and external bodies. In particular, they need to develop further methods for allocating resources and for assessing the performance of the component parts of their institutions. There will be calls for greater accountability by heads of academic departments for the use of resources allocated to them, and for the introduction or strengthening of procedures for staff development, appraisal and accountability. Inevitably there will be a continuing demand for performance indicators, which will aid these processes, and for relevant financial, quantitative and qualitative information for planning, decision-making and control.

Within institutions it will be necessary to balance the pressure for increased *efficiency* in the short-term with actions that need to be taken if institutions are to be *effective* in the long-term. Economists will be aware of the dangers of pressures for short-term efficiency crowding out long-term effectiveness. Teaching, research and scholarship should be concerned with long-term effectiveness. The

Green Paper is also concerned with long-term effectiveness, i.e. contributing to the improvement of the performance of the economy; matching competition in producing more qualified scientists, engineers, technologists and technicians; developing the ability to adapt to change, etc. Demands on funding bodies for a concerted effort to be made to develop and obtain agreement with institutions on their objectives, strategies and academic policy for the next decade flow from this emphasis on long-term effectiveness.

Many would argue that institutions should examine the environment in which they will be operating and attempt to identify the needs of a post-industrial, knowledge, service and information society, which is also responding to rapid advances in information and manufacturing technology. Some institutions consider that, because they cannot plan very effectively in the short-term at the present time, there is little point in attempting long-term planning; there are too many complexities and uncertainties. They call for a longer-term planning and funding horizon. However it should be recognized that, whilst it is reasonable to expect the government to have, and to enunciate, broad policies, strategies and guidelines, it is less realistic to expect a longer-term funding horizon which does not carry with it a considerable degree of uncertainty. If long-term effectiveness is the primary measure of performance, such uncertainties should not excuse the need to examine the impact of long-term trends on an institution's portfolio of activities and to develop a strategy for its long-term development, which is responsive to these trends.

If they can be mobilized, the expertise and resources required to undertake *scenario analysis* are likely to be available within institutions, and economists can play a significant role. Institutions have to decide whether it would be worthwhile. If they decide not, there is a danger that excessive weight will be given to historical data when developing strategic plans and making selective priority decisions. Furthermore, if policy makers cannot be convinced that institutions are willing to respond to the changing needs of society they are likely to opt for a more inventionist approach towards higher education. At the present time they still need convincing, hence the concern expressed in the Green Paper that universities in particular need to develop a greater ability to adapt to change.

Such a consideration of the long-term trends and factors is likely to indicate that post-industrial society will require a different mix of outputs and outcomes from universities. Whilst there will be opportunities to generate alternative sources of revenue from applied research, consultancy and continuing education opportunities, many of the new developments in teaching and research will have to be funded by redeployment of existing resources. This will necessitate hard choices which implies the careful evaluation of trade-offs. Thus, institutions will need to plan for resource mobility and for research in anticipation of new course demands, research and consultancy opportunities, and services to the community. Therefore should effectiveness be measured not only in terms of outcomes/benefits/impacts but also in terms of responsiveness to the changing needs of society? Should performance indicators be developed to measure an institution's progress in developing and implementing its strategy for resource mobility and responding to these changing needs?

One starting point in the process of responding to changing demands is to analyze the institution's current portfolio of courses and research programmes. Some institutions have now recognized the need to assess their performance potential by evaluating

(a) their strengths and comparative advantages in various subject areas and research programmes relative to other institutions; and

(b) the future attractiveness or centrality of subject areas and research programmes,

so as to identify priority areas for future growth, consolidation and rationalization. Such analyses can provide a starting point for internal discussions on the institution's long-term strategy for resource mobility and for the development of department mission statements. Certainly decentralized structures require institutions critically to study and evaluate themselves; if they are to preserve their autonomy and academic freedom universities have to find internal solutions to retrenchment and redeployment. However, under conditions of financial stringency and changing needs of society it is not sufficient to rely on faculty and department self-evaluation.

It is the nature of an organization to guard itself against change, at all events against changes which are not in accordance with the dominating internal value system of the organization. The author's ongoing research into the management of financial reductions in universities is supportive of his knowledge of self-evaluation exercises in other countries; they tend to break down under conditions of financial stringency and contraction. There is a general reluctance to face reality and make hard choices. Institutional managements should recognize that under these conditions there is a need for academic and financial planning and resource allocation to be more centralized and integrated, but they should ensure that there is extensive consultation with academic departments and units. As Sizer (1982), the Jarratt Report (CVCP, 1985) and the Green Paper emphasize, both the consultative and decision making process will be strengthened if reliable and consistent performance indicators are available.

If a central organization is established to develop *inter-institutional comparisons of performance indicators*, it would be wise to recognize at the outset that no two institutions, departments or subject areas within institutions, are strictly comparable. There are likely to be good reasons why an institution or part of an institution should not conform with national norms. Therefore a centrally organized inter-institutional comparison scheme should enable the management to determine *where* and possibly *why* its performance differs from that of other institutions but it will not necessarily tell it how to improve it. Have economists a role to play in the development of such schemes?

One of the major problems facing those who wish to produce inter-institutional comparisons either side of and across the binary line of financial performance indicators for the research and teaching functions in higher education is the unscrambling of joint costs of research and teaching functions and the central services. The UGC has argued, in the context of inter-sectoral comparisons, that the lack of any necessary connection between research expenditure and student numbers means that any discussions in terms of unit cost or unit of resource obscures the true issues. The same argument can be applied to comparisons of cost per FTE and staff/student ratios by subject areas across institutions. If the research being undertaken by Professor Keith Clayton from the DES fails to produce an acceptable methodology for analyzing expenditure, should economists consider undertaking further work on the *efficient frontier*, i.e. the sub-set of institutions which are, in a geometrical sense, on the frontier of the set in such a way that they dominate the set taking all the inputs and outputs into consideration? Lindsay (1982) has reviewed work in this area, which has constituted the first steps in the development of an overall ranking criterion for multi-objective, multi-dimensional institutions of higher education and departments within institutions, but the author remains to be convinced of its practical value.

Given the complexities and difficulties surrounding the objective setting and planning process and the application of nonperformance evaluation techniques and multi-dimensional analysis, Sizer (1982) has argued that it is not surprising that there is a tendency to recognize those parts of the institution that can be measured and monitored with a considerable degree of precision, i.e. to develop partial performance indicators. It will be recognized that with *partial performance indicators* there is always the danger that optimizing the parts does not necessarily optimize the whole, and that excessive emphasis will be placed on short-term quantitative input, process, and immediate output measures and performance indicators. Inadequate attention may be given, because of the measurement problems, to the quality of outcomes and long-term impact and benefits. As the author anticipated (Sizer, 1982), and the Green Paper confirms, questions concerning the quality of outcomes and their impact on society are bound to be raised by a government determined to get better value for public expenditure in higher education. Despite the serious methodological problems, should economists renew their attempts to assess quality of outcomes/benefits/impacts and the social value of different disciplines?

Kronig (1978) has examined the possibilities of financing institutions on the basis of performance indicators. He argued that it would be necessary to construct cost curves reflecting cost-volume relationships not for the university as a whole but for particular performance areas: '. . . there is after all no point in trying to work out a single standard financing value for any imaginary average student'. Thus he made the important distinction between financing based on average unit costs and based on cost curves. Studies by Bottomley *et al* (1971) in the late 1960s were concerned with construction of such cost curves. The German Federal Ministry of Education and Science has sponsored research on financing universities on the basis of performance indicators. In their report Beckeroff *et al* (1980) recommend the use of indicators for the financing of universities for both teaching and research. Elstermann and Lorenz (1980) conclude it is impossible to determine separate indicators for teaching and research which would be accurate enough to serve as a basis for an independent funding of teaching and of research, because it is difficult to formulate a creditable and reliable process of quality assessment.

Swinnerton-Dyer (1985) has described the new resource allocation process employed by the UGC to determine the distribution of recurrent grants for the period 1986–87 to 1989–90. The three major components are:

T — resources to be distributed on teaching-based criteria;
R — resources to be distributed on research-based criteria;
S — resources for special factors.

R comprises four sub-components, including resources selectively distributed on judgment (JR). S is further broken down into allowances for non-departmental special factors (NDS) and for departmental special factors (DS). The resources assigned to each cost centre, i.e. thirty-seven departmental groups, covered T, R and DS, and the relevant sub-committee advised on the division between these components. Once the total figure for T was settled it was divided among institutions in proportion to each one's share of the planned student load for the cost centre. The load was weighted differently for undergraduates, taught postgraduates and research postgraduates, but was not varied between institutions within a cost centre.

Thus the model does not employ cost curves, the variable unit of resource being derived from the weighted average historical costs with central overheads absorbed into the departmental cost centres. Teaching resources are allocated within a cost centre directly proportionately to changes in weighted student load. The model could provide a separate grant for teaching and research, but in fact the outcome of the process is still a block grant, and responsibility for deciding how it should be spent remains with the institution. The Committee has disclosed the research ratings by cost centre for each institution but not the teaching load weightings, the units of resource, nor the division between T and R, and the sub-components of R. Nevertheless, regardless of the extent of the disclosure, the knowledge of the components is likely to influence the resource allocation processes within universities. Economists may wish to update Bottomley's work, examine the implications of the UGC's model for institutional resource allocation models, and give further consideration to the cases for and against separate grants for teaching and research.

Whilst developing and applying criteria and partial performance indicators for the evaluation of subject areas and research programmes is a first stage in self-evaluation, this only provides a starting point from which difficult managerial judgments have to be made. The fewer the criteria the greater the gap that has to be bridged by such judgments. No' matter how sophisticated and detailed the analysis the gap will remain a substantial one. This is particularly true in the area of *research performance evaluation*.

Governments in many European countries are concerned to secure the best value for the public money they commit to research in universities. This has led to pressure for greater selectivity in the allocation of funds for research externaily *between* and internally *within* universities, and thus for criteria for evaluation of research performance. The most commonly-used criteria include grants and contracts, peer evaluation, published papers, citation analysis, and prestige awards. Citation analysis, including recent developments in co-citation and co-word analysis, may be of particular interest to economists as current work at the Science Policy Institute is being supported by the ABRC. In the area of citation analysis it is important to distinguish between quality, importance, and impact. Citation counts are primarily a measure of impact, though these may also reflect quality and importance. However it is not possible to obtain any absolute or direct measure of the relation between quality, importance and impact. The number of citations is a partial indicator of impact and can be a valuable monitoring device for research managers and science policy makers. By its very nature much of university research and scholarship is long term, but if the careful use of a range of partial performance indicators yields consistent results over a longish period they should be extremely useful in determining a university's research policy and priorities. The task of evaluating research and scholarship performance is a difficult and complex one, but at the present time too important to ignore. Economists might come to the same conclusion and may wish to undertake further research on benefit, impact and outcome measures.

When developing strategies for resource mobility and redeployment, hard choices will have to be made particularly in respect of *small, weak departments.* As the UGC explained in its recent strategy advice to the government, universities in the UK will have to accept that there is a choice to be made between covering many subjects patchily and covering few subjects adequately. Criteria acceptable to academics have to be developed for identifying small, weak departments. Small departments are not weak and expensive *per se*, but increasingly the onus will be upon such departments to demonstrate that this is not the case. Because the weighted teaching unit of resource is strictly variable within the UGC's resource allocation process, whilst cost functions for most academic departments are semi-variable, it may exacerbate the problem of small departments. This may particularly be the case in small universities with a large number of cost centres containing departments below average size, and in universities with a large number of below average size departments within a number of cost centres. If these small departments are to be adequately funded they may have to be cross-subsidized by large departments. Should economists examine diseconomies of small size, optimal department sizes, and the impact of the UGC resource allocation process on the economics of small departments and below average size universities?

The strategy that might emerge from an evaluation of universities' subject areas, departments and research programmes might distinguish between *existing and emerging growth* areas, *consolidation* areas, and *withdrawal and redeployment* areas. Should the agreed strategy be translated into a detailed action plan including *mission statements* for academic departments and units, which not only define the role of departments but also the performance measures towards which they should be striving? Do these statements provide the link between the institution's development plans, resource allocation processes and accountability? The allocation processes have to be consistent with the development plans, if centres of excellence are to be preserved and subject area and research programme strategies implemented. Planning, resource allocation and accountability will need to be linked in the way envisaged by the Jarratt Committee. Whilst the internal resource allocation process should not necessarily mirror the UGC's model, it will have to provide for the selective allocation of research funds to centres of excellence and emerging priority areas in a manner which is consistent with the institution's research plans and priorities. Can economists assist their institutions in reviewing their resource allocation models and procedures?

Sizer (1982) and the Jarratt Report (CVCP, 1985) have made the case for the appointment of high quality managers who can apply their professional management expertise to create an environment which will lead to positive responses to institutional self-evaluation and secure participation in strategy formulation and implementation. As well as suggesting how economists might assist with their demanding tasks, this chapter has identified a number of possible areas for future research.

Efficiency and the Market Mechanism in Further and Higher Education

Rob Cuthbert

Introduction

This chapter has two broad aims: to review recent studies of efficiency in further and higher education, and to examine the conceptual underpinning of such studies, which has remained largely implicit. This will lead to the exposition of a conceptual framework in which these efficiency studies can be located, and through which their practical implications can be clarified. It will be argued that the drive for efficiency and the current interest in market mechanisms are intimately related, though not in the way usually suggested by current government policy statements.

The Drive for Efficiency

There has in recent years been a particular drive to improve efficiency in post-secondary education focussed, in particular, on the work of the Audit Commission in the so-called 'public sector' and the Jarratt studies in some universities. This section briefly reviews these recent studies.

The antecedents of the recent initiatives can be traced at least as far back as the 1972 Pooling Committee memorandum which commended to local authorities a particular method of calculating student-staff ratios for colleges and polytechnics, and suggested target SSRs for different kinds of work. This initiated a concern for cost measurement which was emphasized by the Layfield Committee's report on local government finance in 1976:

It is difficult to make valid comparison of unit costs or other comparative measurements of the performance of different authorities. Nevertheless, the need to develop and apply the best measures which can be devised is of outstanding importance.

The background to these developments was, of course, the successive rounds of financial cuts which began in the mid-1970s. The Audit Inspectorate (as it then was) began studying non-advanced further education (NAFE) in the late 1970s and issued reports and guidance for auditors from 1981 onwards (Audit Inspectorate, 1981, 1983a, 1983b, 1983c; Audit Commission, 1985a). These were part of a more general thrust by the government to improve 'value for money' in the public sector, an understandable concomitant of a policy of reducing overall expenditure (Lord, 1984).

The audit studies in FE and the polytechnics have been extensively reviewed elsewhere (Cuthbert and Birch, 1982; Cuthbert, 1985a; Birch and Latcham, 1985b). Alongside the later audit studies came other initiatives, notably the Jarratt studies of selected universities (CVCP, 1985). Although more restricted in scope than the parallel Audit Commission studies, the Jarratt studies were welcomed by the Secretary of State, who has subsequently asked the National Advisory Body (NAB) to conduct similar investigations of 'Good Management Practice' in public sector higher education. Meanwhile NAFE efficiency studies are also being undertaken by the Department of Education and Science and the local authority associations.

One of the central thrusts of Audit Commission reports has been to recommend improved marketing of FHE services. This echoed a need already recognized (Cuthbert, 1980b) and partly met by course provision at the Further Education Staff College, where marketing courses had for some years been strongly supported by college managers. The need to improve marketing has been rhetorically endorsed by government spokesmen; this is, of course, congruent with the declared governmental preference for increased use of market mechanisms.

Perhaps the most significant change in post-secondary education in the last ten years has been the growing role of the Manpower Services Commission (MSC), with the Youth Training Scheme (YTS) as its major innovation. It could be argued that the YTS, with its variety of managing agents, has made a significant contribution to the fragmentation of 16–19 provision. Fragmentation is likely, other things being equal, to increase the role of market mechanisms, even if it has not as yet brought about privatization of education and training on any significant scale.

In sum, the dominant features of central government activity in further and higher education in the last ten years have been, in the context of the broad drive to reduce public spending, attempts to increase efficiency and value for money, and to improve marketing and the operation of market mechanisms as means of control.

The Concept of Efficiency

One of the main criticisms of the Audit Commission's most recent publication (Audit Commission, 1985a) is that it lacks an overall conceptual framework (Birch and Latcham, 1985b). By this is meant that the various performance indicators espoused by the Audit Commission to measure 'value for money' are not connected in a coherent pattern:

> In neither the guide nor the report is there any indication of the relative importance to be accorded to the 14 performance indicators identified in Appendix A of the report. This suggests that the Audit Commission has not yet developed a conceptual framework within which to assess 'value for money' in further education. It seems instead to be firing from the hip at everything in sight. (p. 123)

Since the 1985 report contains charts outlining the relationships between the key ratios (pp. 16–17) it is all the more surprising that these relationships are ignored in the selection of material for a press release about the report (Audit Commission, 1985b). The ensuing press coverage about 'underemployed lecturers' was a predictable consequence of the Commission's own press release. This suggests that the Commission either believed that the best way to obtain better value for money was to orchestrate an attack on the diligence of teachers, or alternatively that the main concern of the Commission was political opportunism to secure the Commission's own position in governmental esteem. In any event it becomes particularly important to examine the conceptual framework and assumptions which underlie these and other studies, to determine the extent to which such activities can promote efficiency, and in what sense.

Efficiency is defined by the Audit Commission as follows:

Efficiency is measured by the ratio of inputs to outputs. The approach assumes that college inputs are represented by
— lecturers' contact hours with students, widely interpreted;
— attendance hours of all academic staff, technicians, professional, administrative and clerical staff;
and that college outputs are indicated by
— student hours (registered and taught). (Audit Inspectorate, 1983a)

The term 'efficiency' is used in a broadly similiar, if less narrow, way by most commentators and analysts. This has its origins in a systems perspective which differentiates effectiveness from efficiency: effectiveness relates to the extent or quality of an achievement, i.e. to outputs alone; efficiency is the ratio of output to input, i.e. it refers to the cost of a particular achievement (Cuthbert, 1984). As Drucker put it: effectiveness is doing the right thing, efficiency is doing things right.

The simple clarity of the basic concept may be misleading. A number of commentators have distinguished between what is variously called process or procedural efficiency, and the efficiency of outcomes (Leblebici, 1985). The distinction rests on varying degrees of concern with process against product, or alternatively with means rather than ends. This distinction is often helpful in particular cases, but I prefer in general to maintain the simplicity of the core concept of efficiency, and to specify where necessary the outputs and inputs concerned, and the focus of interest in the means-ends chain. This involves also identifying those people whose interests and definitions of output and input are particularly significant in any particular context.

There is another, perhaps more fundamental, difficulty with the concept of efficiency so defined when applied to education. This stems from the difficulty of specifying educational outcomes. It can be argued that education is an open-ended developmental process whose outcomes are therefore to some extent unpredictable. This means that at the least, efficiency in education is a variable and contestable concept, and that debates about efficiency are inevitably bound up with debates about the values and purposes of education. More seriously, if outcomes are sufficiently unclear it may be that efficiency itself is an unhelpful concept, and analysis should deploy different concepts. However the implication of this relatively extreme stance is that educational spending becomes entirely an act of faith. Furthermore this view must confront the practical test of deciding how much should be spent on education.

By recognizing the political nature of the concept of efficiency we emphasize that decision-making processes and the modes of governmental and managerial control in education are also a focus of enquiry into value for money. It is through these processes that, whether explicitly or implicitly, costs and outcomes are defined as important or as negligible, different interest groups are represented or ignored, and negotiated concepts of value for money emerge.

This puts a different perspective on the move towards greater use of market mechanisms. It becomes clear that we should ask: how will such a move affect the prevailing definitions of efficiency, and the balances of power in existing structures of control? To explore these and related questions I propose to use an economic perspective on organization theory, which uses efficiency as a central explanatory concept to account for the occurrence of markets, bureaucracies and other forms of organization.

The Transactions Cost Approach to Understanding Organizations

An economic perspective on organizations has been developed by Williamson (1975) and Ouchi (1980), in which organizational forms are explained by reference to the costs of the necessary transactions between the participants. The economic antecedents of this perspective are comprehensively reviewed by Jackson (1982). Ouchi (1980) differentiates three major mechanisms for regulating transactions — markets, bureaucracies and clans.

> In this view, an organization such as a corporation exists because it can mediate economic transactions between its members at lower costs than a market mechanism can. Under certain conditions, markets are more efficient because they can mediate without paying the costs of managers, accountants, or personnel departments. Under other conditions, however, a market mechanism becomes so cumbersome that it is less efficient than a bureaucracy. This transactions cost approach explicitly regards efficiency as the fundamental element in determining the nature of organizations. (pp. 129–30)

Ouchi suggests that two variables are particularly significant in determining the relative efficiency of different organizational forms: these variables are the ambiguity of performance evaluation, and the extent of agreement (goal congruence) between the parties concerned.

> Put this way, market relations are efficient when there is little ambiguity over performance, so the parties can tolerate relatively high levels of opportunism or goal incongruence. And bureaucratic relations are efficient when both performance ambiguity and goal incongruence are moderately high. (*ibid*, p. 135)

However, when performance ambiguity is very high, Ouchi suggests that a third form of organization becomes most efficient, provided that goal congruence is also high. This third form of organization Ouchi calls a 'clan', an organization in which people are strongly socialized and where they share many values and beliefs. The model is summarized in the following table:

Table 1: Ouchi's Model of Organization Forms

Mode of control	Normative requirements	Informational requirements
Market	Reciprocity	Prices
Bureaucracy	Reciprocity Legitimate authority	Rules
Clan	Reciprocity Legitimate authority Common values and beliefs	Traditions

Source: Ouchi, 1980, p. 137.

The norm of reciprocity is argued, following Gouldner (1961), to underlie all exchange relationships. Performance ambiguity, if sufficiently high, may make a structure based on legitimate authority more efficient than a market as a means of regulating transactions, since there are effectively economies of scale in shared mechanisms for regulating transactions with diffuse outcomes. When even an authority structure is inadequate, because performance ambiguity is so high, only an organization whose members share beliefs and values can efficiently regulate transactions between its members. This echoes the argument above that under certain circumstances education might be supported for its own sake, as an act of faith (belief), rather than for any clear evidence of its outcomes (performance).

There are also echoes in Ouchi's argument of an earlier set of categories advanced by Lindblom (1977), who also distinguished three broad mechanisms of control. For Lindblom these are the market, based on exchange relationships, government, based on authority relations, and a preceptoral system (exemplified by Maoist China) based on persuasion. Lindblom cites Williamson, though not as a major source, but Ouchi appears to have been unaware of Lindblom's analysis.

Ouchi's framework has been refined and extended by Leblebici (1985), who suggests that three additional concepts — future value, allocation of rights, and uncertainty — are necessary to support the transactions approach. This is neatly encapsulated in Leblebici's definition of the concept of transaction:

> Transaction . . . is a process within which the future value of exchange is determined, the resources available to the parties are allocated, and the rights and obligations of the parties with respect to future behaviour are specified within the framework of collective rules, which constitute and regulate the process of transactions. (Leblebici, 1985, p. 103)

However, there is one further unacknowledged gap in the framework, which does not consider circumstances in which both performance ambiguity and goal incongruence are high. (This is a situation which I will argue below prevails in some parts of post-secondary education at present.) The theory suggests that neither markets, bureaucracies nor clans are efficient forms of organization under such circumstances. It seems reasonable to suppose that the combination of high performance ambiguity and high goal incongruence is inherently unstable, and will tend to evolve towards one of the more stable sets of conditions treated by the model. This hypothesis will be examined below in the light of some practical illustrations.

Efficient Organizational Forms in Further and Higher Education

In this section I will use the conceptual framework sketched above to reinterpret the developments described previously. It first becomes clear that we need to differentiate between two broad strategies for increasing efficiency, one which involves reducing operational unit costs without changing organizational forms, and the other which begins by changing organizational or governmental structures to create conditions in which unit costs can be reduced. This serves immediately to differentiate the Audit Commission recommendations from the Jarratt studies. Jarratt falls clearly into the former category, since no significant organizational changes were recommended in the final report: indeed, such changes were effectively excluded by the terms of reference of the studies. However the Audit Commission, through its emphasis on marketing, could be said at least to pave the way for major change in the structure of relationships between colleges and their various clients (however defined). I have argued elsewhere that the audit studies pose fundamental challenges for LEAs, especially for the way in which LEAs conceive their responsibility for determining the 'general educational character' of their colleges (Cuthbert, 1985b). Thus the Audit Commission's activities pose an altogether more radical challenge to prevailing structures of control than do the apparently similar studies of universities. It must, of course, be acknowledged that it is not the Audit Commission alone which is promoting such change. Rather it can be said that the overall impact of recent changes in NAFE allows for radical structural change in the relationships between colleges, LEAs, the MSC and employers.

We should then consider, for NAFE but also for other sectors of further and higher education, which structural forms for the sector as a whole are likely to be most efficient, that is, are likely to minimize transaction costs. The theory suggests that the crucial variables are the levels of performance ambiguity and goal incongruence among key participants. It was argued above that education is characterized by generally high levels of performance ambiguity. Support for this proposition is likely to be strongest among educationists, and may be significantly weaker among employers and politicians more disposed to take a narrowly instrumental view of the purposes and value of education. To put it another way, employers and government may feel more able to evaluate educational performance as adequate or not for their purposes, while educationists are more likely to stress the multidimensional nature of educational achievement.

If performance ambiguity is perceived to be low then the theory suggests that market mechanisms will be the most efficient form of organization. Thus the theory would predict that those who take an instrumental view of education would (rightly, in their terms) favour the replacement of bureaucracies by markets as a means of controlling education efficiently. If, on the other hand, performance evaluation is held to be more problematic, then bureaucratic or clan modes of control would be preferred unless there are major disagreements between key actors.

Although this analysis has some plausibility, it undoubtedly oversimplifies the situation. It seems likely that the 'pure' organizational categories of the theory are ideal types rather than observable phenomena, and real structures may display the characteristics of more than one structural type. I have argued elsewhere that public sector higher education has effectively two sets of control structures, one relating to academic control and one through which financial control is exercised (Cuthbert, 1979 and 1980a). This raises the possibility that different structures of control may coexist. For academic control, exercised through validating agencies and professional bodies, high performance ambiguity but relatively low goal incongruence might be assumed. Indeed, the shared values and beliefs of professional organizations are cited by Ouchi as an example of clan structures, and it can be argued that clan forms predominate in the academic control of higher education. In contrast, financial control involves more straightforward judgments of performance — not 'Does this examination performance merit a 2.1?', but 'Has this money been spent on the purposes for which it was intended?', and 'Does the student-staff ratio for this department fall within the target band?'. Academic judgments tend to be qualitative and complex, while financial judgments tend to be quantitative and relatively straightforward. Thus market mechanisms might well be the most efficient means of controlling financial performance. There is some support for this in the growth of 'management by league table' in public sector higher education and other sectors of education and local government.

However, the coexistence of such different forms of control clearly poses problems for managers who must reconcile these differences in practice. The continuing difficulties for the NAB and the CNAA in finding a *modus vivendi* exemplifies this problem, and Lewis (1982) has pointed out the fundamental differences in approach of the two agencies. There seem to be two possible ways of reconciling such differences in control structure. The first is that one or other of the structures takes precedence. Thus it could be argued that the 1960s and early 1970s were a period when academic and educational considerations were pre-eminent, and have since given way to a period in which financial considerations predominate; indeed, a number of critics have argued that present government policy for education is finance-led. The second possible reconciliation is the supervention of a new form of control which overrides the differences between market and clan structures. This might come about when, for example, the academic consequences of a finance-led policy become unacceptable and precipitate very high levels of goal incongruence between educationists and government. This illustrates the possibility identified above as a gap in Ouchi's framework, when high levels of performance ambiguity and goal incongruence coexist.

It was suggested above that such conditions are inherently unstable. As an example consider the recent development in so-called 'work-related NAFE'. Growing government dissatisfaction with the responsiveness and performance of NAFE led to the unilateral announcement by central government of a switch of 25% of NAFE funding to central control through the Manpower Services Commission. This precipitated direct conflict with the local authorities, with a prolonged period of non-cooperation followed by the gradual evolution of new bureaucratic forms (the Harding group, the NAFE Implementation Group, etc.) and the development of new rules for financial control (such as the formulation of NAFE development plans). The key to this process is a rapprochement between central and local government, that is, a reduction in goal incongruence. The political conflict is first regulated by general-purpose political structures of central-local discussion and consultation. These discussions then give rise to an emerging special-purpose bureaucratic organizational form. The theory suggests that, if performance ambiguity remains high, then a clan form will be more efficient. In other words, the success of the new structures may depend on the development of shared values and beliefs between the MSC, LEA and college staff concerned.

Some Implications for Practice and for Future Research

The analysis suggests that control structures in further and higher education display and will continue to display the characteristics of markets, bureaucracies and clans in uneasy coexistence. These different mechanisms of control may be only loosely coupled, and their reconciliation may in practice be confronted only at the level of college principal or lower, where financial and academic considerations are equally visible to managers.

One possible direction for future research would be to reconstrue some recent developments so as to assess the potential for change in the structures of control. For example, it seems probable that the assessment of educational performance will usually be highly ambiguous, so that clan structures will normally be most efficient. External examinerships in the university sector, and the working of the CNAA, each provide examples of clan structures in operation: bureaucratic forms imbued with common goals and professional values, whether stressing academic autonomy in the universities or peer review in the 'public sector'. But financial performance may be, or be perceived as, less ambiguous. Thus if the NAB were to succeed in establishing clear norms for 'unit of resource' for different parts of public sector higher education, then there would be scope for more market-based controls and a move away from the more rigid control of numbers by programme and institution which currently exists. Note however that a prerequisite for such a move is the existence of 'prices' (unit costs) which would suffice to regulate transactions between the funding agency and the institutions, in place of the 'rules' (planning procedures) which currently operate.

The recent developments in the debate on student loans versus grants for higher education can also be partly reconstrued. It becomes clearer that the major structural change is not in the student-institution transactions, which already are regulated by a market mechanism. The major change is in the relationship between student and government; in principle, or at least in intention, some costs would be privatized, but without any increased use of market structures for regulation. It is, of course, a matter of debate whether a switch to loans would improve the working of the market which already exists.

To take one final illustration, LEAs face a choice in managing their 16–19 provision between market and bureaucratic mechanisms for deciding on the location of different kinds of work (Cuthbert, 1985b). A bureaucratic mechanism involves an LEA policy which lays down which subjects shall be offered in which colleges, whether schools and/or colleges may run particular types of course, and so on. A market mechanism might, for example, provide that schools and colleges may offer any courses they choose, subject to overall resource constraints and perhaps other kinds of 'price control' (for example, minimum numbers for enrolment). The workability of market mechanisms can then be hypothesized to depend on the level of performance ambiguity. If the focus of performance evaluation is on quantitative criteria (for example, number of places provided, employment rates of students after leaving school/college, unit costs etc.) then a market mechanism may be more workable (efficient). If qualitative criteria of a general educational kind are more prominent then a market mechanism is likely to generate significant additional transaction costs, for example, in greatly increased effort devoted to explanations of why unit costs were higher than the norm, or why enrolments were lower than the target.

There is scope for empirical research to investigate situations of this kind, but it would be important for any such investigation carefully to identify which costs, to whom, should be taken into account for the purposes of analysis. In any case it is clear that the theory does suggest testable (falsifiable) propositions.

To summarize, the pursuit of efficiency in further and higher education may proceed either through a tightening of resource levels without structural change, or through changes in control structures which alter the prevailing balance of market, bureaucratic and clan structures. Such structural changes may be evaluated according to their implications for transaction costs between the parties. The efficiency of different structural forms depends on the ambiguity of performance evaluation and the degree of goal congruence among the participants. This analytical approach can be used to reconstrue some recent debates in post-secondary education, and to assess the probable success of future changes.

Sceptical Reflections on Public Intervention in Company Training

Keith Drake

Company Training as an Object of Public Policy

A careful specification of the nature of training is required more often than it is offered. In some firms, training is inextricably combined with personnel functions like staff selection, evaluation and promotion. Inter-firm training costs may differ considerably according to the inclusion or exclusion of these personnel costs and also induction costs. Both selection and induction are resource-consuming activities. They are unavoidable costs of efficient company operation. There is no substitute for them. For training other than induction there may be an alternative, but it is impossible to substitute for the firm's commitment of resources to induction the purchase of a ready-made product — such as an appropriately trained worker — on the external labour market. Many of the benefits from selection and induction are spread throughout and largely captured by the firm. So firms do not seek to share the cost of these activities with employees or taxpayers, as is often the case with forms of training other than induction.

In addition, there are well-known definitional problems caused by the high visibility of off-the-job training relative to the almost invisible but frequently interrelated on-the-job training and on-the-job experience learning. Substitution is often possible between learning which takes place at different points along the spectrum of formality between off-the-job, off-site training and on-the-job learning by trial and error. What counts as training is frequently limited to a rough and ready assessment of whatever activities in aid of learning happen to fall within the most formal, off-the-job segment of the formality spectrum.

In so far as they have public data systems on company training,

European countries have failed to operationalize a consistent definition of training which copes adequately with these definitional problems. The European Community's Labour Force Survey is only a very partial and modest attempt to do this. For this reason alone, generalizations about the distribution of training activity between firms, or between firms and education and training systems, are no more than tentative approximations. In practice, company training is often defined as what companies call training, and that can vary dramatically even between companies in the same business. A series of studies in recent years have thrown light on the practice of company training, as it relates to external labour markets and national education systems (Maurice *et al*, 1979; Lutz, 1981), as it relates to work organization in matched industries and firms (Sorge and Warner, 1980), to the quality of manpower, machinery and productivity in manufacturing plants (Daly, Hitchens and Wagner, 1985) and to personnel management and training markets (Méhaut *et al*, 1978). One consequence of these investigations is to demonstrate how urgent it is to dig deeper, for example through multi-disciplinary study of the key dimensions of corporate life which influence what is learned, how it is learned, by whom, and with what consequences for productivity, socialization and life chances. 'Training' is clearly as protean a concept as 'democracy'. But if the struggle to identify and tie down the multi-faceted effort to manage, accelerate and resource work-related learning is shirked, then most studies are doomed to a frustrating discussion at cross purposes between parties who mean different things by 'training'.

To make matters still more difficult, there are often reasonable alternatives to many types of company training. When skills are not completely specific or where they are, in Becker's terminology, general skills, firms have a choice from up to five alternatives to training. They may be able to (i) change the product; (ii) contract production out; (iii) change the task (for example, by substituting capital for labour); (iv) reorganize job contents; or (v) hire skilled workers from the external labour market. When there are five possible substitutes for training the response of a firm to loss of workers, product innovation, new technology or expansion of capacity is uncertain. The effect of public policy interventions designed to influence company training is uncertain for the same reason.

Company reaction to public intervention can become quite vicious. Although public authorities generally work closely and constructively with employers, there is not always unanimity between them concerning the most appropriate type of training, especially for young people who do not yet have any occupational identity. For example, the British construction employers openly attacked the Youth Training Scheme introduced in Autumn 1983, on the grounds that it would produce 'a general handyman, expensively trained by the taxpayer, turning up on site and giving the services of a Jack or Jill of all trades and a master of none' (Pike, 1983, p. 10). These companies objected that the training was too broad-based. The Chairman of the Construction Industry Training Board talked of concentrating Board operations and levy income 'on the kind of training wanted, instead of prostituting ourselves to obtain Exchequer financial support by complying with ridiculous criteria' (*ibid*).

The Distribution of Training Costs

To take one sample area, it is very difficult to tell what is really happening to the distribution of the burden of financing training (whatever that is). It may be that the burden of financing the training of young people and the unemployed is shifting more onto the taxpayer (for example, France, the United Kingdom, Ireland, Belgium) and away from employers and households, though counter-examples may be found within the European Community. At the same time the burden of training employed adults may be moving in the opposite direction, away from the taxpayer and onto employers and employees — through market financing and intermediate organizations. The factual question is whether this switch is happening, and to what extent, in member states of the Community. The supplementary question is whether this is accidental or intentional, and precisely why it is occurring.

It has often been an object of public policy on training to change the distribution of training costs between employers, employees and taxpayers. At the same time, successive publicly-financed initiatives have made it more and more difficult to establish the incidence of training costs. Public subsidization of company training and increased public spending on special programmes have helped to make tax-for-price substitution into a major issue in the financing of training.

In most countries very little is known about the overall incidence of training costs. There are limited public data which are the by-product of administration, or of surveys monitoring production costs, and a few case studies. In West Germany, the Edding Commission's work on training costs has recently been updated by another one-off study, from the Federal Institute for Vocational Training (Noll *et al*, 1983). Net cost to the employee is difficult to establish without good data on net earnings foregone during training, training levies paid by employees and uncompensated financial costs borne by employees. Net cost to the firm requires comprehensive data on gross training costs which few firms have in their accounting systems, on the value of trainee output, and on corporate tax savings from writing-off training expenditures as a production cost. Net cost to the taxpayer includes not only exhaustive expenditures and transfer payments, but tax reliefs, this total being reduced in the case of the unemployed by savings which arise when training reduces social security payments and leads to increased output and tax revenues.

European governments have tended to take the view that the volume, quality and distribution of training would be increasingly inadequate to meet the needs of the economy if the financing of training were left entirely to firms. In some smaller countries, such as Denmark, a good deal of training financed by firms in larger countries has always been tax-financed. Governments cannot afford to take over from firms very much of their financing of employees' training. Some governments have even levied employers and employees to help finance training for the unemployed, and to reduce the drain on central tax funds.

One governmental tactic has been to force firms to spend more on training. In France, and in the United Kingdom up to 1982, firms spending below a prescribed level on approved training might have to pay a penal tax, the proceeds of which could be used to subsidize training outside that firm. The scope of the British levy-grant-exemption system has recently been reduced until it now covers only about 30 per cent of the workforce, but the French version applies much more widely. In other countries, such as Sweden and Denmark, payroll taxes are used to help finance training, while in West Germany employers and employees are levied to provide both for unemployment benefits and for further training and retraining for the unemployed. Up to 1982 Industry Training Boards in Britain had their operating costs financed out of general taxation and did much tax-financed work on an agency basis for the Manpower Services Commission, so that disentangling cost to firms and cost to taxpayer was not always easy. In Germany, the Federal Institute for Employment acts as treasurer for the fund to which employers and employees contribute, but that fund can also be topped up from general tax funds if unemployment benefits drain it too severely. Some dedicated institutions act as relatively straightforward mechanisms to collectivize employers financing, for example, the Training Insurance Funds in France, the Industry Training Boards in the United Kingdom since 1982 and the Arbejsgivernes Elevre-fusian in Denmark. Others have received admixtures of tax funds on a regular basis (for example, ITBs before 1982) or on an occasional basis, for example, the Federal Institute for Employment in West Germany.

With so much training being tax-financed in the regular public education and training systems and through special measures such as Britain's Youth Training Scheme, it could be that in most West European countries' tax funding of training has been increasing absolutely. The outstanding public policy problems with respect to training finance are to decide

(i)   what constitutes an adequate level and distribution of non-public, including company training;

(ii)   how to design a financing regime which responds quickly to change while supporting an adequate volume of training;

(iii)   what forms of public intervention will not inhibit non-tax financing, will be neutral in their repercussions, or will stimulate increased funding by firms and households;

(iv)   how to reduce the sensitivity of the level of company training to the business cycle, with minimal interference to the production autonomy of firms and to the occupational and intersectoral mobility of labour;

(v)   how to design public interventions in training which underpin other public policies, for example, on regional industrial development.

The Continuing Importance of Company Training

There are Community countries where large increases in tax-financed training have been the most obvious response to the crisis of the last ten years or so: in part France, certainly the UK with respect to youth training and certainly Belgium. In Belgium (see Leroy, 1984) ONEM — a decentralized employer/worker organization despite being called the National Employment Office — has the second largest budget for training outside schools, amounting to one-third of all such public spending. Its schemes have grown fast and are predominantly, but not exclusively, aimed at the unemployed, with two-thirds of its trainees aged 25 or less. They are 93 per cent tax financed. But the less obvious company training remains extraordinarily important in many member States.

In the Federal Republic, the Noll Report (1983), for all its methodological difficulties, offers some of the best-grounded estimates available anywhere of the changing net costs of firm-based training. Variations in unit costs between training sectors are considerable. But, averaged across forty-five heavily frequented occupations requiring formal training, the specifically occupational training costs increased by around 33 per cent 1972–80. Moreover, the biggest rate of increase among the main cost elements in total training costs was in the cost of training staff, up from a 10–25 per cent share in most occupations in 1972 to a 35–45 per cent share by 1980. Since the increase in cost of trainee remuneration was generally less than the rise in total and net costs, there was a clear shift in the structure of training costs away from trainee remuneration and towards costs of employing training staff. In the Federal Republic it is contrary to the fundamental principles of federal training policy for central government to intervene in the financial responsibility of training firms. The Federal government and the Länder may finance training workshops and full-time vocational schools and even a range of subsidiary programmes, but the total government effort remains puny by comparison with the increasingly costly training effort of employers and employees. One recent estimate (Grunewald, 1984, figure 6), which excludes the Federal Law on the Promotion of Vocational Training, suggests that in 1980–81 training firms met 53.3 per cent of all training costs, trainees 34.6 per cent, the Federal Institute of Labour (from employer and employee cash flow) 1.9 per cent, and the Federal government and Länder combined a mere 10.2 per cent. In France (Rose, 1984, table 5) government financing of continuing training (which excludes apprenticeship) rose 1972–82 from 37.75 to 42.9 per cent of the total and by employers (including the Fonds D'Assurance Formation) fell from 62.2 to 57.1 per cent. Nevertheless, employers were channelling a rising proportion of wage costs into training: a percentage increase from 1.35 in 1972 to just over 1.8 in 1978. Once the schemes for young people are set on one side — and even there employers pay the *tax d'apprentisage* — it becomes clear that even in France employers still dominate training by financing over half of it.

In Denmark (see Koefoed, 1984), there has long been a much

higher degree of public financing than in France or the United Kingdom or the Federal Republic. But two powerful new financing instruments, the Arbejdsgivernes Elevrefusian or AER (1977) and the Arbejdsmarkedets Uddanelsfond or AUD (1983) have brought about a major shift of the financing burden of special training programmes from the taxpayer and onto the cash flow of employers and, to a lesser extent, of employees. The AER has collectivized the payment of wages to apprentices or Efg students — and held up the number of training places in firms — by requiring all private employers to contribute a payroll-based levy: in 1984 432 Danish crowns a year per full-time worker. By contrast, the AUD levies employees and employers in both public and private sectors — 972 Danish crowns a year per full-time worker from both employer and employee in 1984, and both levies tax deductible. These AUD funds are used to finance five types of labour market training:

(i)   for unskilled workers;
(ii) complementary training for skilled workers in industry, commerce and administration;
(iii) retraining for new skills;
(iv) EIFU, which are introductory courses for young people;
(v)   EIFL, which are introductory courses for people who have been unemployed for a long time.

Of all types of training programme, 1976–81, those with the highest rates of increase by value were not publicly financed. In descending order of increase, they were in-firm training courses, training by tax-exempt foundations and associations, by private commercial suppliers, by employers' organizations and by wage earners' organizations (Koefoed, 1984, figure 1.11).

The United Kingdom remains a mystery. One recent attempt to provide an overall first estimate for 1982–83 (Drake, 1984) suggested that about 54 per cent of funds were committed to public training and 44 per cent were being allocated to training by non-government employers directly from their cash flow. But the extreme fragmentation and sheer lack of data make such estimates very unsafe except as a starting point for better estimates. They are produced by so much prorating that margins of error tend to be large where they are not actually indeterminate. Tax-financing of post school training, especially of the Youth Training Scheme, has greatly increased, but there is evidence of a clear government intention (DE/DES, 1984) to reduce overall public spending on adult training and push financial responsibility back towards employers and employees. In most Community countries, apart from youth training, employer-financed training in the production system remains a very large component of overall training. Governments are often unwilling to let its level and character be freely determined by employers. They are inclined to intervene to alter its level and character. One problem with the interventionist strategy is to know what is an optimal or even a better level and character of training. A second problem is to find instruments of intervention which will move company training in the desired direction when so little is known about the in-firm factors governing work-learning and the factors governing company choices between training and non-training options for coping with change. Until governments have a better understanding of the effects of intervention on learning and on choices, such intervention is blind. It may be possible to produce more data on what appears to be company training, but if the relation of that training to learning is unknown, and probably very variable, the meaning of the data will be uncertain.

Evaluation of the NAFE Initiative

Rachel Britton

Introduction

Concern that Britain's economic performance has been held back compared to that of our rivals in international trade, because of a lack of trained competence in the work force, has led the government to undertake a number of initiatives in the education and training field. These have focussed on firms, on individuals, and in the case of the NAFE initiative, on providers of vocational education and training. Projects relate to redesigning qualification structures, introducing flexible learning mechanisms, pre-vocational preparation, adult training, improving information flows about training needs and opportunities, and a variety of other issues.

Because so many initiatives are underway at the same time, all aiming at improving the quality and focus of training, it is very hard to separate out and evaluate the influence of any one of them. And even without the impact of government initiatives, colleges were, and would be, changing in response to the changing demands made on them.

Nevertheless, when resources are limited and needs are urgent, judgments have to be made. Judgments will be made both on the degree to which particular initiatives have achieved their objectives, and on the degree to which the various initiatives cohere into an overall strategy — though this chapter is only concerned with the former more limited evaluation. If such judgments can be based on relevant evidence, so much the better. So in the case of the NAFE initiative, what evidence would be relevant, and how much of it can become available? These questions have to be seen in relation to the objectives of the initiative, the way in which it is being implemented, and the information systems which are or could be in place to provide feedback on results.

Objectives of the NAFE Initiative

The government White Paper *Training for Jobs* (DE/DES, 1984) published in January 1984 set in motion what came to be called 'The NAFE initiative'. The White Paper spoke in terms of a 'Market-orientated approach to training' (paragraph 41) being required. It stated that 'public sector provision for training and vocational education must become more responsive to employment needs at national and local level', (paragraph 43) and in the same paragraph went on to say that 'The public sector needs a greater incentive to relate the courses it provides more closely to the needs of the customer and in the most cost effective way'.

To encourage action on this front, the government transferred funds to the Manpower Services Commission from the Rate Support Grant. Together with existing funds, this gave the MSC control of about a quarter of what was estimated as being spent on work-related non-advanced further education. Roughly half this amount was already allocated to direct purchase of training of various sorts. So the total funds transferred to the MSC under the NAFE initiative represent something like one-eighth of the funds publicly available for work-related NAFE — and of course, a much smaller propor-tion of the total budget for NAFE, and an even smaller proportion still of the money spent by FE colleges over the whole range of their AFE, NAFE and adult education provision.

No extra funds were envisaged in the initiative, which repre-sents a management change within existing budgets; an economic evaluation would strictly speaking therefore have to weigh any net extra 'management' costs against any resulting gain in responsive-ness to employment needs or in the cost-effectiveness of work-related NAFE.

The White Paper requested the MSC to use these resources 'to support vocational education and training at NAFE level closely geared to labour market needs' (paragraph 48), and to give priority to provision for newly-emerging skills, and to arrangements for course and staff development. It also asked for 'reasonable continui-ty of provision' to be maintained.

The Policy Group

After almost a year of disagreement, a joint MSC/Local Authority Associations Policy Group was set up, in early 1985, to review work-related NAFE and to draw up future arrangements for implementing the initiative. Despite initial difficulties, the Policy Group agreed a set of objectives for work-related NAFE, and a mechanism for integrating the MSC in the process of planning and developing work-related NAFE.

Objectives shared by LEA and MSC representatives on the Policy Group include facilitating efforts

(i) to make work-related NAFE more responsive to labour market needs, especially at the local level; and

(ii) to improve the quality of information available on work-related NAFE to allow for improvements in the cost-effectiveness of provision to be achieved and demonstrated (paragraph 2.2.2 of the Policy Group report).

The other six agreed objectives can be taken as particular aspects of improving responsiveness to labour market needs. Improving the quality of information available has come to be seen as a key item both to allow active management of work-related NAFE at the college and LEA levels, and as a secondary matter, to make evaluation of any changes a possibility.

Development Plans

The mechanism unanimously recommended by the Policy Group for involving the MSC in work-related NAFE was collaboration in the production in each LEA of a three-year LEA development plan.

This development plan approach was originally approved by all parties for a one-year period; it was reconsidered in July 1986 in the light of achievements in the previous year, and the agreement was extended for a further year.

The essence of the development plan approach is that the MSC is not cast in the role of a 'discriminating purchaser' who, for instance, steers funds towards LEAs whose development plans are approved of, or particular courses that meet requirements. Rather, each development plan involves the MSC as a collaborative partner from the start, (with local employers, unions and others), so that by the time the plan comes to the table for agreement, it is a failure in the process if all partners are not equally happy with it. It is the collaborative negotiation of the plan between customers and providers of training which is seen as the 'engine for change' and not the allocation of funds. Two qualifications to this are: first, that there are provisions for withholding funds *pro rata* for agreed elements of a planned programme which are not forthcoming, if the need for such changes cannot be agreed; and second, that a small proportion of the MSC/NAFE budget is being held as a central reserve, which can be used more directly to facilitate developments.

In these circumstances, evaluation of the initiative has to contend with a rather diffuse responsibility for what happens in practice, as well as the many problems common to any attempt to evaluate progress in education and training. It does not make much sense to work out the 'value for money' obtained for the MSC contribution separately from the 'value for money' obtained from the seven eighths of the funds supporting annual programmes which do not come from the MSC — though the MSC clearly would need to be satisfied that value for money was being obtained.

As I understand it therefore, issues of economy and efficiency in NAFE are still seen at the national level as the responsibility of the Audit Commission and the Department of Education and Science, and at the local level that of LEAs and college management. A Joint Efficiency Group, chaired by the DES and with local authority representation, has been set up to pursue the issues raised by the Audit Commission report *Obtaining Better Value from Further Education* (1985a). This group is currently researching into the reasons for some of the differences in selected FE management ratios between colleges recorded by the Audit Commission. Other issues relating to costs and the data needed to monitor cost efficiency are also being considered in that Group. It is the effectiveness of work-related NAFE (taken as its relationship to clients' needs) which concerns the MSC.

MSC Objectives

The MSC interest is primarily in its responsibility for facilitating 'responsiveness to labour market needs'. Its concern is that each LEA should have available sufficient information to be able to know whether its current provision is in fact meeting labour market needs (or meeting some other objective to which the LEA gives higher priority for certain areas of provision) — and if not, to know in which direction to change and how much change is required.

Because the concern is with local responsiveness, there is no single central solution which can be handed down, and whose implementation can be monitored. Rather, each LEA will plan in its local context and against its own objectives. All the same, in order to plan, all LEAs will need a range of mechanisms which serve similar functions, even if they are not identical, and a core of similar types of information. Development plans will report on the mechanisms, for example for consultation with local employers, unions and other interested parties, and for course and staff development. They will also report in aggregate terms on the inputs, throughputs and outputs for groups of related courses. The information needed for active planning of responsive provision will also be needed to evaluate 'responsiveness'.

As a basis for evaluating changes in processes following the NAFE initiative, development plans are likely to be invaluable. But because of the unsystematic coverage likely in the first year or two of the exercise, they may not provide a comprehensive picture of what college and LEA processes were like to start with — the baseline from which progress can be judged.

Monitoring and evaluation at a national level of changes in processes will require some careful structuring of development plan information, and may require further resesarch to establish an adequate baseline. Each LEA will, of course, be monitoring and evaluating its own progress, with the local MSC and other interested parties.

Outcome Evaluation

Although there is a need to monitor and evaluate process changes which are perceived as linked with 'responsiveness' (such as changes in marketing, in contacts with employers or in course and staff development), it is changes in the labour market relevance of actual training outcomes that are centre stage. Evaluating the impact of the NAFE initiative on the market relevance of training outcomes would ideally require

(i) agreeing what is meant by being responsive to labour market needs;

(ii) specifying observable indicators of responsiveness;

(iii) having in place information systems which allow such indicators to be observed, recorded in comparable form, and made available at appropriate levels in appropriate degrees of aggregation;

(iv) deciding how 'responsive' the system was to start with;

(v)   monitoring change over time;
(vi) looking at the cost-effectiveness of change (it must be possible to be too responsive);
(vii) assessing the impact of the new MSC role in achieving any change observed.

Indicators of 'Responsiveness'

The NAFE Implementation Group (set up to carry through the recommendations of the Policy Group) has suggested a range of performance indicators which might provide some signals about responsiveness. These cover (categorized by type of course and student)

(i)   take-up of available places on courses;
(ii) drop-out rates (and information on why students left courses and where they went to);
(iii) numbers completing and qualifying;
(iv) information on the destinations of leavers, both short-term placing rates and long-term follow-up;
(v)   information on the views of students and employers on the value of courses.

All this range of information would be needed

(a) by prospective students wanting to make a rational judgment about what course to take;
(b) by employers wondering how to up-date the skills of existing employees;
(c) by colleges and LEAs in deciding whether to keep, modify or replace a particular course or group of courses, in the light of a judgment about whether they were serving clients' needs;
(d) by anyone attempting to get some simple indicators of the 'responsiveness' of work-related NAFE overall.

Indicators of this sort, if they were available, would only be the starting point for planning or evaluating NAFE. They need to be considered in the context of the local employment situation and other relevant factors. Other indicators might be the number of full-cost courses commissioned by local employers; or where colleges take a proactive stance, the number of training needs uncovered through college agency which employers were not previously aware of.

Development of Management Information Systems

Even the relatively crude indicators listed above are often not currently available. HMI note the high drop-out rates from some part-time courses and comment 'few colleges analyze the reasons for these losses' (DES, 1984b paragraph 93). The MSC has undertaken over the last few months a small-scale investigation of management information systems in colleges. Our impression has certainly been, in the colleges we visited, that pains were taken with student records of diverse sorts, and with reporting on individual courses. But the main focus seems to be on tracking and helping the individual student. In many colleges, not much of the mass of detailed information on individuals is aggregated and fed into the planning process. And although course tutors often know a good deal about the post-course destinations of their students, when an authority asked for a routine return from all courses giving destination details for students, the results were very patchy. Information is also far from uniform across each college, so that aggregates when available can be unreliable.

Priority is therefore going to systematizing existing informal information gathering, so that simple aggregates can be fed up the management information system to inform planning decisions at the LEA and college level; and to developing ways of collecting information which is not currently collected, in a standard and cost-effective way. The biggest gaps at the moment are in information on the reasons for leaving courses early, and the short and longer term destinations of students. The views of students and employers on the value of courses also seem to be seldom systematically collected and aggregated. Costs of different types of provision are often lacking; though this is an issue for the Efficiency Group to tackle. The labour market information to which college provision could be matched is still very crude.

All this information is primarily needed for management purposes at the college and LEA level. But it is also needed before any systematic evaluation can be attempted.

Evaluation in the Longer-term

When management information systems are in place in all colleges which allow aggregate performance measures to be given for groups of related courses, these will be included in development plans. The plans will also describe changes in college processes aimed at increasing responsiveness to labour market needs. Progress towards agreed objectives can then be monitored and evaluated by each college and LEA with other interested local parties. Any national evaluation will build on these local evaluations.

It is probably impossible to separate out the influence of the MSC in producing any change which is discernible, except for those parts of the system where MSC is a direct or indirect customer. Direct MSC influence can be charted in some of the process changes (for example, in the production of the development plans themselves, in changes in labour market information provided by MSC, in developments directly funded from the central reserve, and so on). But changes in responsiveness to the needs of the local labour market would be unattributable, except via the opinions of people involved.

However, the fact of such changes in responsiveness is more important than its attribution — and getting agreement on the direction and pace of change, its value and its cost, would be major achievements in themselves.

Conclusions

There are many factors producing change in the FE system at the moment besides the NAFE initiative. There are also many divergent aims for work-related NAFE not all of which are explicit in the objectives of the NAFE initiative. Local education authorities have responsibilities which go wider than MSC's aims in its involvement with the system. However, there is considerable agreement between local authorities and the MSC about the need to improve the responsiveness of the system, and the way in which improvements might be made.

The most urgent priorities at the moment seem to be developing management information systems in colleges to the point where active planning of work-related NAFE at the local level is possible, and improving local labour market information. A range of 'output indicators' have been accepted as at least a starting point for judgments about the relevance of training to labour market needs. One important indicator will be information on the use made of the training after the course ends. Very little information currently exists about this, and evaluation will have to wait on the development of the appropriate management information.

The Structure of the Youth Labour Market: Some Implications for Education Policy

David Ashton and Malcolm Maguire

For the past eight years, in a series of four research projects, we have been investigating aspects of the labour market for young people.[1] This chapter will draw on some of the main findings of these studies which have relevance for schools and the curriculum. In particular, it will look at how young people's experience of the labour market after leaving school supports notions of the existence of segmented labour markets. It will also consider employers' recruitment and employment strategies, and assess their implications for the curriculum.

A Segmented Youth Labour Market

Our previous research has led us to assert that the labour market for young people is essentially distinct from that for adults (Ashton and Maguire, 1983). A decisive factor in establishing this differentiation is the type of competition which exists in the labour market between young people and adults for jobs. We have characterized this competition as comprising three modes of entry to the labour market for young people:

(i)   Where competition is restricted to young people.
(ii) Where competition is restricted to adults. At the point of entry to the organization such jobs are closed to young people.
(iii) Where young people compete directly with adults.

The result is a concentration of employment opportunities for young people (16-year-olds) in a limited part of the labour market.

David Ashton and Malcolm Maguire

The youth labour market is further differentiated by the continuance of rigid sex segregation, which is noticeably extensive in manual occupations.

Besides the factors of age and sex, the youth labour market is also segmented in terms of skill level. We have identified four broad occupational groupings of: (a) professional, managerial, administration and technician jobs; (b) clerical, including secretarial jobs; (c) skilled manual jobs; (d) semi-skilled manual, unskilled manual and sales jobs. The consequence of sex segregation is that the specific jobs which comprise each of these segements and the career chances they provide differ for males and females, thereby creating the eight segments. Each of the segments has a distinctive pattern of entry, and, once entered, they have an important influence on the subsequent labour market experiences of young people. Any job movement tends to be confined within the occupational segment (Ashton, Maguire and Garland, 1982; Ashton, and Maguire et al, 1986).

Professional, Managerial, Administration and Technician Jobs

Entry to this segment usually takes place after the age of 18, on attainment of the appropriate educational qualifications. Training tends to be for a lengthy period, and can last for up to five years. Relatively few entrants leave, and those who do tend to enter other jobs in the same segment. Opportunities for promotion and advancement are greater than in the other segments, while the chances of becoming unemployed are relatively small.

Clerical and Skilled Manual Jobs

Again, the training required for these jobs can be substantial. However, there is a greater propensity to move from one employer to another, especially among skilled manual workers. Those who leave their jobs tend to move to others within the segment, although they are more likely to experience a spell of unemployment in the intervening period than those job-changers in the higher segment. There are widespread promotion opportunities for clerical workers, but this is not the case for either males or females in skilled manual work.

Semi-skilled Manual, Unskilled Manual and Sales Jobs

Job-changing is most common in this segment. The average time spent learning the job is very short, long spells of unemployment between jobs are frequent, and, especially for those in unskilled manual and sales jobs, opportunities for promotion or advancement are extremely limited. Males in semi-skilled manual jobs have greater prospects of internal promotion, while only sales work offers such prospects for females. Entrants to unskilled manual and sales jobs may have previously worked in other segments, but those who leave such jobs tend to do so for other jobs within the segment.

When considering the job movement of young people, it should be noted that the degree of 'job-hopping', which was a characteristic feature of the early labour market experience of young people during the 1960s and early 1970s, has now been greatly reduced. Rising levels of youth unemployment have doubtless been partly responsible for this change. However, our study of the work histories of 1786 18–24-year-olds has clearly shown that a major factor in influencing the pattern of job movement is the character of the local labour market. This affects not only an individual's chance of obtaining employment, but also their chance of changing jobs once in employment. In the study, which focussed on four local labour markets, the differences between the localities were seen to be of greater significance than social class differences in determining the level at which young people enter the labour market. Thus, in St Albans, young people from lower working class families had a greater chance of entering white-collar work than those from the middle class in Sunderland. This general pattern also applied with regard to the level of educational achievement, with respondents in Sunderland who had obtained 'O' levels, and even 'A' levels, finding it more difficult to get a job than less well-qualified respondents in St Albans.

The Value of Educational Qualifications

In recent years, research has suggested that the relationship between educational qualifications and employment is more complex than was previously thought (Ashton and Maguire, 1980; Maguire and Ashton, 1981; Lee and Wrench, 1983; Hunt and Small, 1981; Jenkins, 1983; Raffe, 1984). In his study of Scottish school-leavers,

Raffe concluded that the possession of 'O' grades had a strong and positive influence on the probability of being employed, but, beyond that, higher passes had a negligible influence. He also found that, whereas females who stayed on at school after 16 improved their chances of employment, males' chances of obtaining a job were actually reduced by staying on. He suggested this may be because age restrictions on entry, notably to skilled manual jobs, such as the exclusion of anyone over the age of 16 for consideration for an apprenticeship, restricted the value of educational qualifications for those seeking entry to such jobs. Females who stayed on improved their chances because they were competing for entry to a different segment of the labour market. These findings suggest that the segmentation of the youth labour market affects the value of educational qualifications in providing access to that market. This is because the use employers make of them in the selection process differs from segment to segment, in accordance with variations in the qualities they look for in new recruits. This might be expected, given the differences in work experience, training, promotion prospects and susceptibility to unemployment which were identified above.

Educational qualifications are invariably an essential requirement for entry to professional, managerial and technician jobs. This is partly because of the length and intensity of the training involved, and partly because of pressure from professional bodies which are concerned to maintain and enhance the status of the profession. Employers therefore normally specify a number of 'O' or 'A' levels as minimum requirements for entry. Besides performing a screening function, educational qualifications are used as a measure of a candidate's ability to cope with, and benefit from, a lengthy training programme. The criteria on which the final selection is based, from applicants with the stipulated qualifications, are likely to include the candidate's attitude to work, interest shown in the employing organization and the job, and personality. Extra-curricula activities, hobbies, interests and evidence of leadership qualities may be of crucial significance in determining whether or not the person is accepted. Thus, while educational qualifications are often essential they are not necessarily sufficient to ensure success in the labour market.

At the middle levels of the labour market the criteria used to determine entry for males to clerical occupations which offer good promotion prospects are similar to those used in the higher segments. For women, however, specific vocational qualifications, such as secretarial and keyboard skills, are essential. Leadership qualities are usually sought, but other aspects of the personality to do with interest in the job and ability to work with others are the salient ones. Again, educational qualifications are used to screen applicants but it is vocational qualifications which are particularly significant.

Employers recruiting skilled manual workers are looking for an ability to perform manual tasks. Here educational qualifications are considered to be of little value, apart from providing evidence of the general level of ability of the candidates. Employers then focus their recruitment drive on applicants with this level of ability. For example, a job advertisement may specify that candidates 'should be capable of obtaining CSE grade 3 or better'. Job offers are often made before the exam results are known. In many cases the offer will still hold even if the applicant fails to achieve the relevant grades. Some employers do insist on a minimum level of educational qualifications at the behest of local colleges which provide the off-the-job training. Where qualifications are stipulated for jobs in this segment by employers, they tend to be used in symbolic terms. Examination success is seen as being indicative of other personal qualities, such as attitude to work and ability to persevere with tasks. Recent research by Jones (1985) and Furlong (1986) has shown that personal ambition and self-confidence are also important in explaining the entry of young people into jobs at this level. Thus, although the vast majority of young people entering jobs in this segment have educational qualifications, the link between them and entry to jobs is a tenuous one.

Educational qualifications are largely irrelevant for entry into jobs in the lower segment. When recruiting labour for semi-skilled, unskilled and sales jobs, which can be learnt within a matter of a few weeks, the only academic skills which may be relevant are those of basic literacy and numeracy. As almost all potential recruits will have the abilities to master and perform the work tasks (Blackburn and Mann, 1979; Ashton and Maguire *et al*, 1986), the main concern is to establish that the potential recruit is reliable, hardworking and capable of accepting the discipline of routine and often boring work. In these circumstances evidence of personal initiative and leadership qualities are negatively valued, while educational achievement in the form of 'O' levels is sometimes seen as indicative of a desire for advancement at work which would be inappropriate for anyone entering these dead end jobs. Thus, good academic qualifications are at best seen as irrelevant and at worst a disadvantage for people applying for these jobs. In our study of 18–24-year-olds, while educational qualifications were positively related to success in obtaining employment for the sample as a whole, there was little difference in the distribution of qualifications of respondents who had never had a full-time paid job after leaving school, and those of respondents in jobs in the lower segment.

Implications for the Legitimacy of the School

These research findings raise important questions about the relevance of contemporary schooling and the content of the curriculum. As Raffe argues, much of the legitimacy of the school rests on the extrinsic value of the 'O' level (O-grade in Scotland) which is converted into employment in the labour market. More recently, Brown (1986) has shown how this is achieved as young people develop different orientations to school, based primarily on their assessment of the value of such qualifications within the labour market. For some pupils educational success, in the form of the maximum number of qualifications, is a means of leaving the working class; for others, an adequate performance in CSE and 'O' levels, is a way of getting on within the working class and securing a good job. Those who reject the values of the school and the qualifications it offers regard school performance as irrelevant to their future in the labour market. When seen in this context, the legitimacy which the school enjoys is clearly based on tenuous foundations. Indeed, there is already evidence to suggest that, while teachers use the link between certification and employment chances to motivate pupils and maintain control within the school, school-leavers soon become aware of the fragile nature of this link, especially after entering jobs in the middle and lower segments of the labour market. Results from a number of studies (Cuming, 1983; Raffe, 1984; Jenkins, 1983; Ashton and Maguire, *et al*, 1986) have shown that, while young people at school believe qualifications to be important in securing jobs, those with experience of work are less certain. After having experienced the selection process they are far more aware of the significance of personality and attitudinal factors in securing their employment. Those entering the higher segments are in no doubt about the importance of their qualifications in obtaining access to their jobs and in this sense their compliance with the school system is ensured. It is for those entering at the middle and lower levels of the labour market that the problem of legitimacy is likely to become acute.

Local labour markets are particularly important in determining the life chances of these young people, especially those who leave school at 16 or 17 years of age, because they represent the boundaries within which work can realistically be sought. The level of employment in the locality rather than the national level is of crucial importance in determining the young person's experience of the labour market. Thus, in Sunderland, the level of teenage unemployment rose to such heights that the relationship between educational qualifications and employment collapsed (Spilsbury, 1985). It is here that the legitimacy of the school is likely to be called into question by pupils. As the national level of unemployment continues to rise, so the number of areas where the traditional relationship no longer holds is likely to increase.

Implications for the Content of the Curriculum

The tenuous nature of the link between educational qualifications and employment at the middle and lower levels of the labour market has important implications for the design of the curriculum. While academic examinations measure skills and qualities of immediate relevance to the professions and other occupations in the higher segments, the fact that they are only of marginal and symbolic value for employers recruiting at the middle levels means that the curriculum could undergo fairly radical change without it affecting the employment chances of young people. For the less academically able pupils, who are likely to be seeking jobs in the lowest segment, the content of the curriculum, apart from delivering basic English and maths, is largely irrelevant to their chances of obtaining work.

It may be that a more vocationally relevant curriculum, such as that being developed through TVEI, will create stronger links between educational qualifications and employment prospects. However, the existing attitudes of employers towards educational qualifications suggests that such an improvement may only be marginal. Employers recruiting for the middle segments are more interested in a youngster's relative position in the hierarchy of qualifications (Ashton and Maguire, 1980; Raffe, 1984). Reforms of the curriculum will make relatively little difference to their selection criteria. Alternatively, links may be strengthened if employers stipulate that a certain grade in one of the newly introduced subjects is essential for entry. However, given their interest in the person's general level of ability and the significance they attach to attitudes, interests and other personality characteristics, this is unlikely.

For those destined to enter jobs in the lower segment, all the signs are that a more vocationally orientated curriculum, while it may make the content of lessons more interesting, is unlikely to improve their employment prospects. Here the message from employers is that they are primarily concerned with the discipline, reliability and attitudes of young people. Given that the work tasks can usually be learnt in a matter of weeks, the introduction of vocationally relevant subjects in school is hardly likely to ensure the adoption of more appropriate attitudes, or to make a significant reduction in the company's training costs.

If the school curriculum were to prepare young people for the experiences they will encounter on leaving school, a number of useful and important changes could be made. Schools have already responded positively to employers' demands for a basic understanding of computing and keyboard skills. Given the tremendous impact new technology is having in changing the occupational structure and the nature of work tasks, this is improving young people's competitiveness, *vis-à-vis* older workers, in parts of the labour market. However, three other areas where changes could be made are unemployment, career management and family management. On leaving school the majority of young people will experience a spell of unemployment. The introduction of a two-year YTS will only serve to delay this for two years for many youngsters in areas of high unemployment. Those entering unskilled, semi-skilled and sales jobs may experience frequent spells of unemployment, some of which will be of substantial duration. For others the only experience of work will be on government schemes, after which there will be long periods of unemployment. Indeed, some may not experience full-time paid employment in the foreseeable future, as long-term unemployment continues to rise among the 18–24-year-old population. The prospect of unemployment faces the majority of school-leavers of this generation. When asked about how they could have been better prepared at school, our sample mentioned factors associated with coping with unemployment and improving their job search abilities. They required more information on local jobs, more work experience and practical education and better instruction in dealing with the system of social security, in handling officials, being aware of their rights, and knowing how to cope with interviews. The provision of this type of assistance could be supplemented by information on how young people cope with being unemployed and the demands it makes upon them.Some schools are innovating in this area but in general it is one in which many schools are failing to provide adequate preparation (Watts, 1983). One reason for this is that to openly acknowledge that many young people will spend a period of time unemployed is to question the existing legitimacy of the school, based as it is on the claim that educational achievement will significantly affect employment chances.

The effects of changes in the occupational structure, with a massive growth of part-time employment, the development of new forms of recruitment strategies and work organization[2], and the deregulation of the labour market, have meant that fewer school-leavers can look forward to obtaining permanent, full-time secure employment.[3] Responsibility for training and career progression will rest with the individual worker and not the employer. Schools could make a valuable contribution in assisting with the acquisition of the necessary skills to cope with this situation. They could also usefully incorporate in the curriculum an element of preparation for family life, by providing an understanding of handling finances, household management and child-rearing (*ibid*). Of the 24-year-olds in our sample, 56 per cent were out of the labour force, either child-rearing or unemployed.

What we are arguing for is a rethink of the school curriculum to prepare young people for all aspects of their existence. The need is for a more balanced curriculum to prepare young people not just for paid employment but for the other major areas of unemployment and especially family management and child-rearing. The present trend towards a more vocationally relevant curriculum is likely to be welcomed by the young people themselves, but it still leaves large areas of life for which youngsters are badly prepared. By emphasizing the relevance of the curriculum for all aspects of their future existence, such a strategy would lead the schools and their teachers to rely less on the tenuous link between educational qualifications and employment chances as a means of securing legitimacy in the eyes of pupils and parents. Instead, the school could legitimate its activities through offering a preparation for all aspects of life. This would be a much firmer basis of legitimation in view of present prospects for employment which face young people in many localities.

Notes

1 These projects were: Youth in the Labour Market, 1977–80, financed by the Department of Employment; Careers Service and Employers, 1980–82, financed by the Department of Employment; Young Adults

in the Labour Market, 1982–84, financed by the Department of Employment and the MSC; and The Changing Structure of the Youth Labour Market, 1984–86, financed by the ESRC. While the findings referred to are drawn from these projects, the interpretation provided here is our own.

2 In addition to our current research findings, other researchers are reporting the spread of 'core' and periphery' forms of organization. See ATKINSON (1984); Institute of Manpower Studies (1986).

3 JONES, P. (1984) documents the growth of part-time work among school-leavers. COLES (1986) and STERN and TURBIN (1986) discuss the impact of seasonal work on the youth labour market.

Managing the Honeypots

Brian Knight

What is 'Honeypot Management'?

A new force is at work in education — a simple device for allocating funds which gives powerful leverage for change. It is so new that it has no accepted name. I shall use the term 'Honeypot Management'[1] — HM for short — because it catches the image of wafting honeypot odours stirring the slumbering bears into salivated activity.

HM made dramatic impact in November 1982, when the Manpower Services Commission (MSC) offered £7m for ten LEAs whose submissions for the Technical and Vocational Education Initiative (TVEI) best met the required criteria.

It was closely followed by the Low Achieving Pupils Project, with over sixty LEAs competing for funds from the Urban Aid Programme, and by the introduction in 1983 of Education Support Grants. 0.5 per cent of the rate support grant was retained by the DES, to be reallocated for LEAs' successful bids for designated activities such as pilot schemes for records of achievement. More recently, TRIST (TVEI-related in-service training) has appeared, funded by the MSC, but with the significant change that each LEA has been given its proper share providing its submission met the criteria. This more balanced grant distribution seems likely to be followed by the new in-service training arrangements which will operate from April 1987. Here again, the DES will require submissions to meet criteria, but with another refinement — HMI will be used to scrutinize them. Similar trends can be seen in higher education, for example in the financing of 'new blood' university appointments.

Honeypot Management is not entirely new. The MSC has relied on this approach, disbursing funds for job creation or training programmes to independent agencies which tendered for projects or made successful submissions. The Youth Training Scheme (YTS) operates through managing agencies which renegotiate annually with the MSC. The Sports Council and the regional arts organizations have dispensed funds on similar principles. For example, the Sports Council, lays down criteria for grant applications and makes clear its current priorities. However, these earlier schemes, although they have some of the features of HM, lack the dramatic innovation-seeking qualities of TVEI and some of the DES specific grants.

For the future, there is the suggestion in the Green Paper *Paying for Local Government* (DOE, 1986) that 'there may also be a case for some new grants, for example in the education field in support of the government's objective of raising standards at all levels of ability', with the report (*The Guardian*, 22 January 1986) that 'it is understood that the figure under discussion is 10–15 per cent of education spending, or £1–1.5 billion of the £10 billion total'. Even if this does not materialize, the trend of thought is clear.

So the educational world in the span of four years has begun to realize that a new funding mechanism has been developed which can have dramatic and catalytic effects and which can be pointed with precision to large or small targets. The development has come so quickly that there has been little analysis of the characteristics of the new mechanism and its merits, demerits and possibilities. This chapter attempts that analysis.

Definitions

'Honeypot Management' is a financial mechanism which enables an organization, group or individual (the 'donor') to implement policies and achieve change through the disbursing of funds to lower organizations, groups or individuals who bid for them ('bidders') with submissions designed to achieve the donor's objectives. Its essential features are:

1　The purpose is to achieve change.
2　Total funds available are stated.
3　Donors' objectives are stated.
4　Submissions are invited publicly.
5　The donor states criteria by which submissions will be measured.

Other features should be noted:

1   HM can be 'competitive' (only some bidders are satisfied) or 'equitable' (all bidders receive their proper share of the funds providing they meet the criteria).

2   The funds can be additional to those which would normally be available to bidders or can be deducted from them.

3   The criteria are crucial. A criterion is a measure of achievement to determine whether an objective has been attained. It is not, strictly speaking, an achievement or an objective — although loose use of language blurs the distinction. A criterion can be 'met', 'satisfied', or 'fulfilled' — not 'achieved', 'pursued' or 'gained'.

4   Neither objectives nor criteria need — or should — determine methods. So HM should allow considerable scope to bidders to explore alternative approaches and adjust bids to local needs and conditions.

5   HM can be 'formative' — i.e. a submission can be revised after discussion or even rejection.

6   HM is not synonymous with 'specific grant'. It is a specialized form of the specific grant, quite different to other forms.

7   HM can operate in any fund-dispensing operation and at any level. Within the education service there are three main levels[2] where funds are dispensed:

	Donor	**Bidders**
Level 1	Central government	LEAs
Level 2	LEAs	Institutions
Level 3	Managers of institutions	Heads of departments

The Operating Context

Any organization or person dispensing funds, at any level, faces the same problem. How can fund allocation be made with maximum effectiveness and minimum hassle? For HM is only one of many possible mechanisms. So, which is the best? Normally a donor will continue with the mechanisms used previously, unless dissatisfied with them or under pressure to change. In a new situation, such as the MSC has faced, more radical rethinking is likely. In both cases decisions are likely to be pragmatic, although beneath them one can see some general principles operating.

First, donors are torn between two different strategies. On the one hand, they want to ensure that funds are spent according to their own priorities. On the other hand, they want to ensure that client groups retain their vitality and that local initiative and innovation is encouraged. The two strategies tend to conflict.

Donors are also influenced by tactical administrative considerations:

1 *Equity*

They will want to ensure that allocation is based on some principle of equity, so that groups with greater needs receive greater grants. This may be because donors have a rational desire to allocate resources equitably or because they just wish to avoid complaints. But equity is difficult to define and even more difficult to achieve. At level 1 the search for equity lies behind the constant adjustments to the rate support grant, with refinement piled upon refinement until it reaches impossible complexity. At level 2 LEAs agonize over allocation of staffing between schools to allow for falling rolls, small school size, or special needs. Similar problems are faced at level 3 by individuals responsible for allocation of funds within a school or college.

2 *Predictability*

A system which allows organizations to plan ahead is desirable. One of the strongest criticisms of the present rate support grant system is that it makes forward planning impossible.

3 *Simplicity*

Ideally, any system of grant allocation should be simple to understand and easy to operate. It should not require excessive time from donors or bidders.

4 *Value for Money*

Any disbursing organization will look for value for money, and so may wish to monitor expenditure closely. (However, the Audit Commission (1984a) is pressing strongly for increased financial delegation to schools. 'The Commission considers that more delegation of authority and responsibility to the local level will result in better value for money and avoidance of waste ...' p. 49)

5 *Effectiveness*

Any donor will want to ensure that its funds are used effectively to achieve its objectives. This implies evaluation and feedback — notoriously difficult where one is dealing with a non-profit-oriented service and with objectives which are largely qualitative.

There is considerable conflict between these five tactical objectives as well as that noticed earlier between centralized control and local autonomy. For example, any drive for equity will tend to conflict with the desire for simplicity. Similarly, predictability, say using allocation of funds by formula, may conflict with value for money. Financial delegation may conflict with central priorities. The donor's policy will oscillate between these various objectives depending on current pressures.

Alternative Mechanisms

There are a number of alternatives to HM, some of them long established. Each has advantages and disadvantages for which space is not available here.

1 *Grants Without Strings*
This is traditional form of fund allocation in the 'national system, locally administered' of England and Wales. So, the rate support grant once allocated is very much at LEAs' own disposal. At the lower levels, LEA grants to schools for capitation, or division of funds within a school or college among departments, can normally be spent by users according to their own priorities.

2 *Grants with Recommendations*
There is an increasing tendency for central government to suggest to LEAs that funds allocated to them should meet certain needs. For example, the rate support grant is based upon expectation of reduced school premises capacity. At level 2, LEAs may increase schools' capitation allowances on the grounds that, for example, libraries are understocked. But there is no mechanism for monitoring and enforcing these recommendations. The classic example, again at level 1, was Shirley Williams, as Secretary of State for Education and Science, allocating £7m in 1977 for additional in-service training within the rate support grant — and seeing it swallowed up without trace.

3 *Budget Negotiation*
Here donor and bidder negotiate the size and shape of the budget. A good example is the financing of further education colleges, which normally springs from negotiation with the

LEA of the forthcoming estimates. Within a school, capitation allocation can be negotiated by departments with the head or the committee that controls the budget — in extremes from a 'zero-budgeting' position.

4 *Speculative Bidding*

The process by which the donor reserves funds and awaits unsolicited bids: for example, the head from heads of department, or LEA advisers from schools. This procedure is quite different from HM because normally no criteria are laid down, there is no open competition for funds, and often their extent or existence is concealed.

5 *Pools*

A levy on bidders' funds which can be used as a regulatory device to ensure that a minimum amount of finance is allocated for a purpose or that it is disbursed locally against guidelines. Apart from the DES secondments pool, centralized stationery or reprographics funds in institutions fall into this category.

6 *Tendering*

This is similar in some respects to HM, but much more limited in scope, and often not expecting innovation. It is used, for example, by the MSC, DES and the Research Councils to set up research projects.

7 *Refund of Expenditure for Specific Activities*

This is a neat device to ensure that funds are spent for a defined purpose. A good example is the DES in-service training funding initiated by Circular 3/83, which refunds for supply cover for teachers on courses of certain types. This device is quite commonly used at level 1, but seldom at levels 2 or 3. It is similar to HM, in that it enables the DES to control the education system by pulling the purse-strings, but it does not require innovatory bids.

8 *Allocated Specific Grants*

These are direct grants for specific purposes, but not requiring bidders to make submissions. A good example is the current DES specific grant proposal for school lunchtime supervisors.

9 *Payment for Goods and Services Supplied*

10 *Direct Budget Allocations*

Examples here would be the DES allocating money for inservice training in DES courses, or the LEA allocating INSET funds for courses run by its own advisers, or a head allocating INSET funds to the school's professional tutor. This only operates in a line-management situation.

11 *Matching Funds*
Donor provides funds for a specific purpose to match funds raised by bidders.

12 *Tapering Funds*
Donor initially provides 100 per cent of funds for a specific purpose, but reduces the contribution over a short period of years, possibly to zero, while the shortfall is made up by the bidder.

Merits and Demerits of Honeypot Management

HM, like each of the alternative mechanisms, has its own inherent advantages and disadvantages. It has several considerable merits:

1 It concentrates the minds of both parties. The donor has to think out clearly his objectives and criteria. Otherwise the honey will be given away for little return. Equally, the bidder has to think out a convincing set of proposals to meet the criteria. Otherwise no honey. This incentive to think clearly is a substantial gain.

2 It targets the donor's priorities. It is particularly useful for directing expenditure towards newly emerging needs.

3 It encourages innovation. If bidders are to receive their money, they need to make submissions which appeal to the donor — particularly when HM is competitive. So, TVEI for example, has created a great deal of new thinking.

4 It speeds up implementation of policy. Schools change very slowly. Again taking TVEI as an example, the deadlines have been very sharp, and so it has been launched at a speed which previously would have been thought impossible.

5 It enables the donor to direct and implement policy without requiring a full line-management structure. This is a very economical way of operating, comparable to the way companies offload activities to sub-contractors.

6 It provides a good deal of scope for local initiative and adjustment of policy to local conditions, because criteria should not specify the actual method and system to be used.

7 HM can trickle from one level to another. An LEA making a submission may invite competitive bids from its schools or from consortia of them. HM sharpens the 'bidding' skills of LEAs and schools.

On the other hand, HM has a number of substantial disadvantages:

1   It is not well suited to permanent, ongoing policies. If it is used for allocation of grants for a particular feature year after year, the process will become routine, it will be difficult for the bidder to create or even look for innovatory schemes, and indeed it will be unnecessary since the grant will appear almost automatic.

2   It is haunted with the problem of opportunity costs. It is very well for the donor to lay down priorities, but what opportunities are lost which the bidder perceives as more important? This has been a major criticism of TVEI. LEAs have tended to argue that, whatever its value, if they had the money in their own hands they would give it to other priorities and obtain better returns.

3   It can create unrealistic conditions. Bidders will spend donors' money in a way in which they would not spend their own. Some features of TVEI or TRIST are extravagant and would die back if the MSC ceased to fund them.

4   It tends to create or increase inequalities, particularly if used competitively. This again has been a major criticism of TVEI, that it has widened the gap between schools that have benefitted from TVEI and those which have not. Similarly, when educational support grants were introduced some LEAs appeared to be net gainers and others losers. The demand for equity will damp down this tendency — but in this case some of the innovatory force of HM is lost.

5   It can be time consuming. The donor needs time to draw up proposals, assess submissions, check finance has been spent for the intended purposes, and evaluate. Equally, the receiver has to make up the submission — and in a competitive HM situation, a lot of work may be invested for nil result. Further time is required to respond to the donor, report on expenditure and so on.

6   It can create disillusion and lower morale. HM can be seen as a centralizing tendency, taking away power from the bidder, spending on lower priorities, consuming time, destroying local initiative, and even using funds rightfully belonging to the bidder. It need not be so. Much will depend on the skill with which HM is used, and particularly the degree of negotiation between the two parties.

7   It is difficult to monitor and requires skilled evaluators.

More Extended Use for Honeypot Management?

Despite the caveats above, there is still considerable scope for wider use of HM. So far, it has been used pragmatically — by the MSC to act quickly, central government to change emphasis within the education system, and the DES to strengthen its hold upon the system in general. It could be used selectively to implement change in carefully chosen areas. What might have happened had the Bullock Report (1975) been introduced with a substantial HM scheme? The DES could have channelled funds to those LEAs which appeared the most eager or imaginative at developing language across the curriculum in their schools. LEAs could have made funds available to schools who had a convincing and thought out policy for this. Senior management in schools could have done the same in relation to heads of departments. In community education, HM could be ideal for LEA designation of community schools. And so on.

HM is little used at levels 2 or 3. But it would be quite possible for LEAs to withhold part of schools' resources or to grant extra resources and allocate them through HM. This would be a substantial force for change. Take an LEA which wishes to develop personal and social education in all its schools. It has to push for this — issue policy statements, influence heads and teachers, provide INSET, send advisers to shepherd the laggards. But in the face of complacency or resistance, little may happen. But the thought of gaining — or not gaining — extra finance would be likely to influence the most cynical head! HM creates a pull-force to complement the push.

HM also complements the trend towards increased financial delegation. So far this has been for expenditure, not supply. In other words, schools are given responsibility for spending money, *but not for acquiring it*. Schools still receive their resources, in cash or kind, as a hand-out from the LEA. Only in raising funds from the MSC or other outside agencies, or in private fund-raising, do schools show the independence and initiative which they are now being asked to exercise over expenditures. They could be invited to bid for LEA funds, with safeguards.

At the lowest level, a head could find HM a very useful lever for change within a school. Suppose he (or she) sees a high priority for more active teaching methods and greater student participation, does he preach to his heads of department? Or invite them to bid for resources with submissions of department policies to achieve this end? Of course, the same problems could arise here and at level 2 as are already possible at level 1.

Conclusion

'Honeypot Management' is a very powerful device for using allocation of finance to effect change in education. Used intelligently, sparingly, and sensitively, it could be used to create speedier, better directed and more effective change, and encourage innovation and local variation to meet local needs. Used thoughtlessly, extensively, or crudely, it could encourage centralism, distort priorities, weaken morale, and create rapidly diminishing returns.

Notes

1 'Honeypot Management' — term first coined by Alan Lambourne, Deputy Chief Education Officer, Somerset LEA.
2 There are two additional levels for fund allocation — the Treasury to the education service, and local authority (total budget) to the LEA. These have been omitted for simplicity. All levels are described in Dennison (1984). Higher education is also not covered in this chapter, although similar principles in fund allocation and the use of HM operate.

Categorical Funding and its Limitations: The Experience of TVEI[1]

Oliver Fulton

Introduction

After relatively small beginnings, the Technical and Vocational Education Initiative (TVEI) has now become the major post-war experiment in central governmental promotion of curriculum change. It is of great interest not only as a substantive piece of educational reform, but also because of the method by which it has been introduced: central government (but the Manpower Services Commission (MSC) and not the Department of Education and Science (DES)) has used *financial mechanisms* in an attempt to reconcile its desire to promote educational change with the strong tradition of local autonomy in curricular matters; and the method has been hailed as successful, in that by 1986/87 TVEI in its original form will have been taken up by over 80 per cent of LEAs without direct compulsion from the centre. There is every indication that this near-universal adoption of TVEI will encourage (and has done so already) further use of 'categorical fundings' (Harland, 1985) or 'honeypot management' (Knight, in this volume). If so, it is important to look carefully at the achievements and limitations of the new method. In this chapter I draw on research into the implementation of TVEI to examine more closely the effectiveness of categorical funding by the MSC in achieving its desired goals.

As experienced in TVEI, the technique of categorical funding has the following features. In outline, a central government agency allocates a fixed sum of money for a specific activity, which it defines by a set of broad 'criteria', announced in advance. It invites local authorities to bid for an allocation from these earmarked funds, with schemes that have been designed in accordance with the stated criteria, but whose particular shape may be determined by local needs. Formally, the control of education is unchanged and remains local: not only is there no requirement on local authorities to bid for what are usually regarded as *additional* funds, but the detailed planning and delivery of the new programme is still in local hands. However, once the central agency accepts the bid a *contract* is signed, specifying in some detail what will be done in return for the funds provided. Contract compliance, i.e., accountability for the use of the funds, is assured through a built-in system of formal monitoring, which may range from a simple accounting for expenditure incurred to an elaborate evaluation of outcomes against stated aims or criteria.

Does this new mechanism, then, provide not only an honourable way around the unpalatability of central direction, but also an effective way of achieving national goals? Current discussion appears to take for granted the basic assertion that it is possible for central government to draw up clear and unambiguous goals for education and, by using the financial carrot to circumvent political opposition or inertia among local authorities and their schools, to get these goals effectively translated into practice. In this chapter I want to use the experience of TVEI to identify some of the disadvantages as well as the advantages of categorical funding, and to suggest that the route from central policy to local practice has been a little more tortuous than might have been expected. In Williams' (1979) terms, the use of categorical funding has not succeeded in returning educational policy-making and implementation to a 'technocratic' model: indeed, I suspect that if anything it heightens, rather than diminishes, the 'political' nature of the process. From the start, TVEI — like most of the MSC's activities — has had a high political and public-relations profile. Far from being a 'technocratic' policy innovation, in which (in the ideal type) new policies are approved at the high political level and then implemented by the administrative system in a rational and linear-planned operation, TVEI has been constantly adapted and redefined in response to conflicting interests and pressures. Indeed it has been distinctively political, from its origins outside the conventional educational policy-making system, and its sponsorship outside the DES, through its intriguing and exceptionally wide-ranging combination of formal aims, to the organic development — or, less kindly put, the *post hoc* redefinition — which its agile sponsors, the MSC, have adopted as their style.

TVEI — National Policy Development and Modification

The rules of the TVEI game have certainly changed. As is well known (for example, Dale, 1985), it first appeared as a programme which owed more to high-level ministerial discussion than to the customary channels of the 'educational sub-government'. The Prime Minister's announcement, in November 1982, described '... a *pilot scheme* [1], for *new institutional arrangements* [2] for technical and vocational education for 14–18-year-olds, *within existing financial resources* [3], and *where possible, in association with local authorities* [4]' (quoted in Dale, 1985). One might have been forgiven for supposing that (1) a controlled experiment would be set up, (2) with new 14–18 schools/colleges, (4) quite possibly direct-grant or even independent, (3) using funds withdrawn from the normal budget(s) for state education. In fact, the TVEI 'experiment' (i) is being heavily evaluated but not in any tightly controlled fashion (and has been steadily expanded without waiting for the results of evaluation); (ii) has been provided in existing institutions, with relatively modest additional resource centres (roving buses, Welsh castles etc) to enrich the experience of pupils extracted from the classroom for short periods; (iii) has been financed by MSC without any acknowledged withdrawal of resources from the DES/DoE system; and (iv) has been provided entirely via the local authority education service, albeit through managerially unconventional channels. There can be little doubt that these early modifications were largely 'political': both conscious, and due to the larger political imperative to co-opt at least parts of the existing system into support for TVEI; and also, less deliberately, resulting from the fact of co-option — once it had been decided to use existing institutions the initiative was bound to be modified to fit, at least partially, into their existing practices. I shall return to these points below. But it is worth underlining immediately that TVEI did *not* start its life as a limited, clearly-specified programme designed to use categorical funding to achieve a precise set of aims. It began — and continued, as we shall see — no less 'politically' than any other educational reform.

The fundamental decision was that TVEI would be delivered, not 'where possible in association with' LEAs, but exclusively by them. No doubt both political and practical considerations played their part. At the political level, it was obviously preferable — *other things being equal* — that existing institutions should be co-opted into support for TVEI than that the MSC should set up a new framework of schools and colleges which would surely be seen as hostile but well-funded competition; there would be a risk not only of outright failure, the responsibility for which could not be dispersed, but also of damaging conflict. (And the cost per student would have been even higher, and it would have been essential to satisfy the Treasury by removing the funds associated with TVEI students' costs from the LEA system.) Moreover, it is hard to imagine such an externally-designed programme achieving educational credibility. The experience and resources available in-house to the MSC's TVEI Unit were simply not adequate to allow it to perform the work of several major Schools Council projects in a matter of weeks or months. (Its pride in speedy delivery is of course another major, if self-inflicted, constraint on the MSC.) The same consideration ruled out not only direct control but also any idea of developing a tightly-specified design, to be offered on a take-it-or-leave-it basis to LEAs — which might in any case be quite unpopular. Success would depend on making use of local ideas and of the expertise to be found at all levels in the system; and it would be enhanced by the fact that volunteers tend to be as enthusiastic as conscripts are sullen. But decentralization has its price: other things never *are* equal.

There seem to have been two phases of adaptation to political constraints. The first has been described already: the shift from a bare proposal developed at ministerial level (and without the conventional consultations) to one which appeared politically feasible to civil servants and the Commission itself — after consultation with interested parties. At this stage the modifications outlined above must already have taken place, and it was agreed that local authorities would be asked to deliver the Initiative through the existing system, by bidding for contracts as described above. But the next stage, in which the newly-formed TVEI National Steering Group, most of whose members are 'educationalists', must have had a large hand, led to a further series of adaptations before the formal 'criteria' were published — some time *after* the first series of bids had been received.

When compared with the original announcement, the criteria that emerged are startling: and still more so are the interpretations that were ultimately contracted for, explicitly or otherwise, by the MSC. (Like many other educational reforms, TVEI has both its explicit criteria and its hidden curriculum, often expressed in rhetorical 'buzz-words'.) Within the institutions there have been a whole series of expansions and adaptations of the original stated aims. Even the ostensibly central characteristic of TVEI, its emphasis on 'technical' and 'vocational' education, has become one among many aims of the initiative. Both T and V have been not so much demoted as integrated (at the official-rhetorical level) into a wider and still more ambitious scheme, not just to rehabilitate T and V E, but to transform the secondary school/college experience for all.

There has, indeed, been a real enough enthusiasm and encouragement for technical education, most obvious in the proliferation of information technology and other electronic equipment, and in the teachers and technicians to support it, but also in a much wider range of broadly technical subjects. There has also been support for a wider range of 'vocational' subjects than the strictly technical; and there is further a large component of '*pre*-vocational' curriculum, including not only general job-related skills but also work experience, 'life skills', and so on.

However, the aims and criteria of TVEI go much wider. It was quickly expanded to include socially and economically desirable, if also fashionable, aims such as the provision of equal opportunities in access to the whole programme, and the avoidance of sex-stereotyping within it. (Here the resemblance to American federal funding conditions is striking.) And TVEI programmes are further expected to be designed for and recruit from the whole ability range. This latter aim might be taken as an example of TVEI's curricular imperialism, and so it may yet turn out to be, though not all TVEI schemes have been very successful in this respect. (They have, however, differed considerably in the specific ability band(s) to which they have appealed.) But it is undoubtedly also a response to the early suspicion, especially among Labour authorities, that TVEI was an attempt to reintroduce selection in secondary education; while the equal opportunities provisions may be expected to have appealed to the same audience.

There is one other, perhaps even more unexpected, aim: a strong emphasis on 'the new pedagogy', whose chief educational proponents are probably the Further Education Unit (FEU). Its stated purpose is to move from conventional 'chalk-and-talk' teaching to 'problem-solving', 'learning-to-learn', 'experiential' learning, etc. Once again, this has a fashionable element to it; it is economically justifiable in the light of rapid technological change; and arguably it is politically essential in the face of mass youth unemployment when specific vocational training seems farcical. This is not the place to discuss the merits or otherwise of the 'new pedagogy', although it should be noted that while it is often attacked by critical sociologists as an example of creeping 'state social control', it is also very popular among pupils whom more traditional teaching and academic, knowledge-based forms of assessment have failed to enthuse. And it fits well with the more rhetorical statements of employers' organizations about the failings of traditional academic education, if less well with their actual recruitment practices. But it is noteworthy that while strictly T and V E by its very nature excludes much of the traditional secondary curriculum, and as a matter of present-day fact, however unfortunate, also excludes many of the most able students, the 'new pedagogy' is in principle applicable to any subject and any student. Thus the TVEI criteria, or at least the TVEI philosophy, by encouraging the spread of the new pedagogy outside the T and V areas, made a bid for the support of innovative teachers throughout the system.

These adaptations or extensions of the original T and V idea can be interpreted in two, not necessarily competing, ways. On the one hand there is clearly an evangelical strand, with a gospel according to (in no particular order) NEDO, Lord Young, the FEU, and Education for Capability, which aims at the regeneration of the British economy through educational reform. TVEI emerged at least partly from this line of thinking, which has its supporters within the existing educational institutions (many of their leaders being on the National Steering Committee). But on the other hand there may well have been some concern that without more grandiose, and more fashionable, aims than merely inserting an extra T and V element into the existing hierarchical curriculum, TVEI might simply fail to appeal to local authorities, despite the attraction of the cash — or worse still, that it might appeal only to the greedier and/or most impoverished LEAs or schools, who would be more likely to 'take the money and run' than to turn it into a reform that would do credit to its sponsors. A high-profile progressive and evangelical rhetoric, with very wide and diffuse applications, would help to attract innovators and enthusiasts. In other words, cash incentives might not be enough in themselves: financial mechanisms needed to be supplemented by political sensitivity and a determined effort to encourage local authorities to volunteer, by buying off some of the critics and giving them a chance to use TVEI to achieve their own ambitions for innovation. It ought to be added that most observers would agree that TVEI has benefitted from the process.

I have described the early shift from a centrally-planned and managed innovation to a decentralized, categorically-funded method of reform. My contention is that in this basic shift we can see the tension at the centre between the desire for change and the need for political accommodation in order that the change will be successful. The same tension can be further illustrated in the shifting interpretation of TVEI as a 'pilot' programme. TVEI has always been described as a 'pilot' scheme; but the interpretation of the word has slipped steadily from a carefully controlled 'scientific' experiment, through a more 'natural' experimental design, to a definition as a limited-life programme whose effects, it is hoped, may 'ripple' outwards.[2] These shifts are also quite clearly political adaptations. Essentially the MSC began by using the concept of a scientific experiment as a justification for its tolerance of local initiative and the diversity which inevitably followed. Rigorous 'summative' evaluation was to identify the 'best practice', which would be generally adopted at the end of the pilot programme. However, it was quickly decided, again at a high political level, to recruit another large tranche of LEAs in 1984 to join the fourteen pioneers of 1983. At the time when the second round of forty-four LEAs were being selected, the first fourteen schemes had been running for less than six months, and no evaluative conclusions could possibly yet be drawn. The concept of a 'pilot' therefore needed revision. In any case, it was already obvious that the first schemes differed sharply from each other, not randomly but in response to very different local circumstances. As time has gone on, it has become even more clear that there is enormous diversity both in content (for example, in the proportion of time occupied by the TVEI curriculum, in the subjects on offer, the qualifications obtained, the ability and gender balances), and in the number and type of institutions involved, the management structures and so on. And the diversity has emerged from differing local structures, local cultures and local political philosophies. Evaluation may help to tease out the interconnections between some of the variables listed above, and provide ideas for development on a formative basis; but it will not provide the MSC with a single blueprint for future imposition from the centre. (Indeed, as the MSC has also learned, not only is 'summative' evaluation costly, lengthy and generally inconclusive, it is dangerously unpopular with schools and teachers.)

The second redefinition of the 'pilot', however, grew out of the internal dynamic of LEAs and schools, to which I turn below: it soon became clear that successful TVEI projects would be likely to burst their banks. Aside from the fact that this made strict evaluation impossible, since no 'control group' can be found that is uncontaminated by TVEI, it came to seem indefensible to try to restrain the spread of the TVEI philosophy. Thus the 'pilot' was reconceived as a stone in a pool, whose 'ripples' would spread in ever-widening circles beyond those staff and students originally defined as participants. To understand why and where it was spreading, we need to turn to the local level.

Categorical Funding at the Local Level

On receipt in local authorities, messages from the MSC have been seen as a mixture of the permissive and the authoritarian. There has been considerable permissiveness about the *content* of individual TVEI schemes — though the MSC has flexed its muscles over the criteria in the negotiations leading up to the signing of contracts. (Presumably its strength has been greatest at this point: it needed to make TVEI attractive in order to get LEAs to bid, but once the bids were in, fairly tough negotiations coud take place over the precise terms of the contract. After the contracts were signed, however, the leverage diminished again.) But the MSC has consistently been much firmer in matters of management and control, especially on the financial side. The key issue has been 'additionality' — the concern that money intended for a new scheme should not be covertly used to finance part of the authority's existing educational provision — an especially glaring danger when many of the participants are compulsory-age school children in existing schools. If the MSC has been short on in-house educational expertise, and perhaps longer on political and public relations capability, it has certainly not lacked, as TVEI schools ruefully complain, for experienced accountants. LEAs and schools have been asked to provide unprecedentedly detailed accounts of the use of money received, and more than one has been subjected to very severe auditing.

Indeed, it seems inevitable that the use of categorical funding will create a disproportionate emphasis on financial as opposed to educational accountability. There are a number of reasons for this. The first is the absence of comprehensive or reliable output indicators. Although categorical funding has some parallels with government contracts with industry or commerce, there is one key difference: whereas most such contracts are for a given product, TVEI contracts are for an input. A laundry may contract to clean a hospital's sheets and uniforms for a given period, or a defence contractor to build a new submarine; but an LEA agrees to provide a process:

so many pupils to be exposed to a given curricular experience, under certain additional conditions such as equal opportunity of access. Thus while evaluation can try to assess outcomes — but inevitably over the medium to long term — monitoring for contract compliance is virtually forced to focus on inputs. And finance is the most accessible of these, as well as being obviously legitimate in this case as the motive power for change. Secondly, financial auditing provides the most credible leverage for the monitoring agency. Grants can justifiably be withheld in proportion as they have been misapplied: the threat is real. But what is the appropriate penalty for failing to deliver the hoped-for numbers of trained or job-prepared man- and womanpower, or for failing to meet one of the other criteria in full? Rumours are that the MSC has hinted at all-or-nothing treatment: an absolute right to pull the plug if it is dissatisfied. There must be doubt whether this is wholly credible.

For all these reasons, the budget is in fact that most important element in a TVEI contract, and accountability has been concerned largely with control and management of the budget. This has meant that an essential component of every scheme has been an *alternative* financial control and management structure. Each participating LEA and each school or college has been required to appoint a 'coordinator', who has had control over an independent budget outside the normal management channels. Moreover, within schools the disposable TVEI budget available to the co-ordinator may well be larger than that available to the head for the whole rest of the school. Headteachers and LEA officers and advisers have been chagrined to find that their normal powers — to purchase and allocate equipment and supplies, to allocate Burnham points and even to decide on staff appointments, and above all to move pupils — and staff — in and out of classrooms — have slipped from their hands. Inevitably, strains have arisen.

There is, in fact, a fundamental tension (Saunders, 1985) which arises from TVEI's separate funding and management. On the one hand, the pressures of financial accountability, and underlying them the obligation to spend TVEI money effectively and for the purposes for which it was intended, tend to provoke a separatist culture. TVEI develops a strong identity, with rhetoric to match and generous funds to support it, which may well enhance its achievements among its favoured few participating teachers and students, but will be seen by those excluded as inequitable, threatening and in short 'divisive'. Indeed, in some cases any success that a well-planned and coherent TVEI 'enclave' may produce can be outweighed by the hostility it provokes outside — at any level from LEA management to the staffroom, the classroom or the school grounds. This is the dilemma for an institution that adopts what Saunders calls the 'containment' strategy for coping with TVEI. The popular opposite, or 'extension' strategy, would mean that TVEI is spread, as nearly equally as possible, over the whole school — or even LEA. Internal opposition is disarmed and potential opponents — many of whom may be strong protagonists of specific elements such as the 'new pedagogy' within the broad TVEI philosophy — are co-opted into support. The irony is that while 'extending' TVEI in the widest possible ripples may be effective in some respects, it inevitably waters down or distorts the original sharp thrust of TVEI as planned from above; and it is unlikely to be easily shown to be an efficient use of resources. The MSC, and local TVEI management in their turn, therefore face a constant dilemma: how far to accommodate and how far to remain separate and pure. Shifting attitudes to the 'pilot' and to evaluation and monitoring demonstrate that the conflict has not been permanently resolved.

Conclusion

TVEI is, so far, the most expensive (and extensive) use of financial mechanisms by the centre to promote educational change; but it is not the only conceivable model (see Knight, in this volume). It is unusual in many respects: notably in that it has been managed by the MSC and not the DES — government departments that differ not only in their experience of educational issues at the secondary level, but also in their constitution (as line department or *quango*), in their culture and style, and in their history of relationships with local authorities — to name a few. Nevertheless, I believe that the TVEI experience shows that, while funding reforms may alter the rules of play, and may indeed lead to a different result in some matches, the strength of the sides in the game of educational policy making is not thereby radically changed. In the end it is schools and their teachers which have to deliver educational change, and local communities within which they do so, and to which, one way or another, they are responsible. No system of finance or control can send the interested parties off the field.

If this is a warning to central government against excessive optimism, it is also in many ways a comforting one. My own view is that the original conception of TVEI has been enormously improved by the modifications forced on the MSC by the political realities. Its implementation has in fact shown, at a bad time for education, that there is not only a stock of worthwhile ideas throughout the system, but also a great deal of enthusiasm and excitement that can be liberated by injections of hopefulness — and of extra resources.

Notes

1 I wish to acknowledge the help of Michael Leach and Murray Saunders, my colleagues in the Lancaster TVEI Evaluation Programme, whose work and ideas I have drawn on extensively in this chapter.
2 The announcement in July 1986 of a national, expanded but lower-cost 'TVEI Mark II' in effect again redefines the 'pilot' as a 'preparatory' programme before TVEI is made available throughout an authority's schools.

Efficiency and Opportunity in School Finance Autonomy

Hywel Thomas

Introduction

Giving schools greater control over their budgets is an innovation which has a strong appeal for those concerned with securing improvements in the allocation of resources to education. The change, devolving the level at which allocation decisions are taken, is assumed to lead to outcomes which more closely match client needs. This chapter will examine the growing practice of school finance autonomy and outline an approach for testing the validity of this popular assumption.

The next section summarizes the growth of autonomy schemes and briefly considers its development in Solihull LEA, for whom I am acting as an evaluator. This is followed by a discussion which, after clarifying the underlying theory of choice which appears to justify autonomy initiatives, suggests an alternative theory of choice as one which is both more helpful in guiding research into autonomy and in suggesting ways of improving its practice. The fourth section draws on recent interview material with the intention of analyzing the decisions of practitioners. The concluding section suggests approaches for improving the management of autonomy.

The Growth of Autonomy

In addition to the six LEAs which are known to have introduced relatively substantial levels of financial devolution (Hertfordshire, the ILEA, East Sussex, Cambridgeshire, Cheshire and Solihull) several others are actively considering similar schemes. The Audit Commission (1984a) has added its support to the practice and, more recently, the DES in *Better Schools* (DES, 1985a), although both have suggested that schools should exercise more direct control only over some 25 per cent of their financial budgets.

What this direct control or autonomy basically means is that schools are told the size of their budget for the coming year and are allowed to vire between the given heads of expenditure. If allocations for buildings and grounds maintenance are included in the budget, schools obtain quotations and decide upon contractors. Schemes also allow for the carry-over of a surplus or deficit across the financial year. Autonomy means that schools take on new responsibilities for purchasing and accounting with their consequences of extra work-load and for the acquisition of new skills.

In surveying practice across the six LEAs, Hudson (1984) described those features common to all the schemes which, he wrote, were largely a consequence of the general administrative structure of the education service in England and Wales:

(i) The LEA must determine the overall size of the school budget.

(ii) The school must respect the general policies laid down by the LEA. (There may be room for debate about how far these policies should extend, but there would be general agreement that there must be some such policies.)

(iii) The school must respect national agreements on pay, conditions of service and the like.

In commenting upon the schemes, Hudson noted a change of emphasis in the objectives of the four more recent schemes compared with the earlier schemes. For Hertfordshire and the ILEA, the earliest schemes, he suggests that the '... advantage was seen to lie in enhancing the capability of the schools to function as education institutions, while the more recent schemes put greater stress on the aim of securing cost-effectiveness through greater managerial efficiency'. Given that concepts like cost-effectiveness and efficiency are, by definition, tied to considerations of output, the distinction drawn by Hudson is a little problematic, unless it is interpreted to mean that the later schemes have been introduced in order that interests other than the participating institutions are entitled to benefit from their greater efficiency. This was certainly an issue in Solihull.

It was clear from the outset that the different personnel involved in the scheme expected it to achieve its aims in rather different ways. While the principal aim of autonomy is to make more efficient use of scarce resources, a major problem of practice was in agreeing upon who should benefit from increased efficiency. Efficiency can be improved either by achieving the *same* level of output using *fewer* resources or *increasing* the level of output from an *unchanged* level of resources. The political initiative which launched autonomy wanted the benefits of increased efficiency to be shared with the authority and, initially, a bottom line deduction was placed on the budgets. This approach to distributing the benefits of increased efficiency was not shared by the officers and the head-teachers who pressed a 'value for money' argument, where the schools which managed to improve their operating efficiency would reap the benefit by retaining their savings. This view has now prevailed and, like other schemes, Solihull allows the schools to retain the whole of any savings.

How schools use their enhanced power over the budget is certainly an important question, but the fundamental questions are concerned with the assumptions or theories which underlie these schemes. Are they theories which accord with the circumstances of schools, because if they do not adequately reflect the economic and social realities of schools some of the hoped for benefits of autonomy may not easily be realized? The next section discusses the 'theory of autonomy.'

The Theory of Autonomy

Hudson's (1984) summary of recently introduced schemes places an emphasis on the efficiency benefits expected from devolving more responsibility for resource allocation to schools. The general theory of choice here seems to be that the unit managers (heads and senior teachers) are best placed for making choices which will maximize efficiency. There are six main assumptions underlying this quite popular theory. The unit managers are (i) closer to the clients; and (ii) better able than more remotely sited managers to identify the needs of clients. In addition, unit managers (iii) will give primacy to satisfying these needs; and (iv) will also know the best (i.e. most efficient) way of combining available resources to meet as many of these needs as possible. Finally, in making decisions on resource combinations the unit managers will vary the proportions of different resources as (v) production requirements and (vi) relative prices change.

If these six assumptions properly reflect reality, we can conclude that autonomy schemes will give rise to management choices which increase efficiency. However, doubts can be raised about the validity of several of these assumptions. The first assumption of physical proximity begs the question as to who exactly is the client in education. On the second assumption there is certainly no unanimity that teachers have been very successful in identifying client needs; certainly several aspects of central government policy on the curriculum suggests there is considerable doubt in that quarter about the ability of schools to properly identify pupil needs. As to the third assumption, there is certainly empirical work which suggests that, when conflicts over interests arise, some members of professional groups such as teachers do sometimes place the satisfaction of their own interests ahead of those of their clients. The fourth assumption is valid providing teachers have knowledge of different ways of managing teaching and learning. Knowledge here should be understood as including a sufficient understanding of alternatives that rejection is based upon reasoned consideration and is not a reflex action based upon prejudice. It is not uncommon to read HMI reports which criticize schools for the sameness of their pedagogy. The fifth assumption needs to be tested in autonomous schools because they are alone in the maintained sector in having this flexibility, although comparative information could be sought from the private sector, the further and higher education sector and overseas. Finally, because schools are not subject to the cost and price pressures of more conventional markets, there must be some scepticism as to the responsiveness of school-based managers to changes in relative prices.

These remarks are not intended as an argument that none of these six assumptions are valid but to suggest that, taken together, they do mean that a set of quite restrictive assumptions must be fulfilled if we are to be confident that optimal choices are being made in educational institutions. Indeed, there are some parallels with the restrictive assumptions governing the firm in conditions of perfect competition, where the entrepreneur is presented with circumstances in which there is no alternative but to choose the most efficient course of action: it is a nominal theory of choice. It may be that the theory of autonomy as outlined here is also an essentially nominal theory of choice. This matters when the practice of autonomy is evaluated because too much reliance might then be placed in commenting on outcomes, such as the level of virement and the project priorities selected by schools, because these are assumed to represent the decisions of efficiency maximizing managers. Too little attention is likely to be given to the process and act of choice because that is assumed, by definition, to be essentially well informed and efficiency maximizing.

What is needed is a theory of choice which treats as problematic the six assumptions discussed above and more convincingly represents the nature of choices within educational enterprises. What is needed is certainly a view of the school as a unit of production because that is central to an understanding of the principle of autonomy, but it must also be a theory which recognizes uncertainty about production requirements, relative prices and alternative production possibilities, and which is sceptical about the knowledge and interests of educational managers and sensitive to the ways in which particular circumstances affect judgments about perceived opportunities or choices. Such a theory is empirically useful because, in taking so much less for granted, it alerts us to problems which might otherwise be overlooked. In particular, it guides us to the stages at which choices are made and, using Buchanan's (1969) phrase, by examining the 'choice-influencing' factors, provides information which could be useful for understanding and improving practice.

It is this theory of choice associated with Buchanan which is used in the next section and, drawing on recent interview and other material, offers a preliminary and selective attempt at testing the usefulness of the theory as a means of evaluating autonomy schemes. The first part is based upon interviews, carried out in four of Solihull's autonomous schools, exploring the options and constraints of which senior staff were aware when they were reformulating the budget presented to them last summer. The second part shows how the theory makes us more aware of the tiers of choice and decision within schools over the use of resources.

Options and Constraints for School Managers

Opportunities as Seen by Senior Staff

Autonomy is, for the most part, viewed favourably by the staff interviewed in the four schools. Considerable value is attached to the freedom it gives for selecting priorities within a given item of expenditure. For example, the same might be spent on maintenance as budgeted by the LEA but the school can select the projects. Choice on who does the work is also valued because of the flexibility and competition it brings; one school halved the cost of two projects, saving £4000 compared with the quotations given by the Technical Services Department. However, the range of possibilities over which this freedom is seen to apply varies greatly between schools and for different reasons. This is illustrated by first describing and then examining choices over spending on teachers and capitation.

In one school a possibility for the coming year is to recruit one-half teacher below establishment and use the money to employ secretarial help for departments, a proposal which is being discussed with representatives of all staff. This virement away from teaching staff is seen by heads in two other schools as unacceptable, because 'squeezing' staff 'in the present climate is not on', although both seemed to welcome the opportunity it offers for boosting capitation and ancillary help. This pragmatism on the issue of virement away from teaching staff is not shared in the fourth school where it is strongly believed that it is not the head's job to reduce the numbers of teachers in the school.

Two of the four schools have made deliberate choices over capitation this year. One school has boosted spending by £3000 as a contribution to the 'intense' shortage of books and materials. Another school has transferred rather less than £5000 *from* capitation to employ a laboratory and reprographics technician, a change which 'leads to things being done which teachers would otherwise not do' in 'a largely resource based school'.

How do we explain the different choices mentioned here and, as important, sometimes the absence of a view that there is a choice to be made? Within what might be described as the orthodox theory of autonomy they would presumably be taken to represent different ways of maximizing output in an activity where there are legitimate differences over suitable technologies of learning. Within a Buchanan-inspired theory of autonomy such conclusions are not rejected but are subject to rather more questioning.

Why does one head propose to vire from staffing, others rather reluctantly turn away from the option and a fourth barely recognize the choice? At least part of the explanation for the first decision lies with an expected growth in staffing numbers, because it is easier to live without the extra half-teacher who is never appointed! It is not the whole explanation because the same head takes the view that, in circumstances of contraction, it might be desirable to make a greater cut in teaching staff than required by the budget and transfer resources to produce technical and secretarial help to support more self-study. Here seems to be a view that different circumstances require changes in the pattern of resources provided. As to reluctant rejection of virement, the political circumstances constraining choices in a year dominated by strike action in schools need little elaboration. Finally, the absence of a view that viring from teachers is even a possibility is surely not uncommon among teachers. There is a widespread belief in the idea that the way to improve standards in education is to improve the pupil-teacher ratio; in other words, it is unnecessary to go to all the trouble of measuring outputs because an *input* measure (PTR) offers such a reliable guide to the state of educational standards. The efficiency questions raised by cost analyses, such as Cumming's (1971) of classroom spending on teachers and capitation, do not appear to be asked here.

To what extent do the decisions on capitation simply and properly represent different views about appropriate learning technologies? Are the substantially different emphases apparently attached to the place of books for the support of learning a consequence in each case of a reasoned consideration of some alternatives? In one case the interview evidence does not enable me to offer a confident answer. In the other case the interview material suggests that alternatives were not really considered. Those making the decision were confident that, given their budget and their 'choice-influencing' views about its built-in commitments, theirs was the only choice open. During the interview I suggested we discuss possible alternatives to the decision taken and it seemed fairly clear that the only other item on their agenda of alternatives was to have made no change at all from the given budget.

The analysis of these decisions must raise questions, albeit tentatively given the limited data, about the recognition and importance attached by some teachers to production possibilities other than those they currently use. This is highlighted by the next section, which briefly mentions the importance of some of the other decision-makers in schools.

The Choices of Learners

The value of a theory of autonomy which tries to take some account of the nature of the social reality in schools is that it alerts us to the range of people who make choices in schools about the allocation of resources. Schools appear to have some of the characteristics of command economies in which a small group of resource controllers, undoubtedly influenced by external factors, decide upon the allocation of resources to different activities. Senior teachers are very influential in determining the time to be devoted to subjects and exercise great control over the allocation of time of other teachers and children. In classrooms, teachers *attempt* to exercise quite specific control over the way children spend their time. However, unlike a command economy, the restricted choices which remain available to pupils mean that teachers cannot control learner inputs and outcomes. Learners may choose outright rejection of the package (truancy), partial rejection (inattention in class) and commitment (reflected in genuine attempts to complete teacher-determined objectives). This is not the place for an extended discussion of this aspect of *resource autonomy* and its implications for the management of schools (see Thomas, 1986), but it does emphasize the value of suitable theories for identifying important issues of practice. The implications of this material for the management of autonomy and the relationship between economics and education management are discussed in the concluding section.

Autonomy and Efficiency

While there is general agreement that the purpose of autonomy is to get better educational value for our money this chapter suggests that such an outcome must not be taken for granted. An analysis of the assumptions which appear to underlie autonomy implies a view of schools which may not always be borne out in practice. The implications for the management of autonomy of a more appropriate set of assumptions about schools will be discussed here under the headings knowledge, appraisal and training.

Knowledge

Underlying both theories of autonomy discussed here, and the expectations which practitioners have of autonomy schemes, is a view of the school as a productive process, an important and useful metaphor for the social relations within schools but a metaphor nonetheless. Because it is a metaphor it surely follows that many teachers will not necessarily share this view of schools and the implications which follow. For example, assumptions (iv), (v) and (vi) given earlier imply that teachers believe that concepts like efficiency, production functions or product mix are applicable to schools. To the extent that teachers do not share the metaphor of schools as productive processes, the likelihood of autonomy leading to more efficient schools must be diminished.

Where some teachers do share this metaphor, the discussion and evidence of the previous two sections suggest that teachers are not necessarily efficiency maximizers who consider several options before making a choice.

However, even where there is a search for alternatives it is likely that in an activity such as education, as elsewhere, their valuation involves some subjectivity. The importance attached to teachers as against other resources is illustrative. Who makes this valuation must be influenced by subjective factors as well as knowledge about production functions. Might teachers value their own importance as a resource more highly than non-teachers and be more likely to protect that resource at the expense of others, such as the provision of books?

The Buchanan-based theory of autonomy alerts us to context as choice-influencing, and decisions about spending on teachers can again serve as an example. Reluctance to vire away from teachers can partly be explained by the context of one year of strike action in England and Wales. This reluctance may be stronger in some LEAs if teachers believe that policy-makers are not very supportive either of teachers or spending on education.

Hopefully these examples are sufficient to illustrate the consequences for decision-making of the nature of knowledge about schools held by those who practice autonomy. There are also implications for others who have a responsibility for appraising autonomy, particularly the governors, education officers and politicians.

Appraisal

The arguments advanced about knowledge apply just as much to those with a responsibility for monitoring autonomy because, as the stewards of the public education system, it is their responsibility for ensuring that autonomy-related decisions are better in meeting the needs of clients than more centralized decisions. This requires that the process of scrutinizing the resource choices actually made includes both an examination of the forgone alternatives and a discussion of the effects of the choices on educational processes, on the basis that the latter represent an appropriate bench-mark for the evaluation. This may mean that an LEA's inspectorate has a role in the evaluation of autonomy as advisers to governors, officers and politicians.

Training

In circumstances where some of those with a responsibility for autonomy schemes do not attach much value to the metaphor, and its implications, of education as a productive process the prospects for real success must be limited, unless appropriate training is adopted.

In schools where heads and sufficient senior staff are well-informed about the potential educational benefits of autonomy, processes can be created whereby staff can be educated into new perspectives about resources and learning. One school has a committee responsible for setting some of its budget priorities and, through the process of having to make budget choices in conditions of scarcity, it is hoped that staff at departmental level will become more realistic about financial limits and in becoming better managers of their own resources be prepared to consider more radical alternatives.

In schools where heads or senior staff see autonomy as involving teachers in checking invoices, watching meters and spending many hours on budget profiling exercises, all of which take time away from educational issues, training is needed. Some of this should be designed to overcome existing problems in the day-to-day administration of autonomy; it can be handled through the kind of on-the-job training provided in Solihull by an Autonomy Assistant. However, training should also be concerned with developing a view of a school as an economic system in which concepts of efficiency, resource substitution and production functions are relevant. Short and long courses off-the-job presumably have a role here.

In a recent book much influenced by teaching on short and long courses in educational management and administration, Ribbins (1985) suggests that 'If there is to be a profession of education management there must be a body of relevant knowledge in which its practitioners are superior to non-managers. One area in which such a claim might be sustained is a knowledge of organizations.' I agree with this, providing such knowledge is taken to include a view of organizations as economic systems with managers having an understanding of central economic concepts. Such knowledge would not only assist the development of financial autonomy schemes but of schools where more account is taken of the human resource autonomy of learners.

Measuring the Costs and Effectiveness of 'A' Level Teaching: A Professional Approach by Auditors[1]

David Reeson

Introduction

Secondary school pupil numbers will fall from 4.1 million in 1979 to 3.0 million in 1991. The number of 16–19-year-olds in full-time education may continue to fall until the mid-1990s. To cater for this reduction local education authorities (LEAs) need to make difficult decisions about the provision of 'A' level teaching. Not to do so would invite competition between educational establishments for a limited market. This would be valuable if it resulted in 'A' level teaching being retained only in cost-effective sixth-forms and colleges. However, it is more likely to lead to unnecessary costs, for example, through the duplication of teaching provision.

Decision making is usually difficult because of the number of conflicting priorities and the lack of objective information. Educationalists, treasurers and politicians may all fail to agree about objectives and the best ways to achieve them. When such a stalemate occurs politicians may ultimately be forced to take arbitrary decisions. Local authority auditors, whilst recognizing the problems of reaching a consensus, are concerned that decisions are based on as much objective information as can be conveniently gathered.

Measures of the cost and performance of 'A' level teaching should lead to a more informed debate, provided they are practical and capable of being easily understood. To this end, in 1985 staff of the District Audit Service in the West Midlands area collected and analyzed data from four LEAs. In doing so, use was made of the work of Hywel Thomas (1981). This chapter describes some of the more important findings of the district audit's work.

David Reeson

Effectiveness

Most attempts to measure the performance of schools and colleges have relied exclusively on examination results. The district audit exercise has also adopted this general principle. Given the emphasis placed upon examination results by employers and higher education establishments alike (rightly or wrongly) there would seem to be no other realistic alternative. However, it is recognized that a student's 'A' level results alone are not necessarily a good predictor of subsequent academic or career achievements.

Although the principle of using examination results as a performance measure may be acceptable to a local education authority, the precise formula by which to measure effectiveness is a more contentious issue. Analysis of the data collected in the district audit exercise suggested one essential feature of any measure; 'A' level examination results (output) should be related to 'O' level and CSE examination results (input) achieved by the 'A' level cohort being considered. In other words it is better to measure the 'value added' by 'A' level teaching rather than just the outcome.

This principle is especially important if within a local education authority school sixth-forms and colleges have different selection criteria or the 'O' level and CSE results of feeder schools are significantly different. In one authority regression analysis showed that 77 per cent of the variation in 'A' level performance between establishments (using a points system) could be explained by examination results at 'O' level and CSE. False conclusions may be drawn about the relative effectiveness of establishments if 'A' level results are considered alone.

The district audit exercise used a points system to measure examination performance. For example, 'A' level grade A = 7, grade B = 6, . . . 'O' level = 2, Fail = 1). The full system is set out in the appendix. A ratio was calculated as follows:

$$\text{Examination Performance Quotient (EPQ)} = \frac{\text{'A' level points per examination entered} \times 100}{\text{'O' level and CSE points per examination entered}}$$

Many alternative measures were tested. These included more crude measures such as a comparison of the pass rates at 'A' level and 'O' level/CSE, and also more refined measures, such as non-uniform scales with and without cut-offs to exclude failures. The rank order of establishments, as measured by their EPQs, did not change significantly when these alternatives were used. This suggests that the controversy about the make-up of performance measures may be more of interest to the academic than the practitioner.

Arbitrary statistical measures may be used incorrectly to conceal or exaggerate differences in performance between establishments. It is important not to lose sight of what these differences mean in terms of examination results. For example, it was found in one authority that a fifth-former with average 'O' level and CSE results would expect to achieve three D grades at 'A' level in the sixth form with the highest EPQ and three E grades in the sixth-form with the lowest EPQ. In practice this difference may affect the prospects of only a small proportion of 'A' level students.

Two other issues need to be addressed when attempting to measure effectiveness. Firstly, are measures based on a single academic year valid? As described earlier, some of the variability in 'A' level results between years is removed by relating them to the 'O' level and CSE results of entrants. However, changes in staff and curricula (together with some random variation) suggest that relying on a single academic year may be dangerous. Two or three years' data were used in the district audit exercise.

Secondly, 'A' level performance measures may be affected by feeder schools adopting different practices towards entering fifth-formers for 'O' level and CSE examinations. Some may prefer to restrict students to entries where there is a high probability of success. Others may encourage pupils to enter all examinations for which they are eligible. In the latter case pupils may tend to have lower scores per entry at 'O' level and CSE. The district audit exercise did not cater for this. Entries per student at each feeder school is one possible indicator, but this should depend on the general ability of fifth-formers as well as the school's examination entry policy.

The 'value added' principle may apply best to 'A' levels. The input to output relationship may be more tenuous for assessing effectiveness over longer time periods, for example the 11–16 age range, as other factors such as pupils' socio-economic backgrounds may assume greater importance. Such a relationship may also not be appropriate when the teaching environment changes radically, for example from school to university.

David Reeson

Costs

The DES has recommended that, to be economical and effective, a sixth-form should consist of at least 150 students, and 'A' level groups should be about twelve in size. Figure 1 shows the general relationship between average group size and teaching costs per 'A' level, using data from two authorities. The costs of teaching 'A' levels were calculated as follows. The amount of a teacher's or lecturer's salary apportioned to 'A' levels was determined by the formula:

Figure 1 '*A' Levels Cost Per Student and Group Size: Sample Schools and Colleges*

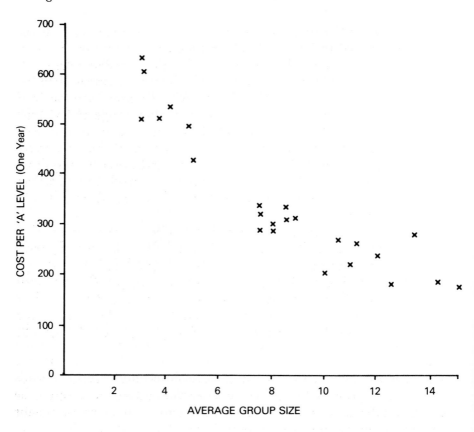

$$\text{Gross salary and NI and superannuation} \times \frac{\text{Formal contact time per week between teacher and 'A' level groups}}{\text{Notional contact time per week}}$$

The notional contact time was fixed for each establishment as the modal number of contact hours of a scale 1 teacher or grade 1 lecturer. Therefore, if the most common teaching time of scale 1 teachers is twenty-five hours per week and the headmaster teaches two hours of 'A' level geography per week, 8 per cent of his employable cost was apportioned to that subject.

The exercise showed that there was a number of ways in which the sizes of sixth forms and 'A' level groups could be increased, and so reduce costs. For example,

(a) In authority A the policy of retaining grammar schools had led to low 'A' level teaching costs. However, in parts of the county there was scope for more common timetabling of subjects on limited offer because numbers had reduced substantially. Where comprehensive schools had been introduced they offered a limited range of 'A' level subjects and were generally below the recommended size.

(b) In authority B, area boards had increased the cost effectiveness of 'A' level teaching in rural areas by requiring students to do a limited amount of travel, but in urban areas there remained a lack of cooperation between schools.

(c) In authority C, four small sixth-forms were teaching 14 per cent of all 'A' levels at 21 per cent of the teaching cost. Three of the four sixth-forms had less than 100 students.

(d) In authority D, there was very little cooperation between establishments and no longer-term planning. Even where a sixth-form college and a technical college shared the same campus the same subject was being taught to small groups in both establishments.

The formula shown above has been used to calculate teaching costs per 'A' level group and teaching costs per 'A' level entry. An example set of results is shown in table 1. A distinction has been made between subjects on general offer i.e. available in all establishments, and those on limited offer, i.e. available in only some establishments. This distinction, although somewhat arbitrary, has proved helpful in pointing to areas where savings might be made. This is because

David Reeson

Table 1: Barnham 'A' Level Teaching Costs 1984–85 (One Year)
(The data is drawn from one authority in the district audit exercise)

'A' Level Establishments	School A	School B	School C	School D	Sixth Form College	Technical College
General Offer Subjects						
No. of 'A' levels	203	153	128	26	2445	465
No. of groups	23	18	17	7	171	35
Average group size	8.8	8.5	7.5	3.7	14.3	13.3
Teaching Cost (£)	63,189	51,509	43,420	13,339	467,835	132,441
Cost per group (£)	2747	2862	2554	1906	2736	3784
Cost per 'A' level (£)	311	337	339	513	191	285
Limited Offer Subjects						
No. of 'A' levels	105	50	41	0	719	740
No. of groups	14	10.5	10	0	64	49
Average group size	7.5	4.8	4.1	0.0	11.2	15.1
Teaching Cost (£)	33,748	24,894	21,863	0	188,881	134,403
Cost per group (£)	2411	2371	2186	0	2951	2743
Cost per 'A' level (£)	321	498	533	0	263	182
All subjects						
No. of 'A' levels	308	203	169	26	3164	1205
No. of groups	37	28.5	27	7	235	84
Average group size	8.3	7.1	6.3	3.7	13.5	14.3
Teaching Cost (£)	96,937	76,403	65,283	13,339	656,716	266,844
Cost per group (£)	2620	2681	2418	1906	2795	3177
Cost per 'A' level (£)	315	376	386	513	208	221

within a sixth-form there are often significant cost differences between the two clusters of subjects.

Figure 2 illustrates the opportunities for reducing teaching costs to cater for falling rolls. Reorganization of 'A' level teaching provision, whether by closures of sixth-forms or specialization of subjects by different schools, should be effective in increasing average group size and reducing teaching costs. There may also be opportunities within an establishment to modify teaching input to 'A' levels, thereby reducing costs and helping to preserve a broad curriculum.

Figure 2: Factors Influencing 'A' Level Teaching Costs

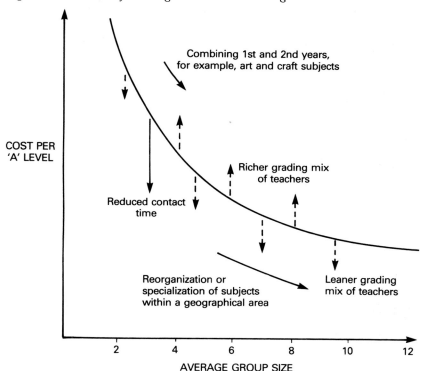

The cost of teaching 'A' levels depends on the grading mix of teachers, the group size and the amount of contact time between teacher and 'A' level group. These factors vary significantly between and within local education authorities. For example, data collected in the district audit exercise suggest that for a sixth-form of 100 students with an average group size of eight, teaching costs can vary by as much as £30,000 per year.

Opportunities to vary the number of teaching staff in any establishment may be limited in the short term. However, in schools, headteachers have some flexibility in allocating staff between the sixth-form and the remainder of the school. Whilst total staff for the school may be allotted on the basis of two different pupil teacher ratios (PTRs), small sixth-forms may have to be allocated more staff than justified by the recommended PTR in order to sustain the curriculum. The audit exercise found that in two authorities classes in the lower school were larger than their recommended PTR because they were effectively subsidizing the sixth form. In one school with a sixth-form of nearly 100 students this subsidy was the equivalent of two scale 1 teachers.

Grading mix of 'A' level teaching staff also varies between schools. For example, table 2 below shows for five schools the proportion of total 'A' level teaching time accounted for by each grade. The average salary of 'A' level teachers (weighted by the time they spend teaching 'A' levels) varied between £11,200 at school C and £12,400 at school E, a difference of 10 per cent.

Table 2: 'A' Level Teaching Time (by grade)

Scale	School A (%)	School B (%)	School C (%)	School D (%)	School E (%)
1	10	20	33	23	23
2	44	38	21	33	34
3	17	13	23	22	28
4	23	29	20	0	13
Senior teacher and above	6	0	3	22	2

Contact time between teacher and 'A' level group is of greater significance in explaining cost differences between establishments. Table 3 below shows the average contact time per 'A' level group at six establishments and that the differences are largely accounted for by average group size.

Table 3: Contact Time Between Teachers and 'A' Level Groups

Establishment	A	B	C	D	E	F
Average group size	14.3	13.5	8.3	7.1	6.3	3.7
Contact time (hours per week)	5.9	5.1	4.9	4.6	4.4	3.2

All establishments appear to be reducing contact time to compensate for small 'A' level groups, but the extent to which this practice is adopted varies. For example, some schools were providing the same teaching input for each subject irrespective of student numbers. Others were reducing contact time if the group size was six or less. Other measures to cater for falling student numbers and to help maintain a broad curriculum include:

(a) Combining the first and second years in the sixth-form into one group and alternating the syllabus between years. This measure is practical only for certain subjects.

(b) Combining 'A' level students with 'O' level students. Again, this is practical only for a few subjects, for example, art and craft, and some educationalists may think it harmful.

Whilst the initiatives discussed above will help reduce 'A' level costs they do not provide an economic justification for preserving small sixth forms.

A different problem is encountered with larger groups. For each subject, the establishment must determine the maximum size of an 'A' level group before it is split into two groups. This is clearly a complex decision because of the trade-off between effectiveness and economy.

Conclusions

The exercises carried out by the District Audit Service have brought together (often for the first time) objective data about the costs and effectiveness of 'A' level teaching in several local authorities. This should assist officers and members alike in assessing what reforms are needed to cater for falling rolls as they affect the 16–19 age group. Analysis of the data has also helped point to the relative importance of factors affecting the costs of 'A' level teaching input and how they might be controlled.

However, as auditors of local authorities it is not our role to make value judgments about the relationship between costs and effectiveness. For example, if school A achieves 20 per cent better results than school B but at 10 per cent greater cost, which school is the more cost effective? Such judgments must be left to local authority members, as advised by their officers.

Appendix

Calculation of Examination Performance Quotients (EPQs)

For any establishment, the EPQ relates the 'A' level results achieved to the quality of the same 'A' level cohort as measured by their examination results at 'O' level and CSE on entry to the sixth-form or college.

Scores have been attached to the grades achieved in each type of examination, as shown below:

Score	'A' Level Grades	'O' Level Grades	CSE Grades
7	A		
6	B	A	
5	C	B	
4	D	C	1
3	E	D	2
2	'O' Level	E	3
1	Fail	Unclassified	4
0			5

Note

1 (Any views expressed are those of the author and not necessarily those of the District Audit Service or the Audit Commission).

The Costs Consultant's Contribution to Planning and Evaluating Third World Education

Christopher Cumming

Introduction

The aim of this chapter is to review the possible contributions which someone with an economics of education training can make to education in the Third World. The content includes two accounts of costs studies undertaken by the writer: in Bangladesh, the entire education system was scanned with a view to forecasting the costs[1] of the primary education system; while, in Kenya, the costs of teaching practical subjects in secondary schools were probed as part of a summative evaluation of an aid-financed project.

In the concluding section two questions are posed: how far do such cost studies meet the needs of public policy-makers?; and what research needs to be done to enhance the contribution of the economics of education to policy formulation in the Third World?

The Future of Education in Bangladesh

Bangladesh is one of the youngest nations. It is also poor ($140 per head in 1982) and incredibly crowded (645 people per square kilometer).[2] The period of field work lasted from mid-April to mid-December 1982. The broad terms of reference were to 'investigate the problem of maintaining or improving the financial status of primary education in Bangladesh'. The costs study was one of four studies included in the IDA fourth education project. Two economists from the University of Dhaka joined the costs study in mid-June 1982. Before leaving Dhaka in December 1982, a draft report was discussed with officials of the Ministry of Education and the

Planning Commission. A final report was available in February 1983.

The terms of reference inferred that availability of data for the forecasting of costs and revenue would be a matter of referring to the Ministry of Education or the various education sector directorates. However, data on the system was at best patchy. Senior officials coped with mountains of paper work, interviewed streams of visitors and laboured prodigious hours at meetings but without the benefit of a common store of intelligence about the gigantic system they were attempting to manage. To exacerbate the lives of officials, postings and re-postings as well as redesignation of responsibility for posts were frequent and abrupt. (From March to December 1982 there were three holders of the post of Director of Primary Education and one of these also had the responsibility for Mass Education.) The mobility of key senior personnel and the degree of centralization must have been main factors in the absence of a secure database.

The Education System

In 1982 there was no effective system of decentralization of government. (A major change is now in progress.) Education, like other sectors, was administered centrally: for instance, McLellan (1983) estimated that as many as 12,000 officers could have direct access to the Director-General (Primary). Beyond primary, there are junior secondary, secondary and higher secondary schools, a 5 + 3 + 2 + 2 structure below higher education. Higher education has, at its apex, six universities: but, there is also a welter of mainly non-governmental degree colleges, affiliated to the universities. Educated unemployment is chronic, as are skills' shortages. True university education is all but free, whereas, in about 98 per cent of secondary schools, fees are charged. The government is involved in supporting many so-called non-government institutions, sometimes to the tune of 50 per cent of recurring expenditure. There is one national language — Bangla — which is the medium of instruction in education up to and including university. Females are 'progressively' underrepresented at all levels.

It was a central plank of the second five-year plan that UPE (Universal Primary Education) should be a national priority target and that by 1985, a staging post, 90 per cent of the 5–9 years age group should have been reached. However, with estimates of the size of the relevant age group based on a census held in 1974 (after the War of Liberation), with the general non-availability of registered births, and with the inconsistency over reports of enrolments in primary schools, forecasting the shape of primary education seemed the more hazardous, the closer I came to the 'data'.

Costing Education in Bangladesh

Only two aspects of the *process* of doing the cost study in Bangladesh are reported here. They are chosen primarily because, on reflection, they may contribute to our understanding of the environment for education policy-making in Bangladesh. These aspects are: (1) the process of detection involved in establishing base data for enrolments and expenditure; and (2) the 'negotiation' of future scenarios for education and education spending.

Detection work on enrolments and expenditure

In the first quarter of 1982 the commonly quoted statistics of enrolments in schools were for 1978. The manual enumeration of enrolment returns for 1981 was in progress. (Data for 1979 and 1980 were not available.) The quality of this data was everywhere doubted: over-reporting of enrolments was said to be common. Detectives need luck: a visit to the Engineer Adviser to the Ministry of Education disclosed that, for roughly 7 per cent of all Thanas (small geographical areas), data had been collected in 1981 for individual schools and this data included enrolment figures — three for each school as well as student and teacher (sic!) attendance data for a particular survey day. All that had to be done was to compile this data into a consolidated statement for each Thana and to request The Bangladesh Bureau of Educational Information and Statistics (BANBEIS) to produce enrolments, for 1981, for the same areas. A comparison was, therefore, possible for certain Thanas between enrolment data collected by the national statistics agency (BANBEIS) and data collected by assistant engineers. While pursuing the question of the validity of the comparison, it emerged that (i) no school list existed for any Thana; and (ii) the source of BANBEIS data was not the school but rather a district inspector or a Thana education officer. It was claimed that the engineers' study included all government schools and as many non-government schools as could be found. The likelihood is that the enrolment data collected by this method was more reliable than that collected from secondary sources.

In only two Thanas, out of seventeen examined, did enrolment of boys taken by the engineers exceed that reported to BANBEIS. In all Thanas girls' enrolments, as taken by the engineers, were lower than those reported to BANBEIS. For seventeen Thanas there was, on average, a 20 per cent gap in reported enrolments. The primary gross enrolment rate for the surveyed Thanas averaged 54 per cent in 1981 while BANBEIS believed that nationally the figure was 71 per cent in 1978. The distance to travel to reach UPE (or to reach 90 per cent of the age group in school by 1985) was clearly uncertain.

The engineer adviser's survey was part of the IDA fourth education project yet it lacked co-ordination with (a) routine statistical surveys; (b) other 'front-line' sources of intelligence, viz. the working of the planning cell (in the Ministry of Education) and the Planning Commission, responsible for sectoral allocations of resources within the economy.

It was officials of the Planning Commission who first set the trail after *actual* expenditure information. Their figures related exclusively to planned and annual allocations of development funds to the various programmes in education. They were cautious about interpreting allocations as actual expenditures. They themselves had no feedback on what happened to their allocations. The trail led round the 'Ministries': the Ministry of Finance, the Bangladesh Bureau of Statistics and the Office of the Accountant General. Actual expenditure on 'development', which covers capital outlays plus projects, fell short by between 21 per cent and 39 per cent of revised allocations for the period 1978–81. Moreover, within the expenditure actually incurred, there were shifts (in favour of the universities) from planned allocations. (Over the period covered by the first two development plans, 1973–1980, universities were *allocated* 12.59 per cent of development funds for education but *received* 26.39 per cent of actual funds released. Primary education received 13.18 per cent against 17.63 per cent allocated (Planning Commission, 1983, Chapter XVI).) (If education policy-makers in Bangladesh thought in terms of rates-of-return would they 'invest' in universities to the detriment of primary education? The differential in unit recurrent expenditures is roughly 100:1.)

It is part of the conventional wisdom of commentators on the costs of education that teachers' salaries make up typically more than 90 per cent of expenditure in primary schools in Third World countries. Certainly, field trips to primary schools suggested that inputs to the pedagogical process other than a teacher were rare. (In 1982, books were supplied by the Textbook Board through the Post Offices where queues of children waited to 'buy' their texts at subsidized rates. The system was not especially effective in ensuring timely distribution (Green, 1983).) Once again officials had no specific information on how the total expenditure on primary education was broken down. Here the benefit of local colleagues becomes evident for, in the 1982/83 detailed budget estimates (printed in Bangla), details of the sub-heads were given. Teachers' salaries apparently accounted for about 70 per cent of the 1980/81 recurrent expenditure of 95 crore Taka (about £27m). Allowances (mainly house rents and medical expenses) paid to *administrative personnel* at the Thana and district levels, amounted to 29 per cent. Other inputs make up the 1 per cent residue. There are other inputs to primary schools, not paid for out of the government's revenue expenditure. These would include some project aid and materials donated free by such bodies as UNICEF. The limitations of publicly available statistics are thus exposed. As one administrator remarked, 'These official figures written up in English are meant for foreigners'. While the language barrier explains, in part, why the non-Bangla reader can get only a partial view of the education system, it does not explain why officials in the operating ministry could not 'off-the-top-of-the-head' respond to enquiries on expenditure in education. It was suggested by McLellan (1983) in his contemporaneous study of management of education that documents including budgets, standing orders and administrative codes were not available in sufficient quantity for the frequently re-posted senior administrators to acquaint themselves with the system they were administering.

Agreeing about the future

If we can agree about the future we can make it less uncertain. (Benveniste, 1977, p. 12)

Having prepared a useable database, the next phase of the work was to produce decade-long forecasts of government spending on primary education and likely revenues for the same sector. The quality of this forecasting work would have been improved had it been possible to collaborate with senior administrators in government. In a strict formal sense the consultancy was under the guidance of the education adviser. However, this official was never seen. A senior administrator in the Ministry of Education did have overall responsibility for coordinating the four consultancy studies: but he, like the professional educators in the various directorates (of primary, secondary and technical education), was loathe to commit himself to any future scenario for primary education. Changes of regime, of minister and of key officials must have contributed to what can only be described as expressions of powerlessness to shape the future. Only with respect to two features of the future did clear parameters for forecasting emerge, and the first of these (targets for UPE) was not made *public* and was not confirmed until after the consultancy.

It is recalled that the major staging post towards achievement of UPE was laid down, in the draft Second Five-Year Plan (SFYP), as 90 per cent of primary school-aged children in school by 1985. Towards the final third of the consultancy, it transpired that official thinking favoured a revision of targets towards 70 per cent of children *enrolled* and 50 per cent of age group *retained* until the fifth and final year of primary school. At the same time the age for starting school was being raised to six so that, in future, the relevant age group for primary education was to be 6–10 years rather than 5–9.

The other aspect of the future which was given definition was the matter of whether the government could tolerate earmarking of revenues for education. The short answer, given by the Board of Revenue, was no! Preliminary investigations of local sources of revenue included suggestions for a supplementary land tax and a graduate tax. The collection cost of the former and the political unpopularity of the latter made them both unlikely sources of increased revenues for primary education. They were killed, however, on grounds of principle at the executive rather than political level: the government had no earmarked taxes and, if allowed to primary education, an unacceptable precedent would be set.

The assumptions that, in the event, had to guide the forecasts were derived partly from the writer's experiences of other developing countries at similar stages of education development and partly from estimates of the economic prospects set out in World Bank papers. A series of forecasts incorporated various data bases and assumptions about the movement of unit costs. Total costs — recurring and development — were seen to be most sensitive to assumptions concerning the government's response to the accelerating requirement for trained teachers. On one scenario, the gap between requirements for teachers and their availability could be of the order of 75,000 by 1992 when, at best, 72 per cent of the 6–10 age group would be in school. The political implications of such dilution of an already poorly professionalized teaching force are obvious.

Costing Practical Subjects in Kenya

This costs study was part of an evaluation of 'industrial education' (IE) subjects which were introduced with Swedish aid into thirty-five Kenyan academic schools. The evaluation was summative and sought to provide the sponsors of the evaluation, SIDA, and the Kenyan government with lessons about the effectiveness of a long term (twelve years) donor assistance programme in diversifying the curriculum. The contribution of a costs study to a fairly broad and illuminative evaluation framework was to quantify the relative unit expenditures on practical and 'classroom' subjects as well as compare expenditures on other existing forms of training and education that could be classified as vocational. The field work on costs was restricted to a little over two weeks in 1984, while the evaluation extended over two years, 1983–85. (The evaluation was published in three volumes: Lauglo, 1985; Narman, 1985; Cumming *et al*, 1985.)

Data Questions

The data to be collected and analyzed was very restricted compared to that required in the sector study in Bangladesh. The study was further helped because the implementation unit for industrial educa- tion (and technical education) was still in existence in Nairobi and because I had worked in the Ministry of Education from 1973 to 1975. Nine years later the scent of usable data could still be fol- lowed! The pleasant surprise was that salary payments to teachers were computerized. Centralization of administration can bring be- nefits. The Teachers' Service Commission (TSC) is an agency of the Ministry of Education, though separate from it geographically and administratively. As in Bangladesh, a lack of coordination of in- formation useful to the two bodies was evident. The officials in the Ministry did not know whether salary records existed for individual schools. In the TSC the data existed on computer file only.

Data on items other than teachers' salaries was available in the Ministry of Education files for each school. On probing, it turned out that the figures were agreed *estimates* and not *outturns* of expenditure. The system of administering secondary schools' finance, unchanged since Independence (1963), involves the Ministry of Education issuing a 'grant' for all the items in the final estimates of expenditure except teachers' salaries. Fees are also taken into account in the contribution of the 'grant' to the school. The head-teacher then pays non-teaching staff, makes purchases of equipment, and pays accounts. The actual patterns of expenditure may differ from the estimates: it is common knowledge, for instance, that heads in boarding schools sometimes spend more on feeding and boarding than estimated. Otherwise the schools would have to close before the end of the session.

The payment vouchers for all the items of construction and initial equipping were available in files in the IE implementation unit. It was a clerical task to determine the actual expenditure for each school.

The two findings from the report (Cumming *et al*, 1985) worth highlighting here were (a) in terms of recurrent cost per student, industrial education is probably twice as expensive as other subjects; (b) in terms of initial development expenditure per student-place, industrial education is as much as ten times more expensive than a talk-and-chalk subject. When it comes to informing government policy, these findings have to be set alongside Lauglo's conclusions that 'IE is valued by parents, pupils, teachers and headmasters. It has entirely adequate status in most schools' (Lauglo, 1985, p. 155).

Conclusions

How far do cost studies meet the needs of public policy-makers? One need that can confidently be ascribed to policy-makers in education everywhere is that of information. The two-volume Bangladesh study, *Education Costs and Finance*, provided a consolidated statement of the largest single element in the education system, namely the primary education sector. The study's status as a resource document was in evidence when I returned to Bangladesh briefly in late 1984. By then, the officials in the DPE and in the Planning Cell had changed. The latter unit was using it as a source book for questions which I posed! The latest in the line of directors of primary education had heard of but not seen the four studies — of management and administration, of curriculum, of textbooks, and of costs and finance in primary education. The latter finding was disappointing but not surprising, given the acceleration of senior administrator through government.

While cost studies of the kind carried out in Bangladesh have potential to provide policy-makers with some key input to their thinking, as long as the questions which cost studies attempt to answer are not posed by policy-makers (but rather by donors), impact on policy-making is likely to be unpredictable. A possible second barrier to use of cost studies lies in the administrators' suspicion that economists, with their concentration on measuring inputs, ignore outputs. One then has to ask whether a thorough-going cost-benefit approach would have been more attractive to policy-makers. I have in mind the kind of study well illustrated by a recently reported cost-benefit analysis of a Harijan Education Program (HEP) in Kerala State in India (Marar and Fraser, 1986). Their evaluation, was intended to show whether the spending on a disadvantaged group by means of affirmative action programmes was worthwhile. They show that the net present value of the HEP was negative. Ministry of Education officials might be willing to accept the broad sweep of findings of the human capital school such as those brilliantly summarized by Psacharopoulos (1973 and 1981). But how ready will they be to suspend judgment, based on an apparently 'scientific' result (a negative return on the HEP program), in favour of vague 'social and political advantage'? All too ready perhaps to do just that for these are exactly the considerations that do shape goals, policies and programmes in education without the injection of much hard data referring either to the present or the past.

In short, the adoption of a cost benefit approach to educational policy-making in the Third World (and maybe elsewhere) may add a spurious dimension of sophistication while leaving administrators unprepared for the hard work of portraying various scenarios for the future. Even Psacharopoulos admits that the popularity of cost benefit or rate of return analysis in education is due to the American PhD market. Do we know which, of all the cost benefit studies that have been effected in the field of education, have contributed to policy making and how they have done so?

What research needs to be done to enhance the contribution of the economics of education to Third World policy formulation?

We must beware of assuming that the public cycle in Third World countries is a reflection (albeit a faint one) of that typical in industrialized democracies.

> In the management literature there are numerous unques-
> tioning extrapolations of organizational solutions beyond
> the border of the country in which they were developed.
> This is especially true for the exportation of management .
> theories from the United States to the rest of the world ...
> Management itself is very much an American concept, just as
> earlier the entire discipline of economics was very much an
> Anglo-Saxon discipline. (Hofstede, 1984, p. 253)

Though the World Bank and other aid donors would like to imagine
that information is information and economics is economics where-
ver the context, it is definitely not the case in countries with military
regimes, unstable economies, government control of press, an
'opposition' that is at best muted, a civil service that must be
cautious above all else, and where there is no tradition of open
challenge and debate concerning public policy. Yet, for all that,
there is in such countries educational development. Policies do
emerge; constraints dissolve; new hurdles appear. What needs to be
done by the countries themselves is to trace the practice of public
policy-formulation and make it explicit as far as possible within the
tenets of the prevailing political philosophy. Planning the future of
their economies and education systems can only be aided if the
broader context for public policy making is understood. The plans
may not be consultative; they may not reflect the state of the art of
economics; and they may look irrational to the outsider. Plans, like
organizations, are culture-bound.

Notes

1 Costs is used synonymously with expenditure and does not include
  income foregone.
2 All these statistics are taken from The World Bank (1985).

The Research Seminar: Economics and Education Management, University of Birmingham, 24–25 April 1986: List of participants

David Ashton	University of Leicester
Brian Atkinson	Preston Polytechnic
Rachel Britton	Manpower Services Commission
Dr. John Calvert	Loughborough University
Bernard Cullen	Department of Education and Science
Dr. Christopher Cumming	Moray House College of Education
Rob Cuthbert	Further Education Staff College, Coombe Lodge
Keith Drake	University of Manchester
Derek Esp	Chief Education Officer, Lincolnshire
Tony Fitzgerald	University of Birmingham
Oliver Fulton	University of Lancaster
John Gretton	*Public Money*
Andrew Gurney	Department of Education and Science
Dr. Jim Hough	Loughborough University
Professor Meredydd Hughes	University of Birmingham
Brian Knight	University of Exeter
Ken Lambert	University of Birmingham
John Mace	University of London Institute of Education
Gordon Macnair	Manpower Services Commission
Malcolm Maguire	University of Leicester
Judith Marquand	Manpower Services Commission
John Pratt	North East London Polytechnic

Participants at the Research Seminar

David Reeson	District Audit Service
Peter Ribbins	University of Birmingham
Dr. Paul Ryan	King's College, Cambridge
Tim Simkins	Sheffield City Polytechnic
Professor John Sizer	Loughborough University
Dr. Michael Strain	University of Ulster
Jason Tarsh	Department of Employment
Hywel Thomas	University of Birmingham
Barry Wakefield	Department of Education and Science
Peter Watt	University of Birmingham
Professor Gareth Williams	University of London Institute of Education
Maureen Woodhall	University of London Institute of Education

Bibliography

ACSET (1981) *The Future of the Teacher Training System*, ACSET 81/24, London: DES

AHAMAD, B. and BLAUG, M. (Eds) (1973) *The Practice of Manpower Forecasting*, Amsterdam: Elsevier

ARROW, K. (1973) 'Higher education as a filter', *Public Economics*, July

ASHTON, D.N. and MAGUIRE, M.J. (1980) 'The function of academic and non-academic criteria in employers' selection strategies', *British Journal of Guidance and Counselling*, 18, 2, July

ASHTON, D.N. and MAGUIRE, M.J. (1983) 'Competition between young people and adults: A research note on the structure of the youth labour market', *International Review of Applied Psychology*, 32, pp. 263–9

ASHTON, D.N., MAGUIRE, M.J. *et al* (1986) *Young Adults in the Labour Market*, Department of Employment, Research Paper 55

ASHTON, D.N., MAGUIRE, M.J. and GARLAND, V. (1982) *Youth in the Labour Market*, Department of Employment, Research Paper 34, March

ASHWORTH, J. (1985) 'What price an ivory tower? University-industry relationships', *Higher Education Review*, 17, 2, Spring

ASTIN, A.W. (1982) 'Let's try a "value-added" approach to testing', *Chronicle of Higher Education*, 28 July

ATKINSON, J. (1984) *Personnel Management*, August

AUDIT COMMISSION (1984a) *Obtaining Better Value in Education: Aspects of Non-Teaching Costs in Secondary Schools*, London: HMSO

AUDIT COMMISSION (1984b) *Economy, Efficiency and Effectiveness*, London: HMSO

AUDIT COMMISSION (1985a) *Obtaining Better Value from Further Education*, London: HMSO

AUDIT COMMISSION (1985b) *75,000 more students can receive further full-time education — at little extra cost*, Audit Commission press release 85/8, 20 June

AUDIT COMMISSION (1986) *Towards Better Management of Secondary Education*, London: HMSO

AUDIT INSPECTORATE (1981) *Study of Further Education Colleges: Final*

Report, London: Department of the Environment

AUDIT INSPECTORATE (1983a) *Colleges of Further Education: Guide to the Measurement of Resource Efficiency*, London: HMSO

AUDIT INSPECTORATE (1983b) *Registers and Control Information in Colleges of Further Education*, London: HMSO

AUDIT INSPECTORATE (1983c) *Education: Polytechnic Expenditure*, London: HMSO

BACON, R. and ELTIS, W. (1978) *Britain's Economic Problem: Too Few Producers*, London: Macmillan

BATES, A.W. (1970) 'The administration of comprehensive schools' in MONKS, T.G. (Ed) *Comprehensive Education in Action*, Windsor: NFER

BAUMOL, W.J. (1967) 'Macroeconomics of unbalanced growth', *American Economic Review*, 57, 3, June, pp. 415–26

BAUMOL, W.J. (1985) 'Productivity policy and the service sector' in INMAN, R.P. *Managing the Service Economy: Prospects and Problems*, Cambridge: Cambridge University Press

BAUMOL, W.J., BLACKMAN, S. and WOLFF, E. (1985) 'Unbalanced growth revisited: Asymptotic stagnancy and new evidence', *American Economic Review*, 75, 4, September, pp. 806–17

BAUMOL, W.J. and BOWEN, W.G. (1966) *Performing Arts: The Economic Dilemma. A Study of Problems Common to Theater, Opera, Music and Dance.* New York

BAUMOL, W.J. and WOLFF, E. (1983) 'Feedback from productivity growth to R&D', *Scandinavian Journal of Economics*, 85, 2, pp. 147–57

BEARD, R. (1970) *Teaching and Learning in Higher Education*, Harmondsworth: Penguin

BECKEROFF et al (1980) *Hochschulfinanzierung auf der grundlage leistungsorientierter kennziffern*, Munchen: Gersbach, Bundesminister fur Bildung and Wissenschaff, Schriftenreihe Hochschule 33

BENSON, C.S., MEDRICH, E.A. and BUCKLEY, S. (1980) 'A new view of school efficiency: household time contributions to school achievement' in GUTHRIE, J.W. (Ed) *School Finance Policies and Practices: 1st Annual Yearbook of the American Educational Finance Association*, Lexington, MA: Ballinger

BENVENISTE, G. (1977) *Bureaucracy*, San Francisco, CA: Boyd and Fraser

BERG, I. (1970) *Education and Jobs: The Great Training Robbery*, Harmondsworth: Penguin

BESSANT, J., GUY, K., MILES, L. and RUSH, H. (1985) *IT Futures: What Current Forecasting Literature says about the Social Impact of Information Technology*, NEDO, NEDO Long-Term Perspectives Group

BIRCH, D. and LATCHAM, J. (1985a) 'Measuring college performance', *Coombe Lodge Report*, 18, 3. FE Staff College

BIRCH, D.W. and LATCHAM, J. (1985b) 'The Audit Commission and FE: Value for money and the audit ratios', *Coombe Lodge Report*, 18, 3

BLACKBURN, R.M. and MANN, M. (1979) *The Working Class in the Labour Market*, London: Macmillan

BLAUG, M. (1969) 'The productivity of universities' in BLAUG, M. (Ed) *Economics of Education 2*, Harmondsworth: Penguin

BLAUG, M. (1970) *An Introduction to the Economics of Education*, London. Allen Lane

BLAUG, M. (1972) 'The correlation between education and earnings: What does it signify?', *Higher Education*

BLAUG, M. (1976) 'The empirical status of human capital theory: A slightly jaundiced survey', *Journal of Economic Literature*, 14, September, pp. 827–55

BLAUG, M. (1985) 'Where are we now in the economics of education?', *Economics of Education Review*, 4, 1 (version of a paper originally written in 1982)

BOGUE, E.G. (1982) 'Allocation of public funds on instructional performance/quality indicators', *International Journal of Institutional Management in Higher Education*, 6, 1

BOSWORTH, D. and FORD, J. (1985) 'Perceptions of higher education by university entrants: An exploratory study', *Studies in Higher Education*, 10, 3

BOTTOMLEY, J.A. *et al* (1971) *Costs and Potential Economies*, Paris: OECD

BOWEN, H.R. (1980) *The Costs of Higher Education*, San Francisco, CA: Jossey Bass

BOWEN, H.R. and DOUGLASS, G.R. (1971) *Efficiency in Liberal Education*, New York: McGraw-Hill

BOWLES, S. and GINTIS, H. (1975) 'The problem with human capital theory — A Marxian critique', *American Economic Review*, May, pp. 74–82

BOWLES, S. and GINTIS, H. (1976) *Schooling in Capitalist America*, London: Basic Books

BRIAULT, E. and SMITH, F. (1980) *Falling Rolls in Secondary Schools* (2 vols), Windsor: NFER

BRINKMAN, P. and KRAKOWER, J. (1983) *Comparative Data for Administrators in Higher Educaton*, NCHEMS

BROWN, B.W. and SAKS, D.H. (1975) 'The production and distribution of cognitive skills within schools', *Journal of Political Economy*, 83, 3, pp. 471–593

BROWN, B.W. and SAKS, D.H. (1980) 'Production technologies and resource allocations within classrooms and schools' in DREEBEN, R. and THOMAS, J.A. (Eds) *The Analysis of Educational Productivity: I Issues in Microanalysis*, Lexington, MA: Ballinger

BROWN, P. (1986) Schooling and the School/Post-School Transition in Urban South Wales, PhD thesis, University of Wales

BROWNE, S. (1984) 'NAB and "quality" in higher education', *Higher Education Review*, Autumn

BUCHANAN, J.M.(1969) *Cost and Choice: An Inquiry in Economic Theory*, Chicago: Markham Publishing

BULLOCK, A. (1975) *A Language for Life* (Report of the Committee of Enquiry into Reading and the Use of English) London: HMSO

BURGESS, C. (1986) *The Impact of New Technology on Skills in Manufacturing and Services*, Skills Series No.1 (Research and Development No.28), London, Manpower Services Commission

BURSTALL, C. (1979) 'A time to mend the nets: a commentary on the outcomes of class size research', *Trends in Education*, Autumn

BUTTERWORTH, I. (1983) *Staffing for Curriculum Needs: Teacher Shortages and Surpluses in Comprehensive Schools*, Windsor: NFER-Nelson

CALLAGHAN, J. (1976) 'The Prime Minister's Ruskin Speech', *Education*, 148, 17, 22 October, pp. 332–3

CARLISLE, M. (1979a) 'Conservative hot in pursuit of excellence', *Education*, 153, 16, pp. 457–8

CARLISLE, M. (1979b) Letter to Education, Arts and Science Committee of House of Commons, 13 December

CARTER, C.J. (1972) 'The efficiency of universities', *Higher Education*, 1, 1

CBI/MSC (1985) *Survey of Skills Shortages in Manufacturing Industry, December 1984*, London: CBI

CBI/MSC (1986) *Survey of Skills Shortages in Manufacturing Industry, December 1985*, London: CBI

CENTRAL STATISTICAL OFFICE (1985) *United Kingdom National Accounts: Sources and Methods*, 3rd ed., London: HMSO

CIPFA (1979) *Statement on Internal Audit Practice — Public Sector*, London: Chartered Institute of Public Finance and Accountancy, July

CIPFA (1984) *Expenditure Reductions in Institutions of Higher and Further Education in the Maintained Sector*, London: Chartered Institute of Public Finance and Accountancy, October

CIPFA (1985) *Block Grant Statistics 1985–86*, London: Chartered Institute of Public Finance and Accountancy

CLARK, B. (1984) *The Higher Education System: Academic Organization in Cross National Perspective*, Berkley: University of California Press

CLARK, J.A. (1986) 'A vintage capital simulation model' in FREEMAN, C. and SOETE, L. (Eds) *Technical Change and Full Employment*, Oxford: Blackwell

COHN, E. (1971) 'Economic rationality in secondary schools', *Planning and Changing*, 1, pp. 166–74

COHN, E. (1979) *The Economics of Education*, Lexington, MA: Ballinger

COLES, R. (1986) 'Sixteen to Nineteen: A Survey of Young People in North Yorkshire', University of York, Department of Sociology

COMMITTEE OF VICE-CHANCELLORS AND PRINCIPALS (CVCP) (1985) *Report of the Steering Committee for Efficiency Studies in Universities* (The Jarratt Report), London: CVCP, March

COOPERS, LYBRANT and ASSOCIATES (1985) *A Challenge to Complacency*, NEDO/MSC

CRAVEN, B.M., DICK, B. and WOOD, B. (1983) 'Resource allocation in higher education in Britain', *Higher Education*, 12, 5

CRICK, B. (1964) *In Defence of Politics*, Harmondsworth: Penguin

CRISPIN, A and PERKINS, R. (1980) 'Appraising staffing standards in schools', *Educational Administration*, 9, 1

CROSS, M. and MITCHELL, P. (1986) *Packaging Efficiency — The Training Contribution*, Technical Change Centre

CULLEN, B.D. (1979) 'Lessons from class size research — an economist's perspective', *Trends in Education*, Winter, pp. 29–33

CUMING, D. (1983) *School-Leavers, Qualifications and Employment*, Nottingham: Nottingham University

CUMMING, C., DAVIES, M., LILLIS, K. and NYAGAH, B. (1985) *Practical*

Subjects in Kenyan Academic Schools: Background Papers, Stockholm: — Swedish International Development Agency

CUMMING, C., ISLAM, T. and HUZ, A.T.H.Z. (1983) *Education Cost and Finance*, Vols. 4 and 5 in 'UPE in Bangladesh Project Related Studies', London: British Council

CUMMING, C.E. (1971) *Studies in Educational Costs*, Edinburgh: Scottish Academic Press

CUTHBERT, R.E. (1979) *The Relationship Between Planning and Budgeting in the Management of Polytechnics*, Sheffield City Polytechnic, Papers in Education Management No. 5

CUTHBERT, R.E. (1980a) 'Costs and quality in higher education', *Higher Education Review*, Summer

CUTHBERT, R.E. (1980b) 'The marketing function in education management', *Coombe Lodge Reports*, 12, 12

CUTHBERT, R.E. (1984) *The Management Process*, Course E324: Management in Postcompulsory Education, Block 3, Part 2, Milton Keynes: Open University Press

CUTHBERT, R.E. (1985a) 'Do we get value for money from value for money studies?', *Coombe Lodge Reports*, 18, 1

CUTHBERT, R.E. (1985b) 'How to ensure value for money', *Education*, 26 April

CUTHBERT, R.E. and BIRCH, D.W. (1982) 'How should auditors be audited?', *Times Higher Education Supplement*, 3 December

DALE, R. (1985) 'The background and inception of the technical and vocational education initiative' in DALE, R. (Ed) *Education, Training and Employment: Towards a New Vocationalism?*, Oxford: Pergamon/Open University

DALY, A., HITCHENS, D. and WAGNER, K. (1985) 'Productivity, machinery and skills in a sample of British and German manufacturing plants', *National Institute Economic Review*, III, February

DAVIES, J.L. and MORGAN, A.W. (1982) 'The politics of institutional change', in WAGNER, L. (Ed) *Agenda for Institutional Change in Higher Education*, Guildford Society for Research in Higher Education

DAVIES, T.I. (1969) *School Organisation*, Oxford: Pergamon

DAWSON, D. (1976) 'Determinants of local authority expenditure', *Report of the Committee of Inquiry into Local Government Finance*, **Appendix** 7, Dept. of the Environment

DELANY, J.V. (1979) *Exploring Data Patterns in Further Education*, Doncaster Association of Colleges for Further and Higher Education

DENISON, E.F. (1962 and 1979) *The Sources of Economic Growth in the United States and the Alternatives Before Us*, New York: Committee for Economic Development

DENNISON, W.F. (1984) *Educational Finance and Resources*, Beckenham: Croom Helm

DEPARTMENT OF EDUCATION AND SCIENCE (1970a) *Output Budgetting for the DES*, London: HMSO

DEPARTMENT OF EDUCATION AND SCIENCE (1970b) *Education Statistics for the UK*, London: HMSO

DEPARTMENT OF EDUCATION AND SCIENCE (1972) *Education: A Framework for Expansion*, Cmnd 5174, London: HMSO.

DEPARTMENT OF EDUCATION AND SCIENCE (1978) *Curriculum 11–16: Working Papers by HM Inspectorate — A Contribution to Current Debate*, London: HMSO

DEPARTMENT OF EDUCATION AND SCIENCE (1979) *Aspects of Secondary Education in England: A Survey by HM Inspectors of Schools*, London: HMSO

DEPARTMENT OF EDUCATION AND SCIENCE (1984a) *Parental Influence at School: A New Framework for School Government in England and Wales*, Cmnd. 9242, London: HMSO

DEPARTMENT OF EDUCATION AND SCIENCE (1984b) *Education for Employees*, London: HMSO

DEPARTMENT OF EDUCATION AND SCIENCE (1984c) *Schoolteacher Numbers and Deployment in the Longer Term*, mimeo, September

DEPARTMENT OF EDUCATION AND SCIENCE (1985a) *Better Schools*, Cmnd 9469, London: HMSO

DEPARTMENT OF EDUCATION AND SCIENCE (1985b) *The Development of Higher Education into the 1990s*, Cmnd 9524, London: HMSO

DEPARTMENT OF EDUCATION AND SCIENCE (1985c) *Education Statistics for the United Kingdom*, London: HMSO

DEPARTMENT OF EDUCATION AND SCIENCE (1986) *Report by HM Inspectors on the Effects of Local Authority Expenditure Policies on Education Provision in England* London: DES

DEPARTMENT OF EMPLOYMENT/DEPARTMENT OF EDUCATION AND SCIENCE (1984) *Training for Jobs*, Cmnd 9135 London: HMSO

DEPARTMENT OF EMPLOYMENT (1985) *New Earnings Survey*, London: HMSO

DEPARTMENT OF ENVIRONMENT (1986) *Paying for Local Government*, Cmnd 974, London: HMSO

DERBYSHIRE, H. (1985) 'How training resources are managed: An employer's view', *Coombe Lodge Report*, 18, 1

DOERINGER, P. and PIORE, M. (1971) *Internal Labour Markets and Manpower Anaylsis*, Lexington, MA: Heath and Co.

DOLPHIN, A.M. (1981) 'The demand for higher education', *Employment Gazette*, July

DOYLE, P. and LYNCH, J.E. (1979) 'A strategic model for university planning', *Journal of the Operational Research Society*, 30, 7

DRAKE, K. (1979) 'Decision-making in the classroom: A micro-economic analysis' in EGGLESTON, J. (Ed) *Teacher Decision-Making in the Classroom*, London: Routledge and Kegan Paul

DRAKE, K. (1982) 'The cost effectiveness of vocational training: A survey of British studies', *Economics of Education Review*, 2, 2, pp. 103–25

DRAKE, K. (1984) *Vocational Training Finance: The UK Focus Study*, Berlin: European Centre for the Development of Vocational Training

DREEBEN, R. and THOMAS, J.A. (Eds) (1980a) *The Analysis of Educational Productivity: I Issues in Microanalysis*, Lexington, MA: Ballinger

DREEBEN, R. and THOMAS, J.A. (1980b) 'Introduction' in DREEBEN, R. and THOMAS, J.A. (Eds) *The Analysis of Educational Productivity: I Issues in Microanalysis*, Lexington, MA: Ballinger

ELSTERMANN, G. and LORENZ, W. (1980) 'Financing universities on the basis of performance indicators', paper presented to the Ninth Special Topic Workshop of the IMHE Programme, Paris: OECD/CERI

EWELL, P. (1984) *The Self-Regarding Institution: Information for Excellence*, NCHEMS

FAY, C.R. (1956) *Adam Smith and the Scotland of his day*, Cambridge: Cambridge University Press

FIELDEN, J. (1982) 'Strategies for survival' in MORRIS, A. and SIZER, J. (Eds) *Resources and Higher Education*, Guildford SRHE/Leverhulme Report No. 8

FORTE, F. and PEACOCK, A. (1985) *Public Expenditure and Government Growth*, Oxford: Basil Blackwell

FOSTER, C.D., JACKMAN, R. and PERLMAN, M. (1980) *Local Government Finance in a Unitary State*, London: Allen and Unwin

FOSTER, P. (1961) 'The vocational school fallacy in development planning' in BLAUG, M. (Ed) *Economics of Education I*, Harmondsworth: Penguin

FREEMAN, C., CLARK, J. and SOETE, L. (1982) *Unemployment and Technical Innovation*, London Frances Pinter

FREEMAN, C. and SOETE, L. (1985) *Information Technology and Employment: An Assessment*, University of Sussex Society Policy Research Unit

FREEMAN, C. and SOETE, L. (1986) *Technical Change and Full Employment*, Oxford: Blackwell

FREEMAN, R. (1976) *The Overeducated American*, New York: Academic Press

FRIEDMAN, M. (1953) *Essays in Positive Economics*, Chicago: University of Chicago Press

FUCHS, V. (1968) *The Service Economy*, New York: Columbia University Press

FURLONG, A. (1986) 'Coming to terms with the declining demand for youth labour', paper presented to the British Sociological Association Annual Conference, Loughborough University

GERSHUNY, J. (1983) *Social Innovation and the Division of Labour*, Oxford: Oxford University Press

GESKE, T.G. (1979) 'Some observations on cost-effectiveness analysis in education', *Journal of Education Finance*, 4, 4

GIBBONS, M. and METCALFE, S. (1986) 'Technological variety and the process of competition', paper presented to a Conference on Innovation Diffusion, Venice, 1–21 March

GIBSON, J.G. and SMITH, P. (1985) *Measuring the Fiscal Pressure on English Local Authorities under the Block Grant System*, University of Birmingham mimeo

GIBSON, J.G. and WATT, P.A. (1986) *The Effect of GREs on Education Expenditure and Budgetary Decision Making by Local Authorities*, Report to the Department of Education and Science, mimeo

GIPPS, C. et al (1983) *Testing Children: Standardised Testing in Local Education Authorities*, London: Heinemann

Bibliography

Gipps, C. and Goldstein, H. (1983) *Monitoring the Children*, London: Heinemann

Glass, G.V. *et al* (1982) *School Class Size: Research and Policy*, Beverley HWS CA, Sage

Goodlad, S. (1983) *Economies of Scale in Higher Education*, Guildford: Society for Research in Higher Education

Gouldner, A.W. (1961) 'The norm of reciprocity', *American Sociological Review*, 25

Gramlich, E.M. (1985) 'Government services' in Inman, R.P. (Ed) *Managing the Service Economy: Prospects and Problems*, Cambridge: Cambridge University Press

Gray, L. (1983) *Resource Management in Primary Schools*, Sheffield City Polytechnic, Papers in Education Management No. 32

Green, B. (1983) *Textbook Studies*, Vol. 3 in 'UPE Project Related Studies', London: British Council

Grunewald, U. (1984) *Financing and Promotion of Vocational Training in the Federal Republic of Germany*, Berlin: European Centre for the Development of Vocational Training

Guthrie, J.W. (Ed) (1980) *School Finance Policies and Practices: 1st Annual Yearbook of the American Educational Finance Association*, Lexington, MA: Ballinger

Hansen, W.L. (1984) 'Economic growth and equal opportunity: Conflicting or complementary goals in higher education?' in Dean, E. (Ed) *Education and Economic Productivity*, Cambridge, MA: Ballinger

Hansen, W.L. and Weisbrod, B.A. (1969) 'The distribution of the costs and benefits of public higher education: the case of California', *Journal of Human Resources*, 4, 2, pp. 176–91

Hanushek, E. (1979) 'Conceptual and empirical issues in the estimation of educational production functions', *Journal of Human Resources*, 14, 3, pp. 351–88

Hanushek, E. (1981) 'Education policy research — An industry perspective', *Economics of Education Review*, 1, 2, pp. 193–223

Harland, J. (1985) 'TVEI: A model for curriculum change', paper presented to the Annual Conference of the British Educational Research Association, September, Sheffield

Harnischfeger, A. and Wiley, D.E. (1978) 'Conceptual issues in models of school learning', *Journal of Curriculum Studies*, 10, 3, pp. 215–31

Harnischfeger, A. and Wiley, D.E. (1980) 'Determinants of pupil opportunity' in Dreeben, R. and Thomas, J.A. (Eds) *The Analysis of Educational Productivity: I Issues in microanalysis*, Lexington, MA: Ballinger

Harrison, A. (1984) 'Auditing the public sector', *Public Money*, 4, 1, June

Hauptman, A.M. (1983) *Student Loan Default Rates in Perspective*, American Council on Education Policy Brief.

Heath, A., *et al* (1985) *How Britain Votes*, Oxford: Pergamon

HM Treasury (1984) *Economic Progress Report*, London: HM Treasury

Hicks, N. (1980) 'Is there a trade-off between growth and basic needs?', *Finance and Development*, 17, 2, pp. 17–20

HILSUM, S. and CANE, B.S. (1971) *The Teacher's Day*, Windsor: NFER

HILSUM, S. and STRONG, C. (1978) *The Secondary Teacher's Day*, Windsor: NFER

HINDLEY, C. and OWEN, C. (1978) 'The extent of individual changes in IQ for ages between 6 months and a year, in a British longitudinal sample', *Journal of Political Economy*, September/October

HINDS, T. (1984) 'Local financial management: A pilot scheme', *Educational Management and Administration*, 12, 1, pp. 21–26

HOFSTEDE, G. (1984) *Culture's Consequences: International Differences in Work-Related Values*, Beverley Hills, CA: Sage

HOUGH, J.R. (1981) *A Study of School Costs*, Windsor: NFER-Nelson

HOUSE OF COMMONS (1980) Education, Science and Arts Committee *The Funding and Organization of Courses in Higher Education*, HMSO, September

HUDSON, J. (1984) *Financial Devolution to Schools*, mimeograph, Education Management Information Exchange, NFER

HUMPHREY, C. and THOMAS, H. (1983a) 'Making efficient use of scarce resources', *Education*, 19 August

HUMPHREY, C. and THOMAS, H. (1983b) 'Counting the cost of an experimental scheme' *Education*, 162, 8, 19 August

HUNT, J. and SMALL, P. (1981) *Employing Young People: A Study of Employers' Attitudes, Policies and Practices*, Edinburgh: Scottish Council for Research in Education

HUSAIN, M.K. (1976) *Institutional Resource Allocation in Higher Education*, Paris: OECD

ILEA (1984) *Improving Secondary Schools* (The Hargreaves Report), London: Inner London Education Authority

INDEPENDENT SCHOOLS INFORMATION SERVICE (1986) *Statistical Survey of Independent Schools — January 1986*, London: ISIS

INMAN, R.P. (Ed) (1985) *Managing the Service Economy: Prospects and Problems*, Cambridge: Cambridge University Press

INSTITUTE OF MANPOWER STUDIES (1986) *Changing Work Patterns*, London: NEDO, July

INTER-DEPARTMENTAL GROUP OF OFFICIALS ON OVERSEAS STUDENTS (1985) *Internal Review of the British Government and British Council Funded Award Schemes*, London, mimeo

JACKMAN, R. and PAPADACHI, J. (1981) 'Local authority education expenditure in England and Wales: Why standards differ and the impact of government grants', *Public Choice*, 36, pp. 425–39

JACKSON, P.M. (1982) *The Political Economy of Bureaucracy*, Oxford: Philip Allan

JADOT, J. *et al* (1980) *Survey on the State-of-the-Art and Likely Future Trends*, Report to Fifth General Conference of the Programme on Institutional Management in Higher Education, OECD, Paris, 8–10 September

JENKINS, R. (1983) *Lads, Citizens and Ordinary Kids: Working-Class Youth Life-Styles in Belfast*, London: Routledge and Kegan Paul

JESSON, D., GRAY, J. and JONES, B. (1984) 'Measure for measure', *Times Educational Supplement*, 3 August

JESSON, D., GRAY, J., RANSON, S. and JONES, B. (1985) 'Some determinants of variations in expenditure on secondary education', *Policy and Politics*, 13, 4, pp. 359–91

JIMENEZ, E. (1986) 'The public subsidization of education and health in developing countries: A review of equity and efficiency', *The World Bank Research Observer*, January, pp. 111–29

JOHNSON, P. (1983) *A History of the Modern World*, London: Weidenfeld and Nicolson

JOHNSTONE, D.B. (1987) *Sharing the Costs of College* Washington DC: The College Board

JONES, D.T.L. (1985) 'Efficient effectiveness in colleges — A practical approach', *Coombe Lodge Reports*, 18, 3

JONES, P. (1984) *What Opportunities for Youth?*, Occasional Paper No. 4, London: Youthaid

JONES, P. (1985) 'Qualifications and labour market outcomes among 16-year-old school-leavers', *British Journal of Guidance and Counselling*, 13, 3

JONES, S. (1984) 'Reflections on a capped pool', *Higher Education Review*, 17, 1, Autumn

JOSEPH, SIR K. (1983) Letter to Sir Edward Parkes, Chairman, University Grants Committee, 1 September

KATZ, D. and KAHN, R.L. (1966) *The Social Psychology of Organisations*, London: Wiley

KOEFOED, E. (1984) *The Funding System for Vocational Education and Training in Denmark*, Berlin: European Centre for the Development of Vocational Training

KOGAN, M. (1986) *Education Accountability: An Analytic Overview*, London: Hutchinson

KRONIG, W. (1978) 'Performance-related budgeting for universities', paper for OECD/IMHE workshop, Paris, June

LAUGLO, J. (1985) *Practical Subjects in Kenyan Academic Schools: General Report*, Stockholm: Swedish International Development Agency

LAYARD, R. and PSACHAROPOULOS, G. (1974) 'The screening hypothesis and the returns to education', *Journal of Political Economy*, September/October

LAYARD, R. and SAIGAL, J. (1966) 'Educational and occupational characteristics of manpower: An international comparison', *British Journal of Industrial Relations*, July

LAZEAR (1977) 'Academic achievement and job performance', *American Economic Review*, March

LEBLEBICI, H. (1985) 'Transactions and organisational forms: A reanalysis', *Organisation Studies*, 6, 2

LEE, G. and WRENCH, J. (1983) *Skill Seekers: Black Youth, Apprenticeships and Disadvantage*, Studies in Research No. 1, Leicester, National Youth Bureau

LEONTIEF, W. and DUCHIN, F. (1984) *The Impact of Automation on Employment 1963–2000*, New York: Oxford University Press

LEROY, R. (1984) *Funding of Vocational Training in Belgium*, Berlin: European Centre for the Development of Vocational Training

LEVIN, H.M. (1975) 'Cost-effectiveness in evaluation research' in GUTTEN-TAG, M. and STRUENING, E. (Eds) *Handbook of Evaluation Research* (Vol. 2), Beverley Hills, CA: Sage

LEVIN, H.M. (1976) 'Concepts of economic efficiency and educational production' in FROOMKIN, J.T., JAMISON, D.T. and RADNER, R. (Eds) *Education as an Industry: A Conference of the Universities-National Bureau Committee for Economic Research*, National Bureau Committee for Economic Research/Ballinger

LEVIN, H.M. (1983) *Cost-effectiveness: A Primer*, Beverley Hills, CA: Sage

LEVIN, H.M., GLASS, G.V. and MEISTER, G.R. (1984) *Cost-effectiveness of Four Educational Interventions*, Project Report 84–A11, Stanford University: Institute for Research on Educational Finance and Governance

LEVIN, H.M. and WOO, L. (1981) 'An evaluation of the costs of computer-assisted instruction', *Economics of Education Review*, 1, 1

LEWIS, R. (1982) 'Funding versus validating' in MORRIS A. and SIZER, J. (Eds) *Resources and Higher Education*, Guildford SRHE/Leverhulme Report No. 8

LIKIERMAN, A. (1983) 'Maintaining the credibility of cash limits', *Fiscal Studies*, 4, 1, March

LINDBLOM, C.E. (1959) 'The science of muddling through', *Public Administration Review*, 19, Spring, pp. 79–88

LINDBLOM, C.E. (1977) *Politics and Markets*, New York: Basic Books

LINDLEY, R. (Ed.) (1981) *Higher Education and the Labour Market*, SRHE/Leverhulme Report No. 1

LINDSAY, A.W. (1982) 'Institutional performance in higher education: The efficiency dimension', *Review of Educational Research*, 52, 2

LOCKWOOD, G. and DAVIES, J.L. (1985) *Universities: The Management Challenge*, Windsor NFER-Nelson

LORD, R. (1983) 'Value for money in the education service', *Public Money*, 3, 2, September

LORD, R. (1984) *Value for Money in Education*, London Public Money/CIPFA

LUTZ, B. (1981) 'Education and employment: Contrasting evidence from France and the Federal Republic of Germany', *European Journal of Education*, 16, 1

MCLELLAN, A. (1983) *Educational Administration and Management*, Vol. 1 in 'UPE in Bangladesh Project Related Studies', London: British Council

MACE, J. (1978) 'Mythology in the making: Is the Open University really cost-effective?', *Higher Education*, 7

MACE, J. (1979) 'Internal labour markets for British industry', *British Journal of Industrial Relations*, March

MACE, J. (1984) 'The economics of education: A revisionist's view', *Higher Education Review*, 16, 3, Summer

MACE, J. and TAYLOR, S. (1975) 'The demand for engineers in British industry: Some implications for manpower forecasting', *British Journal of Industrial Relations*, July

MAGUIRE, M.J. and ASHTON, D.N. (1981) 'Employers' perceptions and use of educational qualification', *Educational Analysis*, 3, 2

MARAR, R.P. and FRASER, S.E. (1986) 'A cost-benefit analysis of the Harijan education program of Kerala, India', *International Journal of Educational Development*, 6, 1

MARRIS, R. (1985) 'The paradox of service', *Political Quarterly*, July

MAURICE, M., SELLIER, F. and SILVESTRE, J-J. (1979) 'The search for a societal effect in the production of company hierarchy: A comparison between France and Germany', *Revue Francaise de Sociologie*, June (French original)

MÉHAUT, P. *et al* (1978) *Formation Continue, Gestion du Personnel et Marche de la Formation: Une Etude Regionale du Systeme Francaise de Formation Continue*, Paris: Editions du Centre National de la Recherche Scientifique

MILES, M.B. (1981) 'Mapping the common properties of schools' in LEHMING, R. and KANE, M. (Eds) *Improving Schools: Using What We Know*, Beverley Hills, CA: Sage

MILLER, G., GALANTER, E. and PRIBRAM, K. (1960) *Plans and the Structure of Behaviour*, New York: Holt

MILLER, S.E. (1985) *Student and Parent Loans: A Growing Reliance*, American Council on Education

MINCER, J. (1984) 'Human capital and economic growth', *Economics of Education Review*, 3, 3

MINGAT, A. and TAN, J.P. (1986) 'Who profits from the public funding of education? A comparison by world regions', *Comparative Education*

MONK, D.H. (1981) 'Toward a multilevel perspective on the allocation of educational resources', *Review of Educational Research*, 51, 2

MONK, D.H. (1982a) 'Alternative perceptions of cost and the resource allocation behaviour of teachers', *Educational Administration Quarterly*, 18, 2

MONK, D.H. (1982b) 'Resource allocation in classrooms: An economic analysis', *Journal of Curriculum Studies*, 14, 2

MONKS, T.G. (1970) *Comprehensive Education in Action*, Windsor: NFER

MORRIS, A. AND SIZER, J. (Eds) (1982) *Resources and Higher Education*, Guildford SRHE/Leverhulme Report No. 8

MSC (1985) *Skills Case Study: Clerks and Cashiers in Banking, Finance and Insurance*, Evaluation and Skills Branch, MSC, mimeo

MSC (1986a) *Skills, Monitoring Report*, MSC, May

MSC (1986b) *Improving Information on Skill Supply and Demand: A Consultative Document*, MSC

MSC/LOCAL AUTHORITY ASSOCIATIONS POLICY GROUP (1985a) *Work-related NAFE: A Guidance Handbook*, MSC

MSC/LOCAL AUTHORITY ASSOCIATIONS POLICY GROUP (1985b) *MSC/ LAA Group on Work-Related Non-Advanced Further Education: Report of Policy Group*, unpublished

MURNANE, R.J. and PHILLIPS, B.R. (1981) 'Learning by doing, vintage, and selection: Three pieces of the puzzle relating teaching experience to teaching performance', *Economics of Education Review*, 1, 4, pp. 453–65

NARMAN, A. (1985) *Practical Subjects in Kenyan Academic Secondary*

Schools: Tracer Study, Stockholm: Swedish International Development Agency

NATIONAL ADVISORY BODY (1985) 'Advice from NAB on 1984/85 allocations to Sir Keith Joseph', 9 December

NATIONAL UNION OF STUDENTS (1985) *Student Loans: The Costs and the Consequences*, London, National Union of Students

NEAVE, G. (1982) 'Cuts, constraints and vexations in European higher education', *Higher Education Review*, 15, 1, Autumn

NELSON, R. and WINTER, S.G. (1982) *An Evolutionary Theory of Economic Change*, Cambridge, MA, and London: Belknap Press

NOLL, I. *et al* (1983) *The Net Cost of Firm-based Vocational Training in the Federal Republic of Germany*, Berlin: European Centre for the Development

NORRIS, G. (1978) *The Effective University: A Management by Objectives Approach*, Farnborough: Saxon House

NORTHEAST MISSOURI STATE UNIVERSITY (1984) *In Pursuit of Degrees with Integrity*, Kirksville, Missouri: Northeast Missouri State University

OECD (1976) *Public Expenditure on Education*, Paris: OECD

OPEN UNIVERSITY (1984) *Report of the Vice-Chancellor 1983*, Milton Keynes: Open University

OUCHI, W.G. (1980) 'Markets, bureaucracies and clans', *Administrative Science Quarterly*, 25, 1, March

OUSTON, J. and MAUGHAN, B. (1985) 'Issues in the assessment of school outcomes' in REYNOLDS, D. (Ed) *Studying School Effectiveness*, Lewes: Falmer Press

PACE, C.R. (1979) *Measuring Outcomes of College*, San Francisco, CA: Jossey-Bass

PATTISON, M. (1980) 'Intergovernmental relations and the limitations of central control: Reconstructing the politics of comprehensive education', *Oxford Review of Education*, 6, 1

PEACOCK, A., GLENNERSTER, H. and LAVERS, R. (1968) *Educational Finance, Its Sources and Uses in the United Kingdom*, London Oliver and Boyd

PFEFFER, J. (1977) 'Power and resource allocation in organisations' in STAW, B.M. and SALANCIK, G.R. (Eds) *New Directions in Organisation Behavior*, St. Clair Press

PIKE, A. (1983) 'Construction chief warns MSC on training scheme', *Financial Times*, 23 November

PISSARIDES, C.A. (1981) 'Staying-on at school in England and Wales', *Economica*, November

PISSARIDES, C.A. (1982) 'From school to university: The demand for post-compulsory education in Britain', *Economic Journal*, September

PLANNING COMMISSION (1983) *Thoughts on the Third Five-Year Plan (1985–90)*, Dhaka: Government Printer

PLEWIS, I., GRAY, J., FOGELMAN, K. and MORTIMORE, P. (1981) *Publishing School Examination Results: A Discussion*, Bedford Way Papers 5, University of London Institute of Education

POPPER, K.R. (1945) *The Open Society and Its Enemies*, London: Routledge and Kegan Paul

PRATT, J. (1971) 'Open, University!', *Higher Education Review*, Spring

PRATT, J. (1985) 'Some issues for a Green Paper' (editorial), *Higher Education Review*, 17, 2, Spring

PRATT, J. and GILL, H.S. (1986) *Responses to Financial Constraint of Institutions of Higher Education in the Public Sector*, London: DES

PRATT, J., TRAVERS, T. and BURGESS, T. (1978) *Costs and Control in Further Education*, Windsor: NFER

PRICE WATERHOUSE (1983) *Report on Polytechnic Expenditure*, Price Waterhouse, June

PSACHAROPOULOS, G. (1973) *Returns to Education: An International Comparison*, New York, Elsevier

PSACHAROPOULOS, G. (1975) *Earnings and Education in OECD Countries*, Paris: OECD

PSACHAROPOULOS, G. (1981) 'Returns to education: An updated international comparison', *Comparative Education*, 17, 3

PSACHAROPOULOS, G., HINCHCLIFFE, K., DOUGHERTY, C. and HOLLISTER, R. (1982) *Manpower Issues in Educational Investment*, World Bank Staff Working Paper No. 624, Washington, DC: World Bank

PSACHAROPOULOS, G. and LOXLEY, N. (1985) *Diversified Secondary Education and Development: Evidence from Colombia and Tanzania*, Baltimore, MD: Johns Hopkins Press

PSACHAROPOULOS, G. and WOODHALL, M. (1985) *Education for Development: An Analysis of Investment Choices*, New York: Oxford University Press, for the World Bank

RAE, J. (1895) *Life of Adam Smith* (reprinted by Augustus M. Kelley, New York, 1965)

RAFFE, D. (1984) 'School attainment and the labour market' in RAFFE, D. (Ed) *Fourteen to Eighteen: The Changing Pattern of Schooling in Scotland*, Aberdeen: Aberdeen University Press

RENTON, T. (1985) *Government Policy on Overseas Students*, First Annual Lecture, London Conference on Overseas Students

RIBBINS, P. (1985) 'Organisation theory and the study of educational institutions' in HUGHES, M., RIBBINS, P. and THOMAS, H. (Eds) *Managing Education: The System and the Institution*, Eastbourne: Holt, Rinehart and Winston

ROBBINS, L. (1935) *An Essay on the Nature and Significance of Economic Science*, 2nd ed, London: Macmillan

ROBERTS, J.K. (1980) *Secondary School Costs*, MBA dissertation, Henley Management College, Brunel University

ROGERS, E.M. (1982) *The Diffusion of Innovations*, 3rd ed, London: Macmillan

ROIZEN, J. and JEPSON, M. (1985) *Degrees for Jobs: Employer Expectations of Higher Education*, SRHE and Windsor: NFER/Nelson

ROSE, J. (1984) *Funding of Basic and Continuing Vocational Training: Trends in France during the Seventies*, Berlin: European Centre for the Development of Vocational Training

ROSSMILLER, R. (1982) 'Productivity and cost effectiveness as financing criteria' in McMAHON, W.W. and GESKE, T.G. (Eds) *Financing*

Education: Overcoming Inefficiency and Inequity, Urbana, IL, University of Illinois Press

RUTTER, M., MAUGHAN, B., MORTIMORE, P. and OUSTON, J. (1979) *Fifteen Thousand Hours: Secondary Schools and their Effects on Children*, Shepton Mallet: Open Books

SADLAK, J. (1978) 'Efficiency in higher education — Concepts and problems', *Higher Education*, 7, 2

SAUNDERS, M. (1985) 'Emerging issues in TVEI implementation', University of Lancaster: Institute for Post-Compulsory Education

SHATTOCK, M. and RIGBY, G. (1983) *Resource Allocation in British Universities*, SRHE and Windsor: NFER-Nelson

SIMKINS, T. (1984) 'Changing the formula: Some managerial implications of curriculum-based staffing for secondary schools', *Local Government Studies*, 10, 4, pp. 25–38

SIMKINS, T. (1986) 'Patronage, markets and collegiality: Reflections on the allocation of finance in secondary schools', *Educational Management and Administration*, 14, 1

SIZER, J. (1982) 'Assessing institutional performance and progress' in WAGNER, L. (Ed) *Agenda for Institutional Change in Higher Education*, Guildford: SRHE/Leverhulme 3

SMITH, D.M. (1975a) 'Headteachers' allocation of salary points in English secondary schools', *Educational Studies*, 1, 2, pp. 113–20

SMITH, D.M. (1975b) 'Points allocation, secondary schools and teachers', *Educational Studies*, 1, 3, pp. 163–70

SNELL, W. (1982) 'Efficiency and productivity in education systems', *Journal of Tertiary Educational Administration*

SOETE, L. and FREEMAN, C. (1984) 'New Technologies, Investment and Economic Growth', paper presented to the Inter-Governmental Conference on Employment Growth in the Context of Structural Change, OECD 6–8 February 1984 (SME/SC(83)7) (Directorate for Social Affairs, Manpower and Education)

SORGE, A. and WARNER, M. (1980) 'Manpower training, manufacturing organisation and workplace relations in Great Britain and West Germany', *British Journal of Industrial Relations*, XVIII, 3, November

SPILSBURY, M. (1985) 'Individual youth unemployment and the local labour market', University of Leicester: Labour Market Studies, Working Paper No. 10

SQUIRES, G. (1983) *Innovation Through Recession*, SRHE and Windsor: NFER-Nelson

STERN, E. and TURBIN, J. (1986) *Youth Employment and Unemployment in Rural England*, Development Commission, Tavistock Institute of Human Relations, London

SWANN, J. (1986) *The Employment Effects of Microelectronics in the UK Service Sector*, London: Technical Change Centre

SWINNERTON-DYER, SIR PETER (1985) 'Weighing out the pots of gold', *Times Higher Education Supplement*, 15 November, p. 20

TARSH, J. (1985a) 'Labour market for new graduates in 1983', *Employment Gazette*, May

TARSH, J. (1985b) 'Trends in the graduate labour market', *Employment*

Gazette, July

THEODOSSIN, E. (1986) *In Search of the Responsive College*, Coombe Lodge: Further Education Staff College.

THOMAS, H. (1981) 'Cost-effectiveness analysis as a method of assessing "A" level performance in different educational establishments', *Educational Studies*, 7, 2, pp. 95–103

THOMAS, H. (1984) 'Teachers in decline? The quality consequences of the management of changing rolls', *Educational Management and Administration*, 12, 1, pp. 1–14

THOMAS, H. (1986) 'Choice in the education market', *Educational Management and Administration*, 14, 2

THOMAS, J.A. (1971) *The Productive School: A Systems Analysis Approach to Educational Administration*, London: Wiley

THOMAS, J.A. (1980a) 'Resource allocation in school districts and classrooms', *Journal of Education Finance*, 5, 3, pp. 246–61

THOMAS, J.A. (1980b) 'Issues in educational efficiency' in GUTHRIE, J.W. (Ed) *School Finance Policies and Practices: 1st Annual Yearbook of the American Educational Finance Association*, Lexington, MA: Ballinger

THOMAS, R.M. (1983) 'The politics of efficiency and effectiveness in the Civil Service', *International Review of Administrative Sciences*, 44, 3, pp. 239–51

THUROW, L. (1972) 'Education and economic equality', *The Public Interest*, Summer

TRAVERS, T. (1986) *Finance, Education Working Paper 2:8, The Future Role and Organisation of Local Government*, INLOGOV, University of Birmingham

UNIVERSITY GRANTS COMMITTEE (1983) Circular Letter 3/83, 10 February

UNIVERSITY GRANTS COMMITTEE (1984) *A Strategy for Higher Education into the 1990s*, London: HMSO

VAN DER WERF, D. (1985) *Work in Europe: Five Possible Scenarios* (CEC/DG XII-FAST/TWE 1–10) FAST (EEC DG XII)

WADDINGTON, J. (1985) 'The school curriculum in contention: Content and control' in HUGHES, M., RIBBINS, P. and THOMAS, H. (Eds) *Managing Education: The System and the Institution*, Eastbourne: Holt, Rinehart and Winston

WAGNER, L. (1977) 'The economics of the Open University revisited', *Higher Education*, 6

WAGNER, L. (1981) *The Economics of Educational Media*, London: Macmillan

WALDEGRAVE, W. (1982) Speech at Bristol Branch of the Association of Polytechnic Teachers, 7 May

WALSH, K., DUNNE, R., STOTEN, B. and STEWART, J.D. (1984) *Falling School Rolls and the Management of the Teaching Profession*, Windsor: NFER-Nelson

WALSH, K., DUNNE, R.D., STEWART, J.D. and STOTEN, B. (1985) 'Staffing the secondary schools', *Oxford Review of Education*, 11, 1, pp. 19–31

WATTS, A.G. (1983) *Education, Unemployment and the Future of Work*, Milton Keynes: Open University Press

WEST, E.G. (1965) *Education and the State*, London: Institute of Econo-mic Affairs

WILES, P. (1974) 'The correlation between education and earnings: The external-test-not-content-hypothesis', *Higher Education*, February

WILLIAMS, G. (1979) 'Educational planning past, present and future', *Education Policy Bulletin*, 7, 1

WILLIAMS, G. (1982) 'The economics of education: Current debates and prospects', *British Journal of Educational Studies*, 30, 1, pp. 97–107

WILLIAMS, G. and GORDON, A. (1982) 'Perceived earnings functions and *ex ante* rates of return to post-compulsory education in England', *Higher Education*, March

WILLIAMS, G., WOODHALL, M. and O'BRIEN, U. (1987) *Overseas Students in British Higher and Further Education 1985: A Survey of Students and the Institutions Where They Study* London: DEAPSIE

WILLIAMS, P. (1981) *The Overseas Student Question: Studies for a Policy*, London: Heinemann, for The Overseas Students Trust

WILLIAMS, P. (1982) *A Policy for Overseas Students: Analysis, Options, Proposals*, London: Overseas Students Trust

WILLIAMS, S. (1979) 'Labour's record of opportunity for all our children', *Education*, 153, 16, 20 April, pp. 456–7

WILLIAMSON, O.E. (1975) *Markets and Hierarchies: Analysis and Antitrust Implications*, New York: Free Press

WINKLER, D. (1984) 'Screening models and education' in Husen, T. and POSTLETHWAITE, N. (Eds) *International Encyclopaedia of Education*, Oxford: Pergamon

WOODHALL, M. (1970) *Student Loans: A Review of Experience in Scandi-navia and Elsewhere*, London: Harrap

WOODHALL, M. (1977) 'Alternatives in the finance of education: Vouchers' in Open University', *Economics and Education Policy* (Course ED 322), Block IV, Milton Keynes: Open University Press

WOODHALL, M. (1978) *Review of Student Support Schemes in Selected OECD Countries*, Paris: OECD

WOODHALL, M. (1982a) *Student Loans: Lessons from Recent International Experience*, London: Policy Studies Institute

WOODHALL, M. (1982b) 'Financial support for students' in MORRIS, A. and SIZER, J. (Eds) (1982) *Resources and Higher Education*, Guildford, SRHE/Leverhulme Report No. 8

WOODHALL, M. (1983) *Student Loans as a Means of Financing Higher Education*, World Bank Staff Working Paper No. 599, Washington, DC: The World Bank

WOODHALL, M.A. (1986) *Financing Education in Developing Countries: An Exploration of Policy Options*, Washington, DC: The World Bank

WOODHALL, M. and BLAUG, M. (1965) 'Productivity trends in British university education 1938–67', *Minerva*, 3, Summer, pp. 483–98

WOODHALL, M. and BLAUG, M. (1968) 'Productivity trends in British secondary education 1950–63', *Sociology of Education*, Winter

WOODHALL, M. and TOWSE, R. (n.d.) 'The cuts in higher education spend-ing: The effect on access and cuts', University of London Institute of

Education, mimeo

WORLD BANK (1985) *World Development Report*, Oxford: Oxford University Press

WORLD BANK (1986) *Financing Education in Developing Countries: An Exploration of Policy Options* Washington DC: The World Bank

YOUDI, R. and HINCHLIFFE, K. (1985) *Forecasting Skilled Manpower Needs*, Paris: International Institute of Education Planning

ZIDERMAN, A. (1978) *Manpower Training: Theory and Policy*, London: Macmillan

Notes on Contributors

David Ashton is a Senior Lecturer in Sociology at the University of Leicester. For the last nine years he has been engaged in a programme of research into the structure of the youth labour market. His publications include *Young Workers* (Hutchinson, London, 1976 (with David Field)) and *Unemployment under Capitalism* (Wheatsheaf, Brighton, 1986).

Rachel Britton works as an Economic Adviser in the Evaluation and Skills Branch of the Manpower Services Commission. She joined the MSCA in 1984 after twelve years at the University of Essex where she taught economics and computing, and analyzed the portfolios of Victorian wealth-holders.

Christopher Cumming teaches at Moray House College of Education. After his doctoral thesis *Studies in Educational Costs* (1971) he went on to be an educational planner in Kenya and a UNESCO specialist in Nigeria. As well as interests in Third World Education he had completed research in Scotland in the field of staff development.

Rob Cuthbert is a Staff Tutor in education management at the Further Education Staff College. He has published more than fifty articles and books on the management of post secondary education, and is an international consultant, working with colleges, universities and governments in the UK, North America, Africa and China.

Keith Drake is Director of Part-Time Education at the University of Manchester. He has undertaken work for the Manpower Services Commission, New York State Education Department, the Organization for Economic Cooperation and Development and the European Centre for the Development of Vocational Training. In 1983 he published *Financing Adult Education and Training*.

Oliver Fulton is Director of the Institute for Research and Development in Post Compulsory Education, University of Lancaster. He holds degrees in philosophy and sociology from Oxford University and the University of California. His research interests include many aspects of higher education (access, employment of graduates and higher education policy generally); and he is co-director of a series of research projects on aspects of TVEI.

John Gibson is Lecturer in Economics, Institute of Local Government Studies, University of Birmingham. He is author of *Block Grant: A Study in Central Local Relations* (Public Finance Foundation, 1986) and has published papers on local government finance in many journals including *Political Studies, Public Finance, Government and Policy* and *Economics Letters.*

Andrew Gurney studied PPE at St. Catherines College, Oxford, graduating in 1984. He then worked at the Department of Education and Science as an Economic Assistant, and is currently employed by the National Institute of Economic and Social Research assisting with their marco-economic research.

Brian Knight was Headmaster of Holyrood School, Chard, from 1964–1985. He is the author of *Managing School Finance* (Heinemann Educational Books, 1983) and has lectured and written articles on school finance, the management of school time and community education. He is currently Honorary Research Fellow at the School of Education, University of Exeter.

John Mace is a Senior Lecturer in the Economics of Education at the University of London Institute of Education. He has written extensively on educational planning and various aspects of the financing of education. He has served as a consultant educational economist in a number of countries, including Tanzania, Bangladesh and Pakistan.

Malcolm Maguire is a Research Fellow in the Sociology Department at Leicester University. He spent six years in industry before undertaking a degree course. Following two years as a Research Assistant at Hull University, he has worked for nine years with David Ashton on a series of research projects concerning the youth labour market.

Judith Marquand is a Senior Economic Adviser at the Manpower Services Commission, in charge until April 1986 of work on Evaluation and on Skills in Training Division, but now on secondment as a Simon Senior Research Fellow at the University of Manchester, where she is writing a book about questions of adaptation and technological change.

John Pratt is Director of the Centre for Institutional Studies at North East London Polytechnic. He has written extensively on education policy, administration and management and has recently completed a major study for the Department of Education and Science of the effect of financial constraint on public sector higher education institutions.

David Reeson is a Special Projects Officer with the Audit Commission. Between 1976–78 he carried out research at the University of Nottingham into the consumer protection services of local authorities. Since then he has spent four years working for the Local Government Operational Research Unit and two years in management consultancy working exclusively for public sector clients.

Paul Ryan is a lecturer in the Faculty of Economics and Politics at the University of Cambridge and Fellow of King's College, Cambridge. He was educated at the London School of Economics and Harvard University. He does research on the economics of industrial training, education and wage/price structure.

John Sizer is Professor of Financial Management at Loughborough University of Technology and a member of the University Grants Committee. He was a member of the Research Advisory Group of the SRHE/Leverhulme Programme of Study into the Future of Higher Education and was Chairman of the Directing Group of the OECD/CERI Programme on Institutional Management in Higher Education from 1980–1984.

Tim Simkins is a senior lecturer at Sheffield City Polytechnic where he is course leader for the MSc programme in education management. He has previously worked as an educational planner in Southern Africa and has taught educational planning and administration at the University of Manchester. His major interests are in policy formulation and resource management in education.

Jason Tarsh has been an Economic Adviser at the Department of Education and Science since the summer of 1986. Immediately before that he was an Economic Adviser at the Department of Employment. He has published several papers on aspects of the demand for higher qualified manpower.

Hywel Thomas is a Lecturer in Educational Administration at University of Birmingham. In addition to applying economics to the teaching of education management, he has written on several aspects of educational policy and planning. He is currently engaged in research on the economic aspects of upper secondary provision and the delegation of financial control to schools.

Peter Watt is Lecturer in Economics, Institute of Local Government Studies, University of Birmingham. He has published papers in many journals including *Applied Economics, Bulletin of Economic Research, Journal of Industrial Economics* and the *Manchester School*.

Gareth Williams is Professor of Educational Administration at the University of London. After graduating in economics from Cambridge he worked at the Agricultural Economics Research Institute in Oxford where his interest in the economics of education was encouraged by its director, Colin Clark. Six years of more practical educational planning at the OECD was followed by five years at the London School of Economics and eleven years as Professor of Educational Planning at Lancaster University.

Maureen Woodhall is Lecturer in Educational Administration at the University of London Institute of Education, where she was previously Senior Research Officer. A consultant to OECD, UNESCO, The World Bank and the Commonwealth Secretariat, she has published widely on the economics of education. Her most recent book (with George Psacharopoulos) is *Education for Development: An Analysis of Investment Choice* (OUP, 1985).

Index

Page numbers followed by 'n' refer to notes.